Table of Contents

Acknowledgments..5
Introduction..6
Section 1: *10*
Chicago, IL to Wilmington, IL (77 miles)
Section 2: *17*
Wilmington, IL to Bloomington, IL (75 miles)
Section 3: *24*
Bloomington, IL to Chatham, IL (72 miles)
Section 4: *30*
Chatham, IL to Missouri State Line (79 miles)
Section 5: *36*
Missouri State Line to Sullivan, MO (90 miles)
Section 6: *43*
Sulllivan, MO to Gascozark, MO (83 miles)
Section 7 ....*49*
Gasozark, MO to Halltown, MO (94 miles)
Section 8 ....*55*
Halltown, MO to Baxter Springs, KS (85 miles)
Section 9 ....*62*
Baxter Springs, KS to Claremore, OK (80 miles)
Section 10 ....*68*
Claremore, OK to Davenport, OK (91 miles)
Section 11..*74*
Davenport, OK to El Reno, OK (82 miles)
Section 12..*80*
El Reno, OK to Elk City, OK (88 miles)
Section 13..*87*
Elk City, OK to Alanreed, TX (86 miles)
Section 14..*93*
Alanreed, TX to Wildorado, TX (82 miles)
Section 15 ....*100*
Wildorado, TX to Tucumcari, NM (89 miles)

Section 16..................................*106*
Tucumcari, NM to Romeroville, NM (117 miles)
Section 17..................................*112*
Romeroville, NM to Golden, NM (98 miles)
Section 18..................................*118*
Golden, NM to Paraje, NM (102 miles)
Section 19..................................*125*
Paraje, NM to Gallup, NM (106 miles)
Section 20..................................*131*
Gallup, NM to Petrified Forest NP, AZ (103 miles)
Section 21..................................*138*
Petrified Forest NP, AZ to Winona, AZ (97 miles)
Section 22..................................*145*
Winona, AZ to Seligman,AZ (85 miles)
Section 23..................................*152*
Seligman, AZ to Kingman, AZ (89 miles)
Section 24..................................*159*
Kingman, AZ to Goffs, CA (98 miles)
Section 25..................................*166*
Goffs, CA to Ludlow, CA (76 miles)
Section 26..................................*172*
Ludlow, CA to Hesperia, CA (85 miles)
Section 27..................................*178*
Hesperia, CA to Duarte, CA (79 miles)
Section 28..................................*187*
Durate, CA to Santa Monca Pier, CA (37 miles)
Index..................................*196*

Bicycling Guide to Route 66

FOREWORD

"Get your kicks on Route 66!"

Who hasn't heard that classic tune and dreamed of traveling from Chicago to Los Angeles on the open highway? The legendary U.S. Route 66 is now more accessible than ever to cyclists with the publication of this cycling-specific guidebook, dedicated to highlighting services, sites, and the Route's historic path.

Bob Robinson captures the essence of this travel experience with all the essential details a traveling cyclist needs to consider such as where to eat, sleep, and see the best sites up close.

Sites include the Gemini Giant, numerous old filling stations, diners preserved with their distinct charms, fantastic bridges, the Blue Whale of Catoosa, OK, the Cadillac Ranch in Texas, museums dedicated to the history of U.S. Route 66, historic districts, the iconic Wigwam Motel in Holbrook, AZ, and the deserts of California, culminating in a celebratory spin down the Santa Monica Pier.

Besides the big hitters of Chicago and L.A., the route includes city highlights such as St. Louis, MO, Oklahoma City, OK, and Albuquerque, NM. When you need a break from the highways, be sure to take advantage of rustic side trips to Sky City on the Acoma Pueblo of New Mexico or the dirt backroads into Winslow, Arizona.

And remember, some of these sites are best taken in after dark, especially the remaining neon signs still advertising great eats, old time movie theaters, and places to rest your head at the end of the day.

Since the original U.S. Route 66 has been overtaken by the Interstate Highway System in many places, the routing used to represent the legendary highway for the purpose of cycling is comprised of bike paths, county roads and state, federal and sometimes interstate highways. Luckily, original sections of U.S. Route 66 still exist and all of it can be best enjoyed at the pace of a cyclist.

As a long time staffer, I would be remiss if I did not mention how the Adventure Cycling Bicycle Route 66 maps and digital data are a natural complement to the efforts Bob has put forth in this guidebook.

So what are you waiting for? Get out there and get your kicks on Route 66!

Jennifer H. Milyko
Assistant Director, Routes & Mapping
Cartographer
Adventure Cycling Association

Bicycling Guide to Route 66

Published by
Spirits Creek
Fort Smith, Arkansas

Copyright © 2016 by Bob Robinson
First printing 2016

All rights reserved.
No part of this book or its content may be reproduced in any form, or by any electronic, mechanical, or other means, without permission in writing from the publisher.

Edited by Nancy Raney

All photographs by Bob Robinson.

Cover photo was taken at the Santa Monica Pier, in beautiful sunny California, the western most end of Route 66.

Library of Congress Control Number: 2016903452

ISBN 978-0-9818952-3-9

This book is dedicated to anyone who has ever selected a bicycle as their preferred vehicle of travel.

Acknowledgments:

I would like to express my appreciation to the following people who contributed to this book: Nancy Raney, the staff at Adventure Cycling Association, (especially Ginny Sullivan and Jennifer Milyko), Sheila Smith, Nathaniel Benoit, Sharon Cole, all the National Park and State Park workers, Sue Oxarart, Brent Hugh, and all the volunteers working at the Tourist Information Centers along the Mother Road. I could not have written the book without your valuable work.

I thank you all.

Introduction

Route 66, the Mother Road, the Will Rogers Highway, Main Street of America, the Road to Riches, the Road of Flight, and the Great American Highway; it has been known by many names since it was first established in 1926. From its inception, the thoroughfare has always symbolized more than a cold slab of concrete, with its legend still being remembered in both song and written word.

Each of the eight states Route 66 passes through have their own story to share about the famous route, being told in the countless historic markers installed along the roadside. Odell, Illinois, for example, where the traffic on Route 66 was so heavy they had to build an underground pedestrian tunnel so citizens could safely cross the street. And there are many other communities who share their rich history with the Mother Road.

Cyclists will also want to stop at the numerous Classic Roadside Attractions (CRA) leftover from Route 66's heyday of having a carnival like atmosphere, when tourist attractions were so plentiful they had to go to such extremes as installing one of the famous giant "Muffler Man" in front of their restaurant or gift shop, in hope that when motorists stopped for the photo-op they would buy something at their establishment. Or, to paint advertisements on the roof of barns across the country to market an attraction that was hundreds of miles away.

You will also bicycle through the same stretch of the Mohave Desert where General George S. Patton secretly trained the US Army in the largest military ground training maneuvers in history, in preparation for the North African Campaign against German General Erwin Rommel's Panzer Division during World War II.

It's an interesting ride, with plenty of unique attractions documenting our nation's varied history. It played a key role in America's great migration west, and not just during the Dust Bowl of the 1930s. For many it was a golden pathway west to a new and better life. That is why this guidebook is designed primarily for a Chicago to Santa Monica Pier tour; because historically that was the direction it is normally associated with. However, the Mileage Logs are also designed to be used for a west to east ride.

The national system of auto routes that resulted in the creation of Route 66 actually began in 1911. This national system of roads grew out of the Good Roads Movement, which in turn was founded in 1880 when bicyclists and bicycle manufacturers formed the League of American Wheelmen. The League advocated for the creation of a system of good roadways for bicycles with their publication of Good Roads Magazine. And now, with the creation of Adventure Cycling Association's Bicycle Route 66, it is only appropriate that

Introduction

the route should once again serve the bicycle traveler.

Upon completion of riding the "entire" documented Route 66 route, contact me via my website, spiritscreek.com, and I will send you the personalized official "Certification of Completion" for your great achievement. I will also post your certificate on my Facebook page, Bicycling Guide to the ...., which I share with my other guidebooks.

Enjoy your Route 66 Adventure!

Using This Guide

This guidebook is a collection of relevant materials for cyclists to use to create their own adventure exploring this historic route.

The route has been broken down into sections. The mileage for each section is not based on the number of miles cyclists should ride each day. Not all cyclists share the same agenda. Instead, each section provides the materials a cyclist needs to create their own daily schedule, and the flexibility to adjust their schedule as needed. Each section includes text, services, a map, and the all-important Mileage Log, which lists turn-by-turn directions. I suggest that you first read the text associated with a section, to familiarize yourself with the route, and any attractions along the way. The services included will help you select a target destination for the day's ride, and the map will provide an overall understanding of the route. Be sure to read the Mileage Log to familiarize yourself with the turns involved in the first part of your ride, and keep it handy as a reference throughout your trip.

Mileage for each section will vary depending on the geographical layout of that particular route. When a route is straight, the section will consist of fewer miles than when there are a lot of turns, which will allow more miles to fit on the map.

Text

The text provides a running account of the route, and points out many of its attractions. It often relates to the rich history of the area, so that cyclists can better appreciate the communities and scenery along the way. When needed, the text also serves to complement the Mileage Log, by providing greater detail for complicated directions or other potential hazards.

At the first use of an acronym within the text I will explain its meaning, such as (Lakefront Trail) LFT. So if you encounter an unknown acronym, thumb back a page or two to locate its meaning. The guidebook does not identify every attraction that Route 66 passes. There remain many more attractions for you to discover on your own.

Introduction

Services

Where services are available, each section in the guide lists camping, lodging, and bike shops. Every possible service is not listed. Those services that are preceded by an asterisk (*) are located immediately along the route.

Mileage Log

Column headings:
  Miles E/W: Accumulated miles for the referenced section, when riding east to west, Chicago to Santa Monica Pier.
  Directions: Instructions and points of interest along the route. Rows beginning with an * are intended as an FYI, such as a town or a turn for an optional side trip.
  Dist: The distance in miles to travel for the associated instruction.
  R: Rating for traffic & road condtions, usng a scale of 1 ideal and 5 very congested, and P for separated paved path.
  Services: C= camping, G = a full grocery store, L = lodging, such as a motel, bed-and-breakfast, lodge, etc., Q = a type of business where cyclists can stop for a quick snack, such as a convenience store, small grocery, etc. R = a restaurant that serves prepared foods. Available services will be listed both for the section of road that they are on, and the town they are located in.
  Miles W/E: Reversed accumulated miles for the referenced section, for cyclists traveling west to east, Santa Monica Pier to Chicago.

Acronyms used in the Mileage Log directions:
  CR: County Road, L: Left, R: Right, SH: State Highway, SL: Stop Light, SS: Stop Sign, YS: Yield Sign.

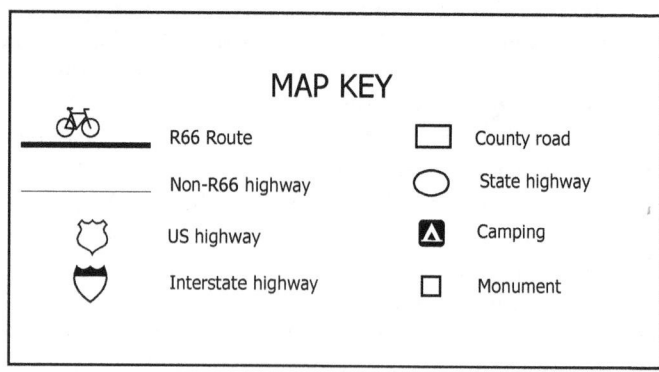

Introduction

Equipment

Like I always say, if you have a bicycle, you can tour. My first bicycle tour was on a 10-speed Huffy® with a daypack strapped to a bolt-on rack. I do admit that touring is a lot more enjoyable with my Fuji® Touring bike and Jandd® Large Mountain Panniers. So, if you would like to improve the chances of your first tour being an enjoyable experience, I recommend that you read one of the many books written specifically about preparation for bicycle touring. Visit the Adventure Cycling Association website for a list of available publications.

Just don't allow your equipment to stop your adventure.

Safety

The list of the roads described in this guidebook as the designated Route 66 route, is not an indication that they are safe for cyclists. When you ride the roads described in this book, you assume responsibility for your own safety. Most of the route of Route 66 follows highways that are used by motor vehicles, and dangers that are normally associated with riding such roads exist while riding Route 66. Be Safe.

Weather: Average High/Low/Rainfall

City, State	Jan Hi Lo Rn	Feb Hi Lo Rn	Mar Hi Lo Rn	Apr Hi Lo Rn	May Hi Lo Rn	Jun Hi Lo Rn	Jul Hi Lo Rn	Aug Hi Lo Rn	Sep Hi Lo Rn	Oct Hi Lo Rn	Nov Hi Lo Rn	Dec Hi Lo Rn
Chicago, IL	31 17 1.73	35 20 1.79	47 29 2.50	59 39 3.38	70 48 3.68	80 58 3.45	84 64 3.70	82 63 4.90	75 54 3.21	62 43 3.15	48 32 3.15	35 21 2.25
St Louis, MO	40 24 2.45	45 28 2.48	56 37 3.36	67 47 4.10	76 57 4.80	85 67 4.34	89 71 4.19	88 69 3.41	80 61 3.38	69 49 3.43	56 38 4.22	43 27 2.96
Tulsa, OK	46 26 1.60	53 31 1.95	62 40 3.57	72 49 3.95	79 59 6.11	88 68 4.72	94 73 2.96	93 71 2.85	84 63 4.76	74 51 4.05	60 39 3.47	49 30 2.43
Amarillo, TX	49 23 0.63	54 27 0.55	62 34 1.13	70 42 1.33	78 52 2.50	87 61 3.28	91 65 2.68	89 64 2.94	82 56 1.88	72 45 1.50	58 32 0.68	50 24 0.61
Albuquerque NM	47 24 0.49	55 28 0.44	62 34 0.61	71 41 0.50	80 51 0.60	90 60 0.65	92 65 1.27	89 63 1.73	82 56 1.07	71 44 1.00	57 32 0.62	31 21 0.49
Flagstaff, AR	43 17 2.18	46 19 2.56	50 23 2.62	58 27 1.29	68 34 0.80	79 41 0.43	82 50 2.40	80 49 2.89	74 42 2.12	63 31 1.93	51 22 1.86	44 17 1.83
Los angeles CA	68 49 3.33	70 50 3.68	70 52 3.14	73 54 0.83	75 58 0.31	79 61 0.06	84 65 0.01	85 66 0.13	83 65 0.32	79 60 0.37	73 53 1.05	69 48 1.91

Route 66
SECTION 1

Chicago, IL to Wilmington, IL (77 miles)

Your Route 66 Adventure begins at Buckingham Fountain in Grant Park. This is one of the largest fountains in the world and makes a great backdrop for a photo op documenting the start of your ride. Before heading out you can sit at Buck's Four Star Grill, located on the promenade circling the fountain, to enjoy a beer and Chicago Dog while you watch the fountain shoot water 150 feet in the air.

There is a lot to do and see in The Windy City. The Chicago Cultural Center, located just north of the fountain, at 77 E. Randolph St, has visitor information to help you plan your visit. The center is housed in the old Chicago Water Works building, one of the few structures to survive the infamous 1871 fire.

Adjoining Grants Park to the north is Millennium Park, which has one of my favorite attractions in the area, The Bean. The official name is Cloud Gate, but most people refer to it as "the bean," mainly because that's what the 110 ton polished steel structure looks like. It provides some awesome views of the city's skyline in its refection.

When you are ready to begin your ride, cross the promenade surrounding the fountain to Buck's Grill then ride down the ramp located beside it. Otherwise, you will have to carry your bike down a series of steps located at the other exits. Once down the ramp, ride east through the park to Balbo Ave. Take a left to cross Lake Shore Drive and then right to begin riding Lakefront Trail (LFT). The LFT is a great example for other cities of how to route cyclists through a large city.

Shortly after beginning LFT you ride right beside legendary Soldier Field, home of "Da Bears". Next to this is the state-of-the-art Field Museum of Natural History, which is the largest museum of this type in the world.

The Northerly Island is also in this area. This is a 91-acre manmade peninsula that has a large portion set aside as a nature preserve, which also includes a section for group camping. In 2017 the area will be turned over to the U.S. Army Corp of Engineers, so I'm hoping they will also allow individual camping. That would be cool, camping with a view of the skyline of the 3rd largest city

Route 66 Section 1

in the U.S.

Most of the LFT routes cyclists right along the lakeshore, with views of sailboats and waves lapping against the shoreline. On the last half-mile at the very southern end of the trail you are pretty much riding on a sidewalk alongside a golf course. Just continue until you reach E 71st St., then curve left around the corner to ride the sidewalk a couple more blocks then cross E 71st St. and begin riding on South Shore Drive.

Photo op at the official beginning of my Route 66 Adventure, Buckingham Fountain!

There will be a short section where you ride on city streets but soon you will be on the Burnham Greenway Trail (BGT). While riding this trail, and also streets in the area, use caution at railroad crossings, some of them are pretty rough.

At the beginning of BGT, as is parallels Indianapolis Ave, there is a good pizza place named Route 66 Pizza. This is the first of many opportunities you have to support businesses linking themselves to the historic route.

Keep an eye out for the Wolf Lake Blvd. turn, there is no sign for it, just use the mileage. The BGT continues a short distance past the turn but you'll want take the route through the park. It is a nice place to stop at a picnic table or use the restroom. It also routes you past an Nike Ajax missile warhead. This was one of 22 Nike Ajax missiles from the Chicago Defensive Area that was located here during the Cold War. It was the largest defensive ring deployed in

Route 66 Section 1

the Continental U.S. Stop along the lakeshore to ponder what the area would have looked like back then.

After exiting Sibley Ave. the BGT routes you through the Forest Reserve District of Cook County, with long wooded stretches of forests bordering the bike path.

Watch for the SH 83 crossing on the Thorn Creek Trail (TCT). A trail also continues straight, however Route 66 (R66) follows the trail that goes across SH 83. If you miss the turn just continue on and cross SH 83 at the stop light to double back on the bike path. You might want to do this anyway if the traffic is bad.

If you turn left at Glenwood Ave. crossing then ride a couple tenths of a mile on Main Street you can eat at the Glenwood Oaks Rib & Chop House. The owners have been serving up good home cooking for over 35 years.

Joe Orr Park is a nice place to take a break with picnic tables, a pavilion, and restrooms. The TCT continues through the park then follows a linear park.

Currently the TCT ends at Campbell Ave., however there are plans to extend the Old Plank Rd Trail (OPT) to join it at this point. But until this happens follow the directions in the book to reach the current trail head of the OPT.

As the OPT approaches Cicero Ave. it zigs to the left, to route cyclists to a safer crossing, then zags right to resume the OPT. You can turn right on Cicero Ave and ride half-a-mile to reach a variety of fast-food restaurants, a mall, and a Walmart. The La Quinta Motel listed in the book is located just behind the Walmart.

About a mile past the Cicero Ave. crossing the OPT routes cyclist thru the Dewey Helmick Nature Preserve. With water on both sides of the trail this is a great place for spotting wildlife.

We ride trails like this and think they are pretty cool, but we need realize all the work required to accomplish achievements like this. The Old Plank Road Trail (OPT) was over 20 years in the making, with the cooperation between both local and state government agencies, plus dedicated involvement of a lot of citizen volunteers. So when we are not riding our bikes we all need to support the programs that make great cycling environments like the OPT happen.

You'll see the Frankfort grain tower before reaching the city limits. This is one of those quaint picturesque small towns that are great to stop for lunch or to grab a beverage at the craft brewery located right on the square.

Say goodbye to the OPT when you reach Washington St. It was sweet while it lasted. There are restrooms at this end of the trail.

Joliet was once nicknamed The City of Spires, due to its

numerous churches. Now it is better known for its casinos.

Washington St. becomes New St. in the downtown area. When New St reaches the train station the road has been converted into a pedestrian walkway. You continue straight on the pedestrian walk to reach Chicago St.

Chicago St. is one way, so west bound cyclists will follow the directions in the book, turning right and circling around, while east bound will be coming in on Chicago St. and turn right on the pedestrian walkway to reach New St.

When you reach the end of Chicago St. for the left turn onto Washington St., if you continue straight on a pedestrian walkway for another couple of blocks you will be in downtown Joliet. It's well worth a side trip to check out the Joliet 66 Diner and the Rialto Square Theater, a restored 1926 vaudeville theater whose lobby was fashioned after the Hall of Mirrors at the Palace of Versailles. At 204 N. Ottawa St., you can also visit the Joliet Area Historical Museum, which includes your first Route 66 exhibit.

After leaving Joliet, R66 routes you through open farmland. You also pass Route 66 Raceway. The old highway legend lives on!

Watch for the left turn off SH 53 onto the unnamed road. Just look for a sign that says to Brown Cemetery and Chicago Rd. It is worth a little trouble to spot this turn because it will get you off of the 4-lane highway for a while.

When you get back to SH 53, you can continue across the highway another half-a-mile for a side trip to the town of Elwood, where you'll find restaurants, convenience stores, and groceries. The town was the inspiration for Blues Brother, Elwood Blues.

Also in Elwood is the Abraham Lincoln National Cemetery. It is located on 982 acres of what was formerly the Joliet Army Ammunition Plant. I wasn't aware that President Lincoln was the founder of the National Cemeteries. He created them as a final resting place for the Civil War dead. This is a well maintained site, and the paved road through it makes for an interesting, but solemn, bike ride.

On my ride on SH 53 the traffic wasn't bad and there is at least a small shoulder most places, but I still rated it 4 because it could potentially be a busy highway, especially with the high speed limits.

North of Wilmington R66 passes through the Midewin National Tallgrass Prairie. In 2016 the U.S. Forest Service plans to release bison to help restore the tallgrass prairie ecosystem. Share your bison pictures on the guidebook Facebook page, Bicycling Guide to the .....

Section One ends in Wilmington, a nice town to end your day, featuring full services.

Route 66 Section 1

Camping (check US Corp of Engineers for possible camping on Chicago's Northerly Island)

Martin Campground Inc
2303 New Lenox Rd
Joliet, IL
815-726-3173

Fossil Rock Rec CG
24615 W Strip Mine Rd
Wilmington, IL 60481
815-476-6784

Lodging

Hostel Internation
24 E Congress Pkwy
Chicago, IL
312-360-0300

La Quinta Inn & Suites
4900A S Lake Shore Dr
Chicago, IL 60615
773-324-3000
(near LFT 6 miles from start)

Chicago Lake Shore Motel
4900 S Lake Shore Dr
Chicago, IL 60615
800-916-4339
(near LFT 6 miles from start)

La Quinta Inn
5210 Southwick Dr
Matteson, IL 60443
708-503-0999

Plaza Hotel
26 W Clinton St
Joliet, IL
815-726-6195

Knights Inn
24001 W Lorenzo Rd
Wilmington, IL
815-476-4271

Bike Shops

Cycle Bike Shop
1465 S Michigan Ave
Chicago, IL
312-997-5554
(less than 2 miles from start)

Bicycle Clinic
2221 E 71st St
Chicago, IL
773-955-2028
(3 blks off LFT)

*Plank Road Cyclery
20 Elwood St
Frankfort, IL
815-469-3594

Chicago to Wilmington (77 miles)

Miles E/W	Directions	Dist	R	Service	Miles W/E
	*Grant Park			R	77
0	S thru park on trail	0.1			77
0	L on Balbo Ave	0.1			77
0	Cross Shore Dr then R on LFT	9.0	P		77
9	R on S Shore Dr/US41	1.3	4	G	68
11	BR to remain on S Shore Dr	0.5	4		66
11	L on 83rd St	0.1	4		66
11	R on Burley Ave	0.5	4		66
12	L on 87th St	0.1	4		65
12	R on Mackinaw Ave	0.6	4		65
12	L on Ewing Ave/US41	1.1	4	GR	65
13	BL to ride under I90 then L on Burnham Greenway Tr (BGT)	0.6	P		64
14	R to cross Indianapolis Ave cont BGT	2.2	P	R	63
16	L to exit BGT then R on Wolf Lake Blvd	0.8	P		61
17	L on Ave O/Burnham Ave	2.9	4	R	60
20	R on Sibley Ave	0.5	4	R	57
20	L on BGT	3.1	P		57
24	S on BGT under I94 then L then R to cross 175th St to cont BGT	1.0	P		53

Route 66 Section 1

25	L to cross Roy St then R	0.1	P		52
25	L at SS on 181st St	0.1	P		52
25	R on Henry St/Grant St	0.1	P		52
	*Lansing (pop. 28,331)			QR	
25	L on Legion Dr	0.3	P		52
25	R at SS on Wentworth Ave	0.2	P		52
25	R at SL on 186th St	1.0	3		52
26	L into parking for Thorn Creek Tr (TCT) then L to begin TCT	1.1	P		51
27	R to cross SH83 to cont on TCT	1.2	P		50
29	S at SL to cross Stoney Island Ave cont on TCT	1.8	P		48
30	S at SS to cross Cottage Grove Ave cont on TCT	2.2	P		47
33	S to cross Glenwood Ave then R and L to cont on TCT	2.2	P		44
35	L to cross Joe Orr Rd then R	1.1	P		42
36	S to cross Chicago Rd to cont on TCT	1.0	P		41
37	R on Campbell Ave	0.6	3		40
38	L on 15th St	1.3	3		39
39	L on Western Ave	0.3	P		38
39	R on Old Plank Road Tr (OPRT)	3.0	P		38
42	BL cross Cicero Ave then R on OPRT	6.2	P		35
	*Frankfort (pop 18,168)			R	
48	Cont S on OPRT	7.0	P		29
55	Cross Cross Haven Ave then L to cont OPRT	4.1	P		22
59	R on Washington St/New St	1.4	3		18
	*Joliet (pop. 147,433)			CLGQR	
61	S on pedestrian walkway	0.1	P		16
61	R on Chicago St then L Washington St	0.1	4	R	16
61	L on Ottawa St, SH6	0.1	4		16
61	BL on R66/US6/SH53	6.2	4	QR	16
67	L on Unnamed Rd then R Chicago Rd	1.2	3		10
69	R on unsigned Mississippi Rd	1.4	3		8
	*Elwood (pop. 2,279)			GQR	
70	L on unsigned SR53/HR66/216th Ave	7.0	4		7
77	*Wilmington (pop. 5,724)			CLGQR	0

Route 66 Section 1

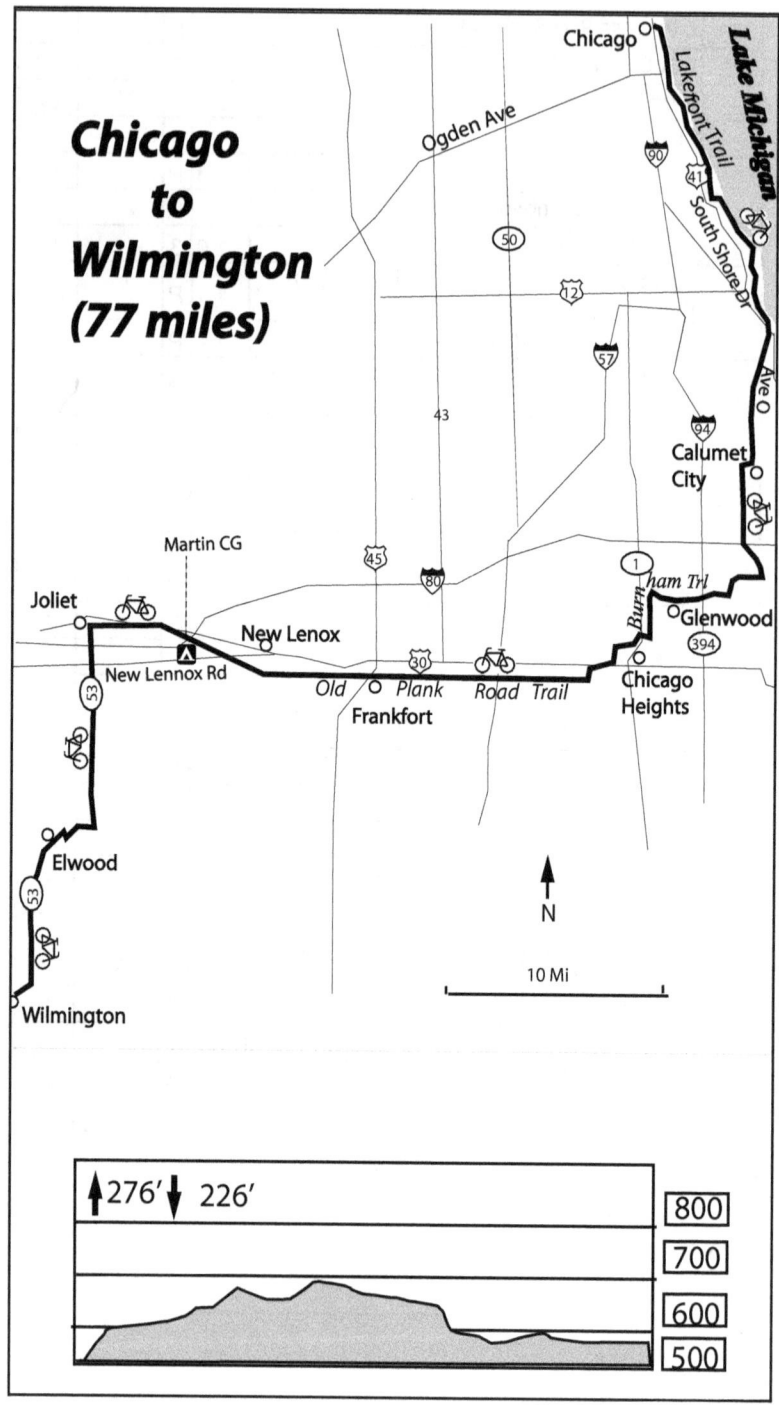

Route 66
SECTION 2

Wilmington, IL to Bloomington, IL (75 miles)

Upon entering Wilmington you will see your first genuine Route 66 icon, the Gemini Giant. Even if you haven't seen any of the 30' tall fiberglass statues, commonly referred to as "Muffler Men" in person, I'm sure you've seen photos. Created by International Fiberglass, in Venice, CA, they caught on in the 60s when businesses would accessorize them with mufflers, hotdogs, or spaceships to attract tourists, in hopes that when people stopped for a photo op, they would also buy whatever product the merchant was selling.

In Wilmington, playing on the popularity of the Gemini Space Program of that era, they dressed their green giant up as an astronaut and named their restaurant the Launching Pad Drive-In. The restaurant was closed when I last rode through, however the Gemini Giant remains, available for your photo op.

Wilmington's Van Duyne's Motel isn't the cleanest or most modern motel, but sometimes you just need a place to sleep that doesn't cost you a wad of money. It is also conveniently located across the highway from Nelly's Route 66 Restaurant.

To reach the Fossil Rock Recreation campground: after leaving Wilmington, as SH 53 takes a left bend, continue straight on Strip Mine Rd. for 2.3 miles, then turn left and ride another .3 miles.

Another classic roadside attraction (CRA) you'll pass on your ride in this section is Braidwood's 1956 Polk-A-Dot Drive In. The traditional food and shakes are reason enough for stopping; however the life-sized statues of legends James Dean, Marilyn Monroe, Betty Boop, Elvis, and the Blues Brothers are what make it classic.

In Gardner if you continue straight on Center St. another block you can visit an interesting old 1906 two cell jail. There is also an old restored Streetcar Diner here (it no longer serves food). If you stop in at the firehouse across the street they will give you a little oral history of the town.

I'm not sure if they were on the road earlier and I didn't notice them, but I began seeing Route 66 emblems painted on the highways through this area.

As you approach Dwight, if you turn right when Dwight Rd. reaches SH 47 and ride half-a-mile, you will reach the Super 8 Motel listed. There are also places to eat and a convenience store in the area of the motel.

Dwight is a good place to tour on a bicycle. You will pass several restored gas stations from the Route 66 era, including Ambler's Texaco Station, which was certified as the longest operating gas station on Route 66, in operation for 66 continuous years. It now serves as a visitor center.

I also encourage cyclists to turn left at Ambler's on Mason Ave. and ride a few blocks to the downtown. A few of the interesting attractions to see are the 1896 Windmill behind Country Mansion, the Fox Development Center to admire its 5 Tiffany-style windows portraying the 5 senses, the First National Bank building which was designed by Frank Lloyd Wright, and the Romanesque railroad depot, now housing the Dwight Historical Society Museum.

As you are leaving Dwight, at the listed turn onto Route 66, there is a picnic area with restrooms.

For the remainder of this section you will pass a lot of the abandoned second set of lanes that Route 66 used when it was a 4 lane highway.

It's difficult to imagine now, but Route 66 was once a very busy highway. The traffic was so busy at one time, several towns had to build pedestrian tunnels under the highway. Odell was one such town to do this and you can still see their tunnel at the intersection across from the church. This is definitely a CRA.

Another CRA in Odell is the 1932 Standard Oil Gas Station. In the late 1940s it was one of nine stations along Route 66 through Odell. You are going to see a lot of Route 66 era gas stations, but this one received the National Historic Route 66 Federation Cyrus Avery Award, so you don't want to miss it. There is also an audio history recording here.

You may be thinking, "Who is Cyrus Avery to have an award named after him?" He was the man known as the "Father of Route 66". Born in Pennsylvania, Avery called Tulsa, OK home.

When working to improve the interstate highway system, Avery realized that an interstate system of highways would benefit his adopted city and state so he became involved in the creation of the Ozarks Trails, a system of roads connecting St. Louis, MO to Amarillo, TX. Through his involvement with this and other highway related organizations, in 1925 he was appointed to the Joint Board of Interstate Highways.

When Congress requested the creation of a cross country

route that would run from Virginia Beach, VA to Los Angeles, CA, which would bypass the entire state of Oklahoma, Avery had something to say about it. He argued for a route that would avoid the Rocky Mountains by directing it through Tulsa and Oklahoma City, and then across the Texas Panhandle, New Mexico, Arizona, and southern California. He also argued that with most of the commerce at that time coming from Chicago, rather than Virginia Beach, the route should turn north after leaving St. Louis.

Congress bought into his arguments and the rest is history.

On the stretch following Odell watch for your first Meramec Caverns barn sign sighting. This marketing campaign is true Route 66. More on this in a later section.

Competition for the tourist dollars was brutal, so advertisement played a big role on Route 66, as you will witness proof of on your bike tour across the country.

The 1926 Old Log Cabin Restaurant you ride past as you enter Pontiac has a unique story. When the previous road that it faced was repositioned to integrate it into the new Route 66, the owners raised the entire restaurant on jacks and rotated it 180° to face the new thoroughfare.

Pontiac is a nice town to get off your bicycle to stretch your legs. Stop by the visitor information center, 115 W Howard St., to pick up a walking tour brochure which will include the Route 66 Hall of Fame & Museum, numerous murals, and other attractions. Also, be sure to stroll across the swinging bridges across the Vermillion River.

Another interesting tidbit: At one time the inmates at Pontiac's state prison manufactured the Route 66 emblems for this area.

On the section of Route 66 following Pontiac keep watch for the metal cutout of a motorcycle cop in front of the old State Police headquarters. He's still standing watch over his stretch of Route 66.

Also keep watch for the sign for the Levington County poor farmers' cemetery. It's just a short .3 mile ride off route, and it is a pleasant setting that I believe the farmers buried there would approve of.

Upon entering Lexington you will pass a turn for the Old Memory Lane. This short section of highway has been preserved in its original condition before Route 66 was rerouted. I recommend riding the abandoned lanes on the opposite side of the current highway that has been converted into a bike path. It only lasts a few miles but unless you are planning to ride through downtown Lexington it makes for a better ride.

Also in this area you will pass Kick's Bar and Grill, which serves up a fish sandwich that has a huge chunk of meat on it.

Riding through Towanda you can take a detour to see "dead man's curve". At one time there was a house located on the curve, however after its front porch knocked off on several occasions and then having a semi-truck knock it completely off its foundation, the owners moved it. BTW, this isn't the only "dead man's curve" you will encounter on Route 66.

And finally, you find the answer to the age old conundrum, "what is normal", when you visit Normal, IL.

In Bloomington Route 66 utilizes the Constitution Trail (CT) system. As it crosses Washington Street you can go off route to visit the place where beer nuts were invented at Beer Nuts, Inc. They even have a gift store and a video tour of their plant.

If you need bicycle repairs watch for the Bloomington Cycling & Fitness store to your right just before the CT crosses Empire St.

The ghost of a state trooper still watching over a long abandoned lane of Route 66.

Camping

Fossil Rock Rec CG
24615 W Strip Mine Rd
Wilmington, IL 60481
815-476-6784

Bayou Bluffs CG
9604 E 2350 N Rd
Cornell, IL 61319
815-358-2537

Route 66 Section 2

Lodging

*Braidwood Motel
120 N Washington St,
Braidwood, IL 60408
815-458-2321

Super 8 Motel
601 S Deerfield Rd
Pontiac, IL 61764
815-844-6888

Comfort Suites
310 Greenbriar Dr
Normal, IL 61761
309-452-8588

Super 8 Motel
14 E Northbrook Dr
Dwight, IL 60420
815-584-1888

America's Best Value Inn
505 Hoselton Dr
Chenoa, IL 61726
815-945-5900

Burr House B&B
210 E Chestnut
Bloomington, IL 61701
309-828-7686

Fiesta Motel
951 W Reynolds St
Pontiac, IL 61764
815-844-7103

Super 8 Motel
Traders Cir
Normal, IL 61761
309-454-5858

Country Inn & Suites
923 Maple Hill Rd
Bloomington, IL 61704
309-828-7177

Bike Shops

Vitesse Cycle Shop
206 S Linden St
Normal, IL 61761
309-454-1541

Bloomington Cycle & Fitness
712 E Empire St
Bloomington, IL 61701
309-820-8036

Wilson's Cycle
424 N Main St
Bloomington, IL 61701
309-829-6824

Wilmington to Bloomington (75 Miles)

Miles E/W	Directions	Dist	R	Service	Miles W/E
	*Wilmington (pop. 5,724)			CLGQR	
0	R on Baltimore St/SR53	4.4	4	GQR	75
4	*Braidwood (pop 6,191)			GQR	71
4	R at SL on Main St then L on Washington St/SH129	3.8	3	Q	71
8	L at SS on Mitchell St (unsigned) then R on SH53/R66	3.0	3		67
11	R on Washington St	0.2	3		64
11	*Gardner (pop 1,463)			R	64
11	L on Center St/R66 then VR on Depot St	0.2	2		64
12	R on Jefferson St	0.1	3		63
12	L at SS on Jackson St	0.3	3		63
12	R at SS on Parker St	0.6	3		63
13	L on R66	6.2	3		62
19	L on Dwight Rd/R66	1.0	3		56
20	L at SS on SH47/McNamara Ave	0.5	3	Q	55
20	*Dwight (pop 4,260)			GLQR	55
20	BR on Waupansie St/R66	1.9	3	GR	55
22	BR on Odell Rd (unsigned)	0.3	3		53
23	L on R66	5.6	3		52

Wilmington to Bloomington (75 Miles)

Miles E/W	Directions	Dist	R	Service	Miles W/E
28	L on N West St	0.9	3		47
29	*Odell (pop 1,046)				46
29	BR at SS then L to cont on West St	0.9	3		46
30	L on R66	8.1	3		45
38	L on Pontaic Rd then L cont Aurora St	0.7	3		37
39	R at SS on Indiana Ave	0.2	3		36
39	L at SS on Main St	0.4	2		36
39	*Pontaic (pop 11,931)			GLQR	36
39	R at SL on Howard St	0.6	3		36
40	L at SL on SR116/R66	0.5	3	QR	35
40	S at SL on R66 as SH116 turns R	9.2	3		35
50	*Chenoa .5 mile offroute (pop 1,785)			LQR	25
50	S on R66	8.4	3		25
58	*Lexington (pop 2,060)			GQR	17
58	S on R66	7.6	3	R	17
66	*Towanda (pop 480)				9
66	S at SS on R66	4.4	3		9
70	S at SL on Shelbourne Dr/R66	1.1	3		5
71	L on Constitution Tr	1.0	P		4
72	*Normal (pop 52,497)				3
72	R at traffic circle on North St	0.1	3	R	3
72	L on Broadway St	0.1	3		3
72	L on Phoneix Ave	0.1	3		3
72	R on Constitution Tr	2.1	P		3
75	L after tunnel on Grove St then R cont Constitution Tr	0.4	P		0
75	*Bloomington (pop 76,610)			GLQR	

Route 66 Section 2

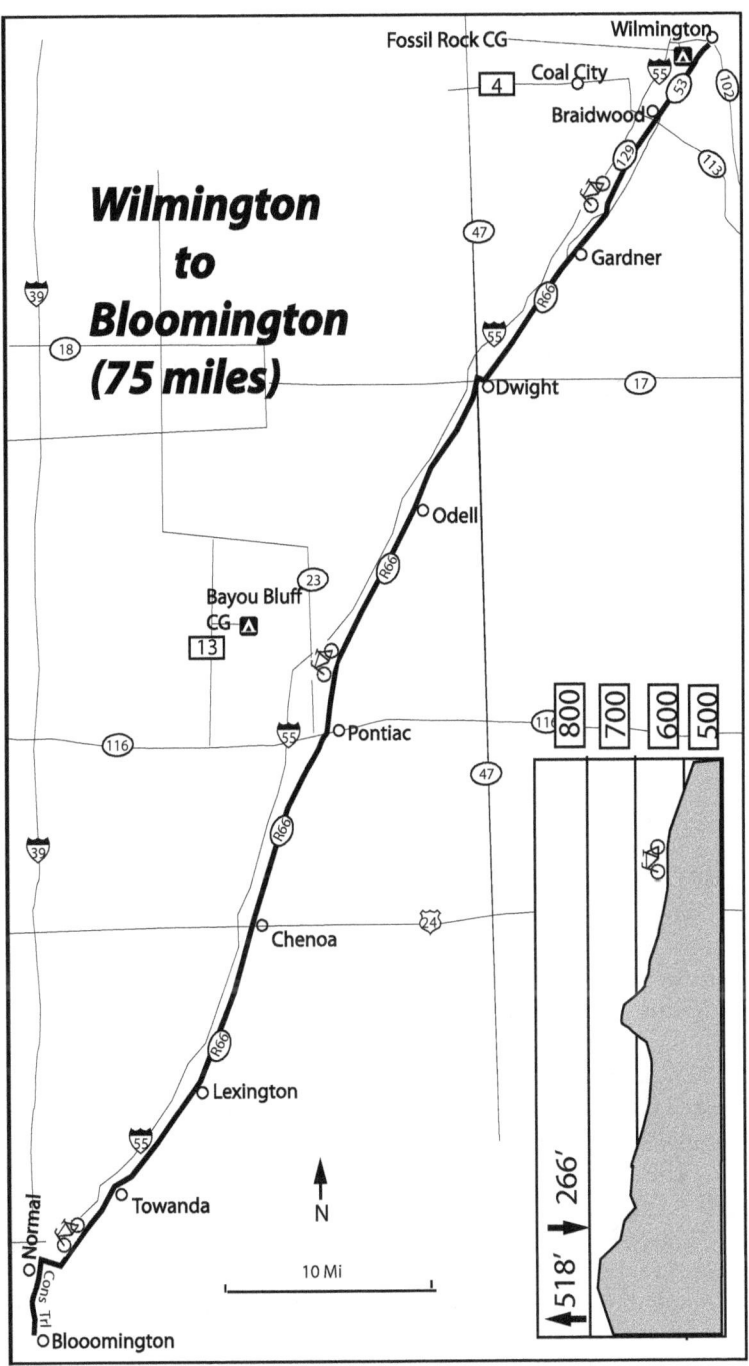

Route 66
SECTION 3

Bloomington, IL to Chatham, IL (72 miles)

Watch for your exit off Constitution Trail because the trail continues on. The exit will be on your left after crossing an overpass. Take the exit, which will parallel the trail a short distance, then turn left on Oakland Ave. Half-a-mile later Oakland Ave. becomes one-way, eastbound cyclists will be using MacArthur Ave.

The Constitution Trail currently ends shortly after you exit it but you will pick it up again a few miles later.

South of Shirley Route 66 takes you past 1920s Funks Grove Pure Maple Sirup Shop (yes, that's the way they spell it). Stop to hear the interesting story of how Iroquois Chief Woksis first discovered this sweet natural concoction. You can also follow the signs to ride about 2 miles off-route to visit the Funks Grove Nature Center, where you will find interpretive trails, a working blacksmith forge the 3rd Saturday of the month, and other nature appreciation/educational related activities.

While riding through Mclean you pass the Dixie Truckers Home, the oldest truck stop in America. Also in Mclean you can stop in front of the Antiques Collectables building for the historic kiosk and a cool metal cutout of a gas station attendant.

Atlanta is another community you might allow time to tour about. Some of the things to see is the 8-sided Public Library with a Seth Thomas hand wound clock tower, Grain Elevator Museum, several nice murals, and the giant Hotdog Man. Another reincarnation of the "Muffler Man", only this one is equipped with a giant hotdog in his grip. Take the time to read the plaque describing the long route the old Paul Bunyon (they seem to enjoy misspelling around here) statue took to reach Atlanta.

The turn for the Camp-a-while campground is less than a mile before reaching Lincoln.

Lincoln has a nice town square, complete with a still operating old movie theater. Stroll around the square to read the interesting plaques and statues associated with the town's namesake (this was the only town to be named for Abe Lincoln before he became

Route 66 Section 3

president). Also check out the phone booth located on the roof of city hall. The booth was installed on this, the highest building in town, during the Cold War as a Civil Defense air raid spotter. Truly a CRA.

Another CRA is the world's largest covered wagon (certified by Guinness World Records), located in front of the Best Western Lincoln Inn. Route 66 is renowned for having the largest, oldest, longest, and any other -est. Think of the old Route 66 as a linear P. T. Barnum Circus.

In Broadwell you pass a plaque commemorating the old Pig Hip Restaurant that opened back in 1937. Shortly following this I encourage cyclists to take a short detour through downtown Elkhart to see another metal cutout. This one is of a waitress serving a small child. You'll need to stop and read who this famous child was that visited the city.

About 2.5 miles south of Sherman turn right on Sand Hill Rd. to reach the Riverside Park Campground.

To properly tour Springfield you'll need a lot more space than I have room for in this book. You can reach the Visitor Center by turning right on E. Jefferson St. then left on S. 7th St. Also, if you continue a couple more blocks beyond the center on S. 7th St. you can visit the Lincoln Home National Historic Site, the only home Lincoln actually owned. Another option for touring Springfield is the Trolley Tours, located 229 West Allen St. There are more Abraham Lincoln related attractions in this town than any other towns or cities in the U.S.

The ride will soon route cyclists past another noteworthy establishment, the 1949 Cozy Dog Drive-Inn, at 2935 S Sixth St. This is where the corndog was invented.

At the intersection 6th St. and St. Joseph St. eastbound cyclists will ride 6th St. following the northbound lanes, then turn right on Myrtle St, and left on 9th St. to rejoin Route 66. I recommend the Route 66 Hotel located at this intersection. It has Route 66 memorabilia and is a great promoter of the Mother Road.

Pedigo Lane dead ends at the Interurban Trail parking lot. Be sure to turn left upon entering the trail. The trail is a nice escape from the busy city environment. It routes cyclists through healthy wetlands and the vegetation provides a buffer from the highway noises. Peaceful.

Camping

Hickory Lane CG
2100 2137th Ave
Atlanta, IL 61723
217-648-2778

Camp-a-while
1779 1250th Ave
Lincoln, IL 62656
217-732-8840
R on Nicholson Rd .8 mile

Riverside Park CG
4105 Sandhill Road
Springfield, IL 62702
217-753-0630
R on Sand Hill Rd .2 mile

Double J CG
9683 Palm Rd
Chatham, IL 62629
217-483-9998

Lodging

Super 8
500 E South St
McLean, IL 61754
309-874-2366

Atlanta Inn
103 Empire St
Atlanta, IL 61723
217-648-2322

*Budget Inn Motel
2011 N Kickapoo St
Lincoln, IL 62656
217-735-1202

Best Western Inn
1750 Fifth St
Lincoln, IL 62656
217-732-9641

Crossroads Motel
1305 Woodlawn Rd
Lincoln, IL 62656
217-735-5571

Flag & Farmstead B&B
500 Old Tipton School Rd
Sherman, IL 62684
217-816-8569

*Route 66 Hotel & Conf
625 E St Joseph St
Springfield, IL 62703
217-529-6626

*The Lodge in Springfield
3751 S 6th St
Springfield, IL 62703
217-529-5511

Super 8 Motel
3675 6th St
Springfield, IL 62703262-
217-529-8898

Bike Shops

Back Alley Bikes
113 Willard Ave
Lincoln, IL 62656
773-743-4201

Velo Mine
301 West Madison Street
Springfield, IL 62761
217-679-2356

Ace Bicycle Shop
2500 S MacArthur Blvd
Springfield, IL 62704
217-523-0188

Route 66 Section 3
Bloomington to Chatham (72 miles)

Miles E/W	Directions	Dist	R	Service	Miles W/E
	*Bloomington (pop 76,610)			GLQR	
0	L after overpass on Oakland Ave	0.4	3		72
0	VR at SS cont Oakland Ave/CR26, EB Oakland Ave joins Macathur Ave	3.1	3	QR	71
4	L at SS on Fox Creek Rd	0.7	3		68
4	R on unsigned Constitution Tr	3.7	P		68
8	*Shirley (pop 378)				64
8	R then L on R66	4.1	3		64
12	*Funks Grove (pop 245)				60
12	S on R66	4.1	3	QR	60
16	*McLean (pop 830)			GLQR	56
16	VL on Steward Rd/R66	0.2	3		56
16	R on Carlisle Rd/R66	0.1	3		56
16	L on Main St/R66	0.1	3	QR	55
17	R on North Rd/R66	0.2	3		55
17	L on SH66	3.9	3		55
21	*Atlanta (pop 1,692)			CGLQR	51
21	R on Arch St	1.7	3		51
22	R on SH66	2.8	3		50
25	*Lawndale (pop 81)				47
25	S on SH66	4.5	3		47
30	L on Kickapoo St/I-56B	1.8	3		42
31	*Lincoln (pop 14,504)			CGLQR	40
31	R on Clinton St	0.2	3		40
32	BL at SS on 5th St	0.8	3	Q	40
32	L on Washington St/Stringer Ave	0.6	4	Q	39
33	L at SS on I-55/Lincoln Pkwy	1.1	3	LQ	39
34	L on frontage Rd/R66	4.4	3		38
39	*Broadwell (pop 145)				33
39	L at SS cont on frontage Rd/R66	3.7	3		33
42	*Elkhart(pop 405)			R	30
42	S cont on frontage Rd/R66	5.5	3		30
48	L on Elm St	0.2	3		24
48	*Williamsville (pop 1,476)			QR	24
48	R on Main St/SR123	0.7	3		24
49	L on Frontage Rd/Outer Rd	4.3	3	Q	23

Route 66 Section 3

Miles E/W	Directions	Dist	R	Service	Miles W/E
53	L at SS on Sudduth Rd	0.3	3		19
53	R at SS on unsigned Sherman Blvd/I-55B	1.0	3		19
54	*Sherman (pop 4,148)			QR	18
54	S at SL on Peoria Rd/I-55B	4.1	4	CQR	18
58	L on Peoria Rd/I-55B/9th St	4.4	4	QR	14
63	*Springfield (pop 116,250)			CGLQR	9
63	R at SL on Laurel St	0.3	4		9
63	L at SL on 5th St/I-55B	1.2	4	GQR	9
64	BR on 6th St	0.7	4	LR	8
65	R at SL on St Joeseph St then L 6th St Frontage Rd	1.3	4	QR	7
66	S at SS on Hazel Dell Rd/Pedigo Ln	0.7	3		6
67	L on Interurban Tr	4.9	P		5
72	*Chatham (pop 11,500)			CQR	0

The latest innovative Cold War Civil Defense air raid spotter.

Route 66 Section 3

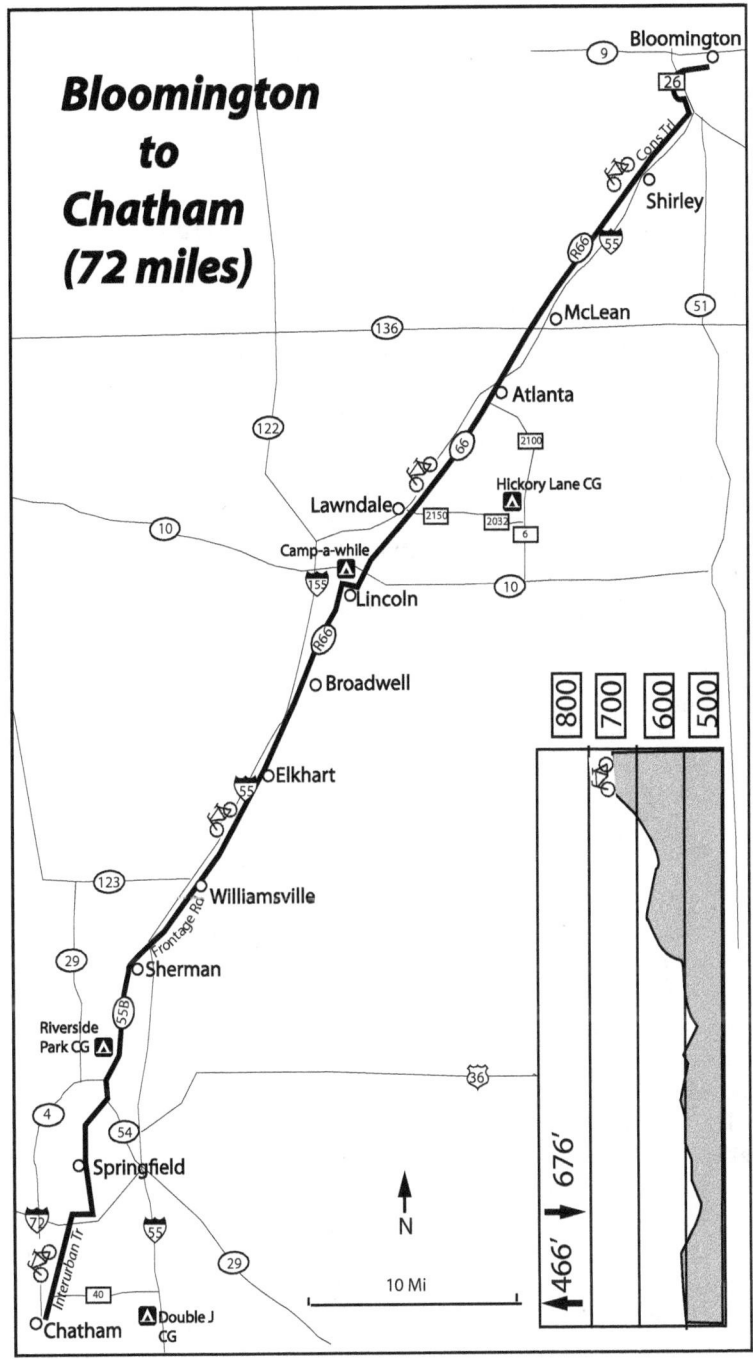

Route 66
SECTION 4

Chatham, IL to Missouri State Line (79 miles)

After leaving Chatham, Route 66 takes you deep into the Illinois rural countryside where in many places your main competition for the highway will be a tractor. There are limited services until reaching Litchfield.

About 8 miles south of Farmersville you pass another CRA, Our Lady of the Highway Shrine. This cararra marble statue of the Virgin Mary was imported from Italy and erected here in 1959 to both honor Mary and ask her assistance guiding travelers safely on their journey. It became a popular attraction as many Route 66 motorists paused to pray for Our Lady to watch over them on their travels. And now she's here to watch over bicycle travelers.

A great place to stop for freshly prepared baklava, while also supporting a member of the Route 66 Hall of Fame, is the Ariston Café in Litchfield. The original restaurant was founded in nearby Carlinville in 1924 by Pete Adam, a Greek immigrant. He relocated it to Litchfield on Route 66 in 1935. It is one of the oldest restaurants on Route 66.

Also in Litchfield, be sure to visit Illinois' Route 66 Hall of Fame, located in the former Vic Suhling Gas for Less station.

When researching this book I found it interesting how, in the same way, Route 66 and Interstate highways influenced the prosperity of the cities they pass through, and how at one time the railroad had a similar impact. Over 150 years ago Litchfield and nearby Hardinsburg were competing to have the railroad pass through their town. Litchfield won out and now you can't even find Hardinsburg on the map. As a side note, however, the citizens of Hardinsburg hedged their bets and built their buildings on skids and wheels, so when they lost they were able to drag them to Litchfield with teams of oxen. Industrious ancestors like these are the ones who made America the great country it is.

In Mt. Olive you can take a short side trip to visit the only union-owned cemetery in the country. The local miner's union purchased the land for the cemetery because no other cemetery in town would allow miners killed in the violent union and law enforcement confrontation known as "Virden Massacre" to be

Route 66 Section 4

buried there. The 22-ft tall pink granite obelisk commemorating Mary Harris "Mother" Jones, the Joan of Arc of the labor union movement, makes the ride worthwhile.

Mt. Olive is also home to another CRA, the restored 1920s Russell Soulsby Shell Station.

Henry's Rabbit Ranch is a must see CRA on your ride through Staunton. I don't want to spoil it for you, but owner, Rich Henry, has found ways to spoof other Route 66 CRAs while using a rabbit theme. Stop off for a visit to see for yourself.

In Staunton, there is a park with restrooms at the start of the Madison County Transit Quercus Grove Trail (MCT). About a mile after this there is break in the trail at State Road 4. The mileage log follows the highway for .6 mile before rejoining the MCT. If you don't mind riding crushed shale, you can continue on across the highway to reach Spangle Rd. and avoid riding on the highway.

In Hamel you pass an old 1930s Roadhouse Grill, currently named Weezy's Route 66 Bar and Grill. The walls are lined with interesting vintage Route 66 memorabilia. This was a regular stop for Al Capone and his gang members. The gangster was a big supporter of Route 66. He wanted good roads for his booze runners.

When the MCT reaches Vandalia St., if you are looking for a place to eat or get supplies, turn right and ride a few blocks to reach downtown Edwardsville.

About half-a-mile into your ride on this segment of the MCT (also called the Nickel Plate Tr. here) the trail passes a trailhead parking lot with restrooms. Just past the trailhead there is another trail off to your right, however you continue straight before bearing left shortly afterward to ride through a tunnel.

Another turn to watch for is the separated 4-lanes of University Drive. There is a paved trail that continues straight prior to this crossing, but you turn right, once across both lanes there is another paved trail leading off to the right, however you continue left here. It's not that complicated once you get there.

Riding Chain of Rocks Rd., when you reach the Canal Bridge, one lane on the bridge is blocked off for bicycles only. Pretty cool.

The Chain of Rocks Canal was built in the early 40s so cargo ships could bypass the 17 miles of rock ledges and shelves extending northeast of St. Louis that were unnavigable during lower water levels. This was the last navigational challenge to overcome on the upper Mississippi River.

After crossing the Canal Bridge you reach one of the main highlights along the entire Route 66. The making of the, now, bicycle/pedestrian crossing is an interesting story. The Chain of Rocks Bridge was built in 1929 to accommodate the increased vehicle traffic as the result of Route 66. The bridge had to be constructed with a 22-degree bend in it to position the foundations around the limited navigable river channels. Operating as a toll bridge the owners filed bankruptcy 1931 and it was then taken over by the town of Madison. Stripped of their tolls when nearby I-274 was built, the bridge was officially closed in 1968. The bridge was scheduled for demolition in 1975, and the only thing that saved it was that the price of scrap metal dropped and the demolition would not pay for itself. Regional bicycle group TrailNet successfully lobbied to have it converted to a bicycle/pedestrian path, and it was reopened 1999.

So, as you pedal across this mile-long architectural wonder be sure to appreciate the history of the bridge. With Route 66 memorabilia lining the bridge, and unique views up and down the Mighty Mississippi, it is a truly unique experience. The bridge provides a close-up view of the massive gothic castle towers built on the downstream side of the river. The first of these stone structures, built in 1890s, was built to pump water into water treatment plants. Tower #2 was built in 1915.

Chain of Rocks Bridge across the Mighty Mississippi River

Route 66 Section 4

Camping

Double J CG
9683 Palm Rd
Chatham, IL 62629
217-483-9998

*MGM Lakeside CG
3133 W Chain of Rocks Rd,
Granite City, IL 62040
618-797-2820

*Kamper Kompanion
18388 E Frontage Rd
Litchfield, IL 62056
217-324-4747

*Trails End RV
3225 W Chain of Rocks Rd
Granite City, IL 62040
618-931-5041

Rustic Acres CG
12246 Binney Rd
New Douglas, IL 62074
217-456-1122
(5 miles off-route)

*KOA Granite City
3157 W Chain of Rocks Rd
Granite City, IL 62040
618-931-5160

Lodging

*Magnuson Grand Hotel
19067 W Frontage Rd
Raymond, IL 62560
217-324-2100

*Super 8-Staunton
1527 Herman Rd
Staunton, IL 62088
618-635-5353

Country Hearth Inn
1013 Plummer D
Edwardsville, IL 62025
618-656-7829

*Quality Inn
1010 East Columbian N Blvd
Litchfield, IL 62056
217-324-9260

Innkeeper Motel Hamel
401 East State Street
Hamel, IL 62046
314-387-3119

*Budget Motel
3220 W Chain of Rocks Rd,
Granite City, IL 62040
618-931-1414

*Super 8 Litchfield
211 Ohren Lane
Litchfield, IL 62056-0281
217-324-7788

* Holiday Inn Express
1000 Plummer Dr
Edwardsville, IL 62025
618-692-7255

*Economy Inn
3228 W Chain of Rocks Rd,
Granite City, IL 62040
618-931-6600

Bike Shops

Wheel Fast Bicycle Co
17 Cottonwood Dr
Chatham, IL 62629
217-483-7807

J & L Blke Shop
303 E Sallee Ave
Litchfield, IL 62056
217-324-3429

Cyclery & Fitness Center
2472 Troy Rd
Edwardsville, IL 62025
618-692-0070

Chatham to Missouri State Line (79 miles)

Miles E/W	Directions	Dist	R	Service	Miles W/E
	*Chatham (pop 11,500)			CQR	
0	L on Walnut St	1.1	4	Q	79
1	R at SL on Gordon Dr	4.6	3		77
6	L on Burnstine Rd	0.7	3		73
6	R on Purdom Rd (unsigned)	0.6	2		72
7	R to cont on Purdom Rd	1.9	2		72
9	L on Ping Rd	1.0	2		70
10	R on Henrietta St	0.5	2		69
10	*Divernon (pop 1,172)				68
10	S on Reichert Rd/R66	8.6	3		68
19	*Farmersville (pop 724)			R	60
19	S at SS on W Frontage Rd	15.1	3	LQ	60
34	L at SS on N 16th Ave	0.2	3		44

33

Route 66 Section 4

Miles E/W	Directions	Dist	R	Service	Miles W/E
34	R on R66/frontage rd	3.4	3		44
38	*Litchfield (6,939)				41
38	S on R66	7.1	3	GLQR	41
45	L on R66 (towards Mt Olive)	1.3	3		34
46	*Mt Olive (2,099)			QR	32
46	S on R66	3.1	3		32
49	L at SS on E Frontage Rd	1.0			29
50	R at SS on Staunton Rd/Main St	2.5	3	LR	28
53	*Staunton (pop 5,139)			CGLQR	26
53	L at SS on Union St	0.4			26
53	S on Madison County Transit (MCT)	1.5	P		25
55	L on SR4		3		24
55	R on Spangle Rd then L on MCT		P		24
55	*Hamel (pop 816)			GLQR	24
55	L on Schroder Ave then R on R66/SR157	0.5	3	R	24
55	L on Trotter Dr then R on MCT	2.5	P		23
58	R on Maple Rd then L on SR157	2.8	3		21
60	R on Hazel Rd	0.3	3		18
61	L on MCT	2.7	P		18
63	L on Vandalia St/SR143 then R at SL on MCT		P		15
63	*Edwardsville (pop 24,293)			GQR	15
63	R on MCT to parallel Springer Ave	0.1	P		15
64	R cont on MCT	1.1	P		15
65	R at intersection with Bryant Ave to cont on MCT	3.0	P		14
68	R to cross University Dr twice then L to cont on MCT	1.6	P		11
69	R on Chain of Rock Rd/R66	4.0	3	LQR	9
73	L on Nameoki Rd/SR203	0.9	4		5
74	R on Chain of Rocks Rd	1.8	4	CLQR	4
76	S to cross Chain of Rocks Canal	0.2	P		3
76	S on Chain of Rocks Rd	1.7	3		2
78	S on Chain of Rocks Bridge	1.0	P		1
79	*Enter Missouri				0

Route 66 Section 4

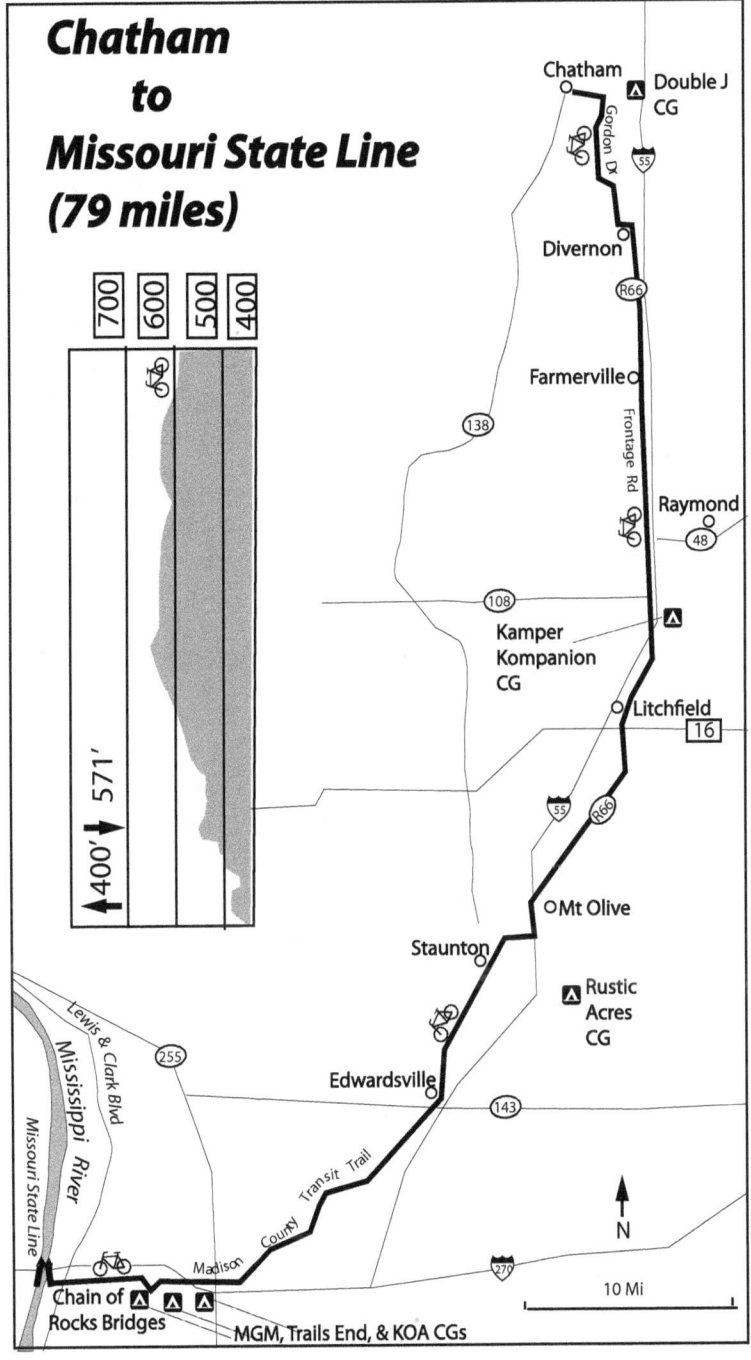

Lake Michigan Trail
SECTION 5

Missouri State Line to Sullivan, MO (90 miles)

Welcome to Missouri, the second state on your Route 66 Adventure.

Once you leave the Chain of Rocks Bridge you will begin riding the Riverfront Trail. Initially it crosses Riverview Drive for a short distance then returns to the riverside, where you will have 9 miles of separated bike trail along the banks and at top the levee of the Mississippi River. It is interesting to see the foreign languages and flags painted on the hull of huge cargo ships from around the world as they cruise along the river to distant destinations.

When the trail ends it drops you off at the base of the world's tallest arch, the 630-foot Gateway Arch in St. Louis. The design for the arch was selected from an open competition. Eero Saarinen's design was selected from the 172 entries in 1948 in large part because it was meant to symbolize the area as the "gateway to westward expansion".

Park your bike on Leonor Sullivan Blvd. to walk up the steep steps leading to the Arch and visit the new visitor center (which was under construction during my last ride through here) to learn more about the history of both the Arch and St. Louis. While you're there, take the tram to the top of the Arch for a fantastic view of the Mississippi River and surrounding area.

Just north of the Arch, on the other side of Eads Bridge (which was the longest bridge in the world at the time of its completion in 1874) you will find a wide selection of interesting restaurants housed in the old downtown district.

If you are a fan of Budweiser beer, when Chouteau Ave. crosses Broadway, you can turn left and ride a couple miles to reach the Anheuser-Busch Brewery (Lynch St. & S 12th St.), which offers tours and tastings. Or you can turn right on Broadway to ride a couple blocks to visit Busch Stadium, home of the Cardinals.

The Forest Park Bike Path is a paved trail that circles 1,300 acre Forest Park, dedicated in 1986 to commemorate the country's 100 years of independence. This is a sweet ride around the park and there are also numerous bike paths crisscrossing the park leading to such attractions as the Missouri History Museum, St. Louis Zoo, the 1904 St. Louis World's Fair Pavilion, several life size bronze statues, and many other interesting sites within the park. Take your time to enjoy this ride through what was once the largest urban park in the country. Another "-est" to add to the growing list of Route 66 credits.

If you are ready for some amusement of an urban variety, turn right on DeBaliviere Ave. and ride half-a-mile to reach "One of the 10 Great Streets in America", the trendy Delmar Loop. This 10 block district is filled with lively entertainment, culture, and fine restaurants.

It isn't until you cross I-270 that you finally begin to leave the St. Louis congestion behind. Manchester, Winchester, and Ballwin kind of all blend in together to form one long megatropolis of strip malls and businesses.

Ignore the Route 66 sign that turns left in Ellisville, our version of Route 66 continues straight here on Manchester Avenue. Shortly after this, State Road 100, which you have been following for a while, continues straight, but you will turn left to continue riding on Manchester Avenue, where you will finally escape the big city sprawl.

As Woods Ave. comes to an end and you turn left onto State Road 109, there is a paved bike path that parallels the road. You can ride this; however you will need to switch onto the highway after about a mile so you don't miss the Alt Rd. turn.

On Forby Rd. you pass a park with restrooms and picnic tables where you can take a break to celebrate putting the big city behind you.

In Eureka, at the turn onto 5th St., you can continue straight on N. Central Ave. to reach Route 66 State Park. This is about a 6-mile ride round trip. The park has hiking trails, a visitor center housed in the old 1936 roadhouse Bridgehead Inn, and other Route 66 memorabilia.

You pass The Six Flags amusement park on 5th Street. There are motels and camping listed in the guidebook that are near if you want to visit the park for an adrenalin fix.

Plan a stop to admire the towering sandstone bluffs that line Route 66 as you enter Pacific. The deep caves in the hillside are from mining that took place back in the 1870s, when the bluff's silica sand was popular for making fine glassware. Pictures of these bluffs were a common scene on many Route 66 postcards. The car wash with the old Beacon Motel neon sign is a good place to view the bluffs.

South of Pacific you begin riding through the foothills of the Ozark Mountains. Keep your eyes out for even more Meramec Caverns advertisements. There are over 5,400 registered caves in Missouri; however thanks to the promotional efforts of Lester Dil, this set of caves is by far the most well-known. Dil drove across the country offering to paint farmers' barns free of charge, if he could advertise the caverns on the roof or sides of the barns. He also invented the bumper sticker to promote the caverns. His campaign paid off, for Meramec Caverns averages over 150,000 visitors annually.

If you have the time, take a side trip in St. Claire to visit the St. Clair Historical Museum. It is housed in the 1899 Odd Fellows building, and has over 32 exhibits which offer a glimpse of the past, from a recreated old general store to a large display of Victorian undergarments from the 1880-1910 eras. Oh, how the times have changed.

Finally, after reading the advertisements for miles, in Stanton you get the chance to visit Meramec Caverns. It is about a 3-mile ride to reach the caverns. There is also a campground and motel in the area, both listed in the guidebook.

Called Missouri's Buried Treasure, this is the largest commercial cave in the state. Between the beautiful colorful underground formations and the guided ranger led tours, this is a very worthwhile stop, and another CRA.

On County Road K in Oak Grove Valley, you have another chance to visit a cave at Fisher Cave. This cave is about a 3-mile ride off-route, and it is located in Meramec State Park. There is also camping at the park. This is another of Missouri's great natural underground wonders, and offers Naturalist-led tours.

Route 66 Section 5

Camping

Yogi Bear's Jellystone CG
5300 Fox Creek Rd
Eureka, MO 63025
636-938-5925
.5 mile from Six Flags

Meramec KOA
74 Highway W
Stanton, MO 63079
573-927-5215

*Historic Route 66 KOA
18475 Old Us Hwy 66
Eureka, MO 63025
636-257-3018
1 mile from Six Flags

*Native Experience Eco CG
1451 E Springfield Rd
Sullivan, MO 63080
573-468-8750

*Pine Oak RV CG & Cabins
1302 State Hwy AT
Villa Ridge, MO 63089
636-451-5656

Meramec State Park
670 Fisher Cave Drive
Sullivan, MO 63080
573-468-6519

Lodging

America's Best Value Inn
1100 N 3rd St
St. Louis, MO 6310
314-421-6556

*Trends Motel
15652 Manchester Rd
Ellisville, MO 63011
636-391-1500

*Gardenway Motel
2958 MO-100
Villa Ridge, MO 63089
636-742-4388

Meramec Caverns Motel
1135 Route W
Stanton, MO 63079
573-468-3166

Hampton Inn-Downtown
333 Washington Ave
St. Louis, MO 63102
314-621-7900

*Super 8
1733 W 5th St
Eureka, MO 63025
636-938-4368
.5 mile from Six Flags

Super 8 St Clair
1010 S Outer Road
St Clair, MO 63077
(636) 629-8080

Baymont Inn
275 N Service Rd
Sullivan, MO
573-860-3333

*The Cheshire
6300 Clayton Rd
St. Louis, MO 63117
314-647-7300

*Quality Inn
1400 W Osage St
Pacific, MO 63069
636-257-8400

Budget Lodging
866 S Outer Rd W
St Clair, MO 63077
636-629-1000

*Comfort Inn
736 S Service Rd W
Sullivan, MO 63080
573-468-7800

Bike Shops

Urban Shark Bicycle Co
1009 Locust St
St. Louis, MO 63101
314-881-0322
(close to OIT)

REI
1703 S Brentwood Blvd
Brentwood, MO 63144
314-918-1004

Big Shark Bicycle Company
6133 Delmar Blvd
St. Louis, MO 63112
314-862-1188

*Maplewood Bicycle
7534 Manchester Rd
Maplewood, MO 63143
314-781-9566

Mesa Cycles
1035 S Big Bend Blvd
St. Louis, MO 63117
314-645-4447

West County Cycles
51 Clarkson Rd
Ellisville, MO 63011
636-227-7266

Route 66 Section 5
Missouri State Line to Sullivan (90 miles)

Miles E/W	Directions	Dist	R	Service	Miles W/E
	*Enter Missouri				
0	L on Riverfront Tr	10.6	P		90
11	*St Louis (pop 319,294)	0.0		GLQR	79
11	S on Lewis St/Leonor Sullivan Blvd	1.4	2		79
12	R on Chouteau Ave/SR100	3.2	5		78
15	BL at SL then BR to remain on Chouteau Ave	0.6	5		75
16	R on bike path to crossover I64	0.8	P		74
17	L on Clayton Ave	0.1	P		73
17	R on Forest Park Bike Tr (FPT) after passing under overpass.	3.4	P		73
20	R on Clayton Rd	0.3	4	LR	70
20	L at SL on Bellevue Ave	1.4	3		70
22	R on Manchester Ave/SR100/R66	7.2	5	GQR	68
29	S on Manchester Ave/SR100 over I270	8.1	4	GQR	61
37	*Ellisville (pop 9,133)			LGQR	53
37	S on Manchester Ave/SR100	1.3	3	QR	53
38	L at SL on Manchester Ave	1.7	3	GQR	52
40	L on Woods Ave	1.5	3		50
42	L at SS on SR109	1.4	3		48
43	R on Alt Rd	2.0	3		47
45	L at SS on Forby Rd	0.8	3		45
46	BL on North St	0.2	3		44
46	R at SS on N Central Ave (unsigned)	0.3	3		44
46	R at SL on 5th St	2.9	4	GLQR	44
49	*Eureka (pop 10,189)			CGLQR	41
49	L at SL on Six Flags Rd to cross I-44	0.2	3	CQ	41
49	R on I-44B/R66/Osage St	4.3			41
54	*Pacific (pop 7,002)			GLQR	36
54	S on Osage St/R66/I-44B	5.0	3	Q	36
59	S at SS on SR100	2.0	3	Q	31
61	S at SL on SR Alt	0.2	3	Q	29
61	BL cont SR Alt	4.5	3	C	29
65	S at SS on Outer Rd (cross SR50)	4.9	3		25
70	L on R66 to cross I-44	0.2	3	Q	20
71	R at SS on Commercial Ave/R66	3.2	3		20

Route 66 Section 5

Miles E/W	Directions	Dist	R	Service	Miles W/E
74	* St Clair (pop 4,724)			GQR	16
74	R at SL on SR30/R66	0.2	3	Q	16
74	R at SS on SR30/R66 to cross over I-44	0.3	3		16
74	L at SS on R66	8.5	3	G	16
83	L at SS on SR W to cross I-44	0.1	3		7
83	*Stanton (pop 34)			CLQR	7
83	R on Service Rd/Springfield Rd	5.2	3	GQR	7
88	*Oak Grove Village (pop 509)			CGLQR	2
88	S on Springfield Rd	2.0	3		2
90	*Sullivan (pop 7,081)			CGLQR	0

The Gateway to Westward Expansion.

Route 66 Section 5

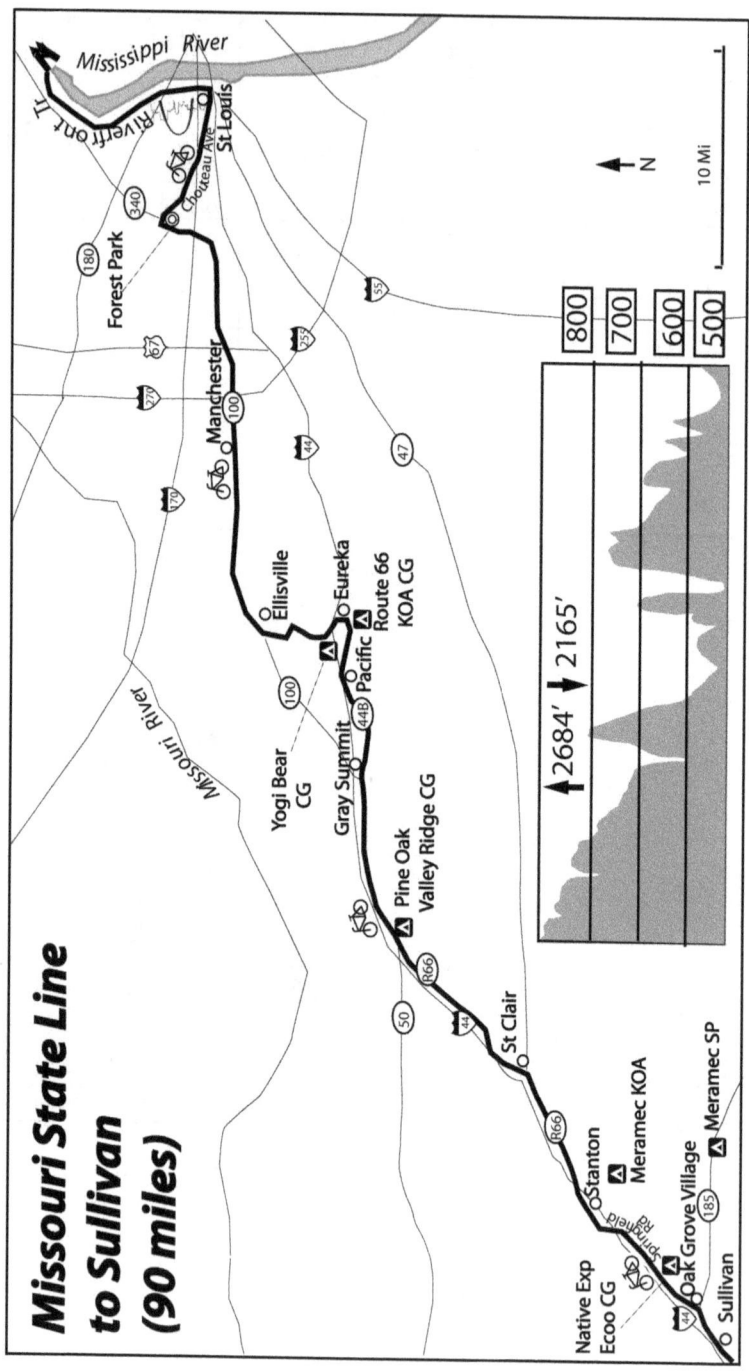

Route 66
SECTION 6

Sulllivan, MO to Gascozark, MO (83 miles)

When riding through Bourbon check out the water tower. Their claim to fame is their tower is the largest bourbon container in the world. Clever.

On the stretch south of Bourbon you pass Belmont Winery. They have an outdoor dining area that makes for a nice setting to sample their wares. Thursday through Sunday they also serve pizza.

Cuba is the "Route 66 Mural City". It makes for a nice tour. They did a good job highlighting some of the town's history with these street paintings, capturing visits by famous celebrities such as Betty Davis and Amelia Earhart, plus scenes of the area's involvement in the Civil War.

Yes, even celebrities drove Route 66. Reading newspaper accounts of a Betty Davis or Clark Gable megastar spotting on the highway lured people to get out and drive the Mother Road. True, at that time it was the best thoroughfare to reach cross country destinations, however, Route 66 became a destination of its own. Everyone wanted to see what all the fanfare was about.

If it fits your schedule, rent a room at the recently remodeled Wagon Wheel Motel before beginning your mural tour. The motel is classic Route 66, with the retro neon sign and individual stone cottages distributed about the courtyard behind it. And after completing the mural tour you can have dinner at Hick's BBQ, right next door to the motel. It will make for a relaxing end of a day of cycling.

South of Cuba you get to experience another Route 66 "largest". The World's Largest Rocking Chair. This thing is so large that when I was cycling past, the structure didn't even register as being the rocking chair I was looking for. I mean this thing is huge, and truly is another CRA.

You pass several wineries on your ride through the Ozarks. The history of grape growing in Missouri dates back to Native Americans. In the early 1800s German immigrants expanded cultivation of grapes and began establishing the state's first wineries. Also, the Civil War exposed German soldiers to the area. Many were so impressed with the wooded hilly countryside they returned to settle down. Before Prohibition, Missouri was the second-largest wine-producing state in the nation. Currently it ranks 8th, but has experienced a big boom in recent years.

Your ride will take you by the largest vineyard in the state, St. James Winery, located at 540 State Route B, in St. James, MO. Stop and pay them a visit to sample their latest awarding winning wines.

In Rolla, while riding past the Missouri University of Science and Technology campus, on Bishop Avenue, keep your eye out to the east for a unique structure, Stonehenge. This 160 ton partial reconstruction of the ancient megalith incorporates many facets of the original structure and a couple of features that even the original structure lacked. In 1984 the National Society of Professional Engineers granted the school one of its annual outstanding engineering accomplishment awards for the structure. Science minded cyclists will want to stop to test the functionality of the structure.

Continue riding Bishop Avenue a few more blocks and turn east on 10th St to see the schools Millennium Arch. The intricate cuts in the thick granite of both this piece and Stonehenge were accomplished using waterjets that were developed by the school itself, with pressure of 15,000 tons psi.

Between Rolla and Springfield, Route 66 roughly follows the same route as the Cherokee Trail of Tears.

In case you were wondering, the answer is yes, the town of Doolittle was named after air-racer and WWII hero Jimmy Doolittle. The unincorporated town grew up as a result of the construction of nearby Fort Leonard Wood in 1941. This was a time when General Doolittle was helping turn the tide of the war, so when they decided to incorporate the town the suggested name was well received. In 1946, Lt. General Jimmy Doolittle himself spoke at the town's dedication.

As I stated earlier, I do not advocate stealth camping, however for those who do, following Newburg the Mark Twain National Forest offers many opportunities.

When you reach the turn on Teardrop Road, you have the option to save a few miles cycling by remaining on State Road Z, because Teardrop Road will rejoin Z later. However you will miss a pair of true CRAs.

The first is Elbow Inn, Bar & BBQ. This place is warehouse

of interesting stories, as the hundreds of brassieres hanging from the ceiling attests to. There is outdoor seating and a stage for live music. It would be a great place to hang out to eat some pretty good BBQ, drink a couple beers, and then find a place to stealth camp on the banks of the Big Piney River. The building for the Elbow Inn dates back to 1929, when it housed the Munger Moss Sandwich Shop.

The old steel bridge across Big Piney River is the other CRA. When Route 66 first came through this area the planning commission utilized many existing highways, like this bridge across the river. However when the country began beefing up the infrastructure to prepare for the WWII war effort, they realized the sharp turn on the approach to the bridge would be a hazard, so they straightened out the road and bypassed the Elbow. But it's a cool old bridge, well worth a looksee.

On your approach into Waynesville, watch for Frog Rock on the west side of the highway. This is a rock formation that has been chiseled into the shape of a frog and painted. The locals have named the structure W. H. Croaker and have the Frogtoberfest each autumn to celebrate the rock.

If you are looking for a place to stop and stretch your legs, Waynesville offers several interesting sites to visit. The 1850s Old Stagecoach Stop Museum has 10 rooms and each room is restored to reflect a different usage the building has had during its history. Also, just prior to crossing the interesting 1923 five span bridge over Roubidoux Creek, there is a park to the left with a memorial marking the location of Cherokee encampments during the Trail of Tears. The park has a one-mile trail with exhibits telling more about the event.

FYI, the turn for the Roubidoux Creek Campground listed in the book is to your right immediately after crossing the bridge.

If you pay close attention on your approach to Gascozark you should be able to see the remains of the 1930s Gascozark Service Station & Café on highway left. It is pretty overgrown with weeds and vines, but you can still see enough of the rock facing to get a feel of what it must have once looked like. The same person, Frank Allison Jones, who built this service station, also built the Gasconade Hills Resort Campground and Cabins listed in the guidebook. Frank was an industrious man and led a very interesting life. Perhaps they will share some stories with you at the resort.

You know, sometimes these Route 66 ruins say more to me than a restored business.

Route 66 Section 6

Check out how small my bike is compared to The Chair!

Camping

Ladybug RV & CG
355 SR F
Cuba, MO 65453
573-885-3622
(may be closed)

*Roubidoux Springs CG
Revere Ln
Waynesville, MO
573-774-6171

Gasconade Hills Resort CG
28425 Spring Road
Richland, MO 65556
573-765-3044
(1.5 mile off route)

Lodging

Budget Inn Motel
55 Highway C
Bourbon, MO 65441
573) 732-4080

*Hampton Inn Rolla
2201 N Bishop Ave
Rolla, MO 65401
(573) 308-1060

*Super 8 St Robert
107 McKinnon St
St Robert, MO 65584
573-451-2888

* Wagon Wheel Motel
901 E Washington BVD
Cuba, MO 65453
573-885-3411

*Sunset Inn Rolla
1201 Kingshighway
Rolla, MO 6540
573-364-4156

*All Star Inn
1057 Old Rte 66
St Robert, MO 65584
800-953-2506

*Economy Inn
102 N Outer Rd
St James, MO 65559
573-265-3256

*Days Inn St. Robert
14125 State Hwy Z,
St Robert, MO 65584
573-336-5556

*Fort Wood Inn Suites
25755 MO-17,
Waynesville, MO 65583
573-774-3670
$39 a night

Bike Shops

Route 66 Bicycles
509 W 5th St
Rolla, MO 65401
573-368-3001

Route 66 Section 6
Sullivan to Gascozark (83 miles)

Miles E/W	Directions	Dist	R	Service	Miles W/E
0	*Sullivan (pop 7.081)			CGLQR	83
0	S a SS on Springfield Rd/Service Rd/R66	4.8	3	GLQR	83
5	*Bourbon (pop 1,632)			GLQR	79
5	S on Chestnut St/R66/CR508	11.3	3	R	79
16	*Cuba (pop 3,356)			CGLQR	67
16	S on Washington Blvd/R66	3.6	3		67
20	S on CR Zz/CR U/ CR Kk/James Blvd	9.9	3		64
30	*St James (pop 3,700)			GLQR	54
30	R at SL on Jefferson St/SR8	0.5	3	GQR	54
30	L at SL on Parker Ln then R on Outer Rd/R66	8.3	3	LQR	53
38	*Northwye				45
38	L at SS on Bishop Ave/US63		4	LQR	45
38	*Rolla (pop 19,559)				45
38	R at SL on Kingshighway/I-44B/R66	0.8	4	LQR	45
39	Exit traffic circle on Martin Springs Dr/CR7100/Eisenhower St	5.5	3	LQR	44
45	*Doolittle (pop 630)			QR	39
45	L at SS on Truman St/SR T/Main St	2.4	3		39
47	*Newburg (pop 470)				36
47	L on Front St	0.1	3		36
47	R on SR T (cross RR)	0.3	3		36
48	R on SR P	8.4	3		36
56	R at SS on SR J	0.6	3		28
57	L on SR Z/R66	3.0			27
60	L on Teardrop Rd	0.3			24
60	*Devil's Elbow (pop 289)			R	24
60	BR to cont Teardrop Rd	1.6	3	LQR	24
61	L at SS on SR Z/R66/I-44B unsigned	3.8	3	LQR	22
65	*St Robert (pop 4,340)			GLQR	18
65	S at SL on I-44B/R66	2.3	4		18
68	*Waynesville (pop 4,630)			CGLQR	16
68	S on I-44B/SR 17/R66	6.2	3	LQR	16
74	L at SS on SR17/R66 to cross I-44	0.2	3		10
74	BR on SR17/SR AB/R66	3.3	3	Q	10
77	S on SR AB/R66	6.2	3	C	6
83	*Gascozark				0

Route 66 Section 6

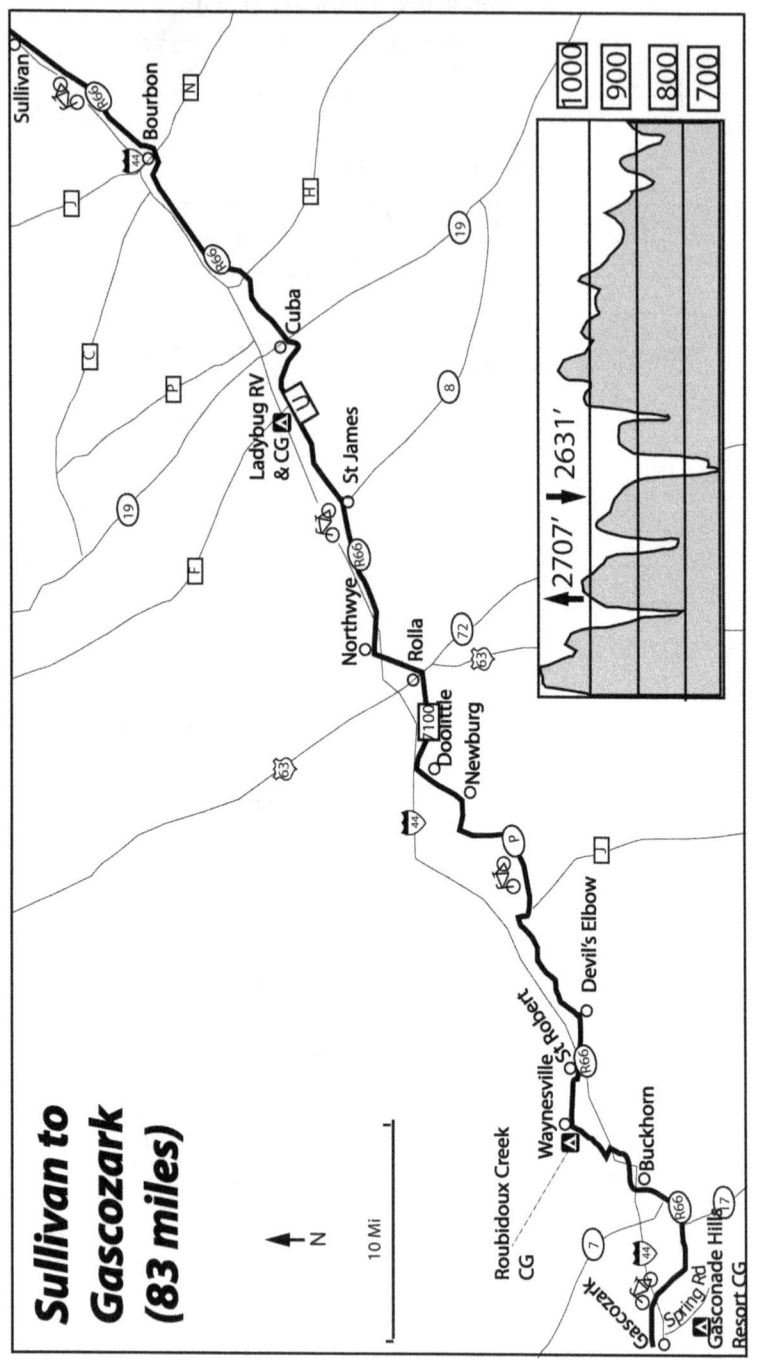

Route 66
SECTION 7

Gasozark, IL to Halltown, IL (94 miles)

There is a convenience store and restaurant in Gascozark, but you'll have to cross over to the other side of the interstate to reach them. It's less than a half mile off-route.

In case you were wondering where the unusual name Gascozark came from, a creative developer in the 1920s came up with it by combining the Gasconade River, which flows through the area, and the Ozark mountains. Mystery solved.

As your ride takes you across the interstate on State Road F, if you turn right on Garden Crest Road and ride less than a mile, you can visit an interesting shop, Ballhagen's Puzzles. Even if you aren't a jigsaw puzzle fan this is an interesting stop. With almost 3,000 puzzles there's bound to be something that interest you, like maybe one of the dozen or so Route 66 related puzzles. It would make a nice souvenir of your ride. Just have them mail it home for you. They have over 250 finished puzzles displayed on the ceiling, including a 7,500 piece New York City puzzle. The people who put this one together were way more patient than I am.

If you plan to stay in this area I highly recommend the Munger Moss Motel in Lebanon. It is a nice motel at a reasonable price, and the owner has been great supporter of Route 66 for many years.

Just down the road from Munger's is another Route 66 landmark, Wrink's Food Market. It was opened in 1950 by Glen Wrinkle.

Lebanon also has a Route 66 Museum housed in its library, at 915 South Jefferson. They have recreated a vintage service station inside the building, complete with gas pumps and 1950s automobiles.

There is a wide selection of places to stay and eat in Lebanon but not much afterwards until you reach Marshfield.

However, on this stretch you will bag another Route 66 "largest". When you cross over I-44 on State Road C you'll pass The World's Largest Gift Store. I was glad I stopped when I saw the huge selection of caramel corn. They had every flavor you could think

Route 66 Section 7

of to choose from, and they are coming up with new flavors all the time. Plus there is a candy factory. And you can eat all you want, because you'll burn off the calories riding your bike all day.

The tourist center is across the street from the gift store.

Marshfield's claim to fame is that it is the home of Edwin Hubble, the American astronomer who the Hubble Space Telescope was named after. They even have an interesting ¼ scale replica of the telescope erected in front of the town's courthouse in his honor.

As you leave Marshfield there is a nice shoulder to ride on. But you soon lose it because they cut the shoulder up with rumble strips. I think the rumble strips would be better positioned in the center of the highway to help avoid head on collisions. Located on the shoulder they are a pain in the butt, literally, for cyclists.

The rolling hills tend to taper off towards the end of this section, as Route 66 reaches the western edge of the Ozark Plateau. The hills are not very tall in the Ozarks, but they will wear on your legs after a while.

Springfield is known as the "Birthplace of Route 66", because it was here, on April 30, 1926 that officials first proposed the name of the new Chicago-to-Los Angeles highway. Your Route 66 ride takes you right past Park Central Square where there is a placard commemorating the city as such.

On your ride into Springfield you pass another CRA, Steak'n Shake. This is a classic 60s style drive-in restaurant, whose franchise has been around over 80 years. The steak in the name comes from the prime cuts of meat they grind for their burgers, and their shakes are hand dipped milk shakes, prepared the old fashioned way.

If you turn right on Jefferson Avenue and ride about 2 miles, you'll reach a unique attraction, the Jefferson Avenue Footbridge. This is a 562-foot long pedestrian bridge, built in 1902, that crosses 13 sets of railroad tracks. It is pretty cool to cross this and watch all the train activity on the tracks. Plus it's the "longest" footbridge in the United States. Another one of those, "You don't get a chance to do this everyday", things.

The route through Springfield, also takes cyclist past one of the city's most recognizable buildings, the Abou Ben Adhem Shrine Mosque. At the time of its construction in 1923, it was the largest auditorium west of the Mississippi River. With its bright terracotta turrets you can't miss it.

And then there's the Bass Pro Shops Outdoor World. It's an outdoors enthusiast's shopping paradise. The 140,000 gallon game fish aquarium and four-story waterfall alone make it worth a looksee. To get there, turn left on Campbell Ave, after circling Park Central Square, and ride for a couple miles to 1935 S. Campbell Ave. While you are there you can also visit World of Wildlife, at 500 West Sunshine St. next door.

It would take too long to cover all of the attractions in Springfield. If you would like to gather more information on the area, stop at the Visitor Center 815 E. St. Louis to learn more.

A little over halfway between Springfield and Halltown, your ride will take you past the remains of a two story stone building on the west side of the highway. This is the Plano Ghost Town, and the cool building is the roofless ivy covered remains of a 1902 general store, built by John Jackson and his family. The store was located on the first floor and the family lived upstairs. The upstairs also had a large room for local gatherings.

Across the highway from the old general store is a building that was once the Tydol gas station. It is has since been converted into a residence.

When the I-44 was built the town went extinct.

Classic 60s style drive-in, still serving up great food.

Camping

Happy Trails RV Park
18376 Campground Rd
Phillipsburg, MO 65722
417-532-3422
(1/2 mile off route)

KOA Route 66 Springfield
5775 W Farm Rd 140
Springfield, MO 65802
417-831-3645
(2 miles off route)

Lodging

*Munger Moss Motel
1336 E Route 66
Lebanon, MO 65536
417-532-3111

*Historic Route 66 Inn
1710 W Elm St
Lebanon, MO 65536
417-532-3128

*Americas Best Value Inn
1830 W Elm St
Lebanon, MO 65536
417-532-3133

Plaza Motel
113 State Hwy W
Marshfield, MO 65706
417-859-2491

Holiday Inn Express
1301 Banning Street
Marshfield, MO
417-859-6000

Super 8 Stafford
315 Chestnut St
Strafford, MO 65757
417-736-3883

*Holiday Inn Express & Suites
1117 E St Louis St,
Springfield, MO
417-862-0070

*Redwood Motel
211 S Market Ave
Springfield, MO 65806
417-350-1234

*Best Western
4445 W Chestnut Expy
Springfield, MO 65802
417-799-2200

Bike Shops

Queen City Cycles
301 W Walnut St
Springfield, MO 65806
417-831-0800

Kingdom Coffee & Cycles
3811 W Chestnut Expy
Springfield, MO 65802
417-864-5988

Sunshine Bike Shop
1926 E Sunshine St
Springfield, MO 65804
417-883-1113

Route 66 Section 7

Gascozark to Halltonw (94 miles)

Miles E/W	Directions	Dist	R	Service	Miles W/E
	*Gascozark				
0	S on Heartwood Rd/R66/Glacier Point Rd	11.3	3	Q	94
11	R on SR F to cross I-44		3		83
11	L on Pecos Dr/R66	3.3	3		83
15	BR on Seminole Ave	1.0	3		80
16	*Lebanon (pop 14,474)			L	79
16	R at SL on ElmSt/I-44B/R66	3.0	4	LQ	79
19	R at SL on SR W/R66	9.2	3	C	76
28	L on SR C to cross I-44	0.3	3	Q	66
28	*Phillipsburg (pop 202)				66
28	R on SR CC/R66	17.4	3	LQR	66
46	*Marshfield (pop 6,633)			GLQR	49
46	S on Hubble Dr/R66	0.8	3	GQ	49
46	R at SL on Washington Ave/SR 38	0.1	3		48
46	BL at SL on Washington Ave/SR OO/R66	13.1	3	GQR	48
60	*Strafford (pop 2,358)			LQR	35
60	L on Peachtree Ln/SR 125/R66	2.9	3		35
62	R on Division St/SR YY/R66	4.8	3		32
67	L on Eastgate Ave	0.9	3		27
68	R at SS on Chestnut Exp/US 65B to ride under overpass	2.2	4	QR	26
70	L at SL on Glenstone Ave/US65B	0.3	4	R	24
71	*Springfield (pop 159,498)			GLQR	24
71	R at SL on St Louis St/R66/Park Central	1.7	4	GLQR	24
72	S on College St	1.1	4	Q	22
73	L at SL on Chestnut Exp/I-44B/SR266/R66	20.8		QR	21
94	*Halltown (pop 173)			Q	0

53

Route 66 Section 7

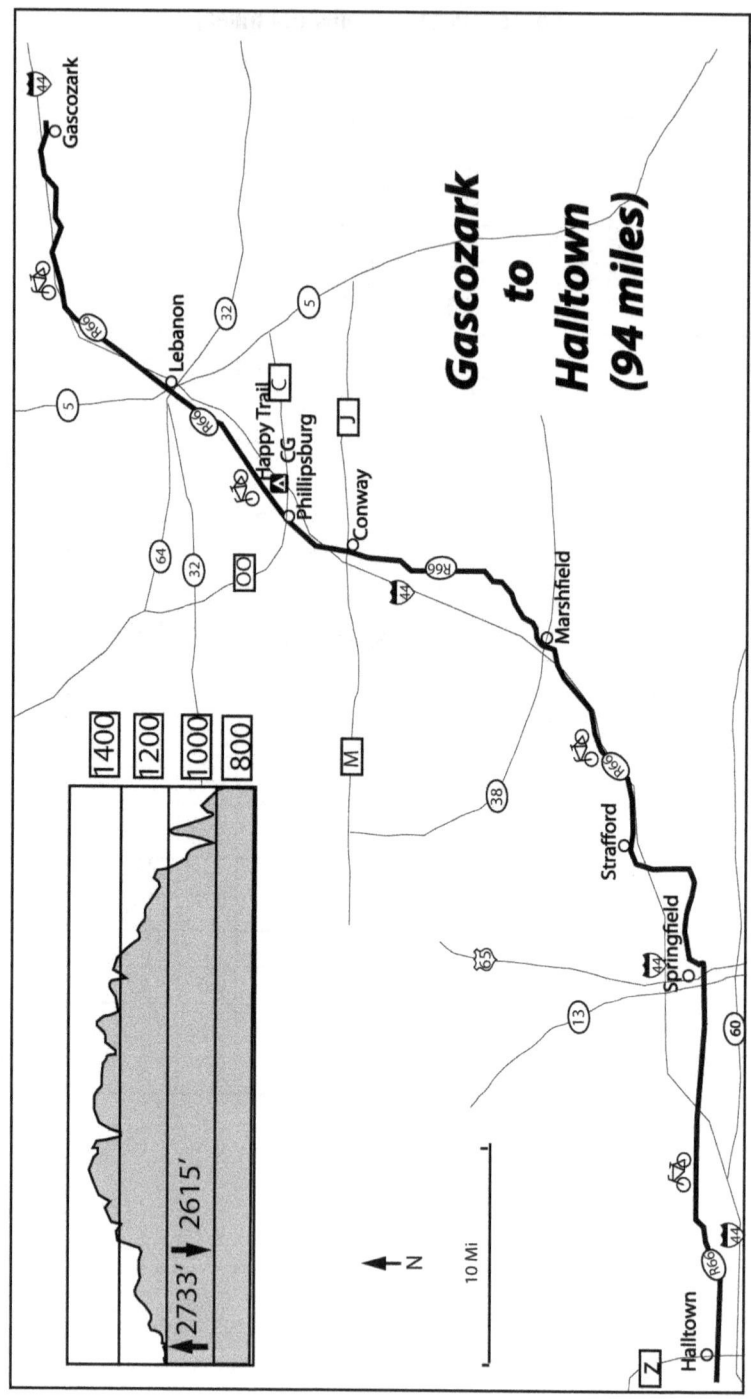

Route 66
SECTION 8

Halltown, MO to Baxter Springs, KS (85 miles)

Shortly into this stretch you'll pass another CRA, Gary's Gay Parita Sinclair Gas Station. Even though this looks like an authentic station motorists would have visited along Route 66, this is actually a replica of the one that was built here in 1930. The original station was built by Fred and Gay Mason. That station burned down in 1955. It was later rebuilt by Gary Turner, and became a favorite stop of many Route 66 travelers.

There have been many stories recorded by visitors about their stop at the station and their visit with Gary. He had a wealth of information about Route 66 and was more than willing to share this with travelers over a soft drink.

Gary has passed away, however the station is still in great condition and worth a stop.

Not much happening on the first part of this section, just some nice bicycling across the Missouri countryside. You've left the rolling hills of the Ozark Mountains behind and it will be pretty flat all the way to the Rockies.

As you are approaching Carthage there is an interesting side trip you can take to Red Oak II. Back in 1987 Lowell Davis began buying up buildings in the small town of Red Oak, where he grew up, and moving them 20 some miles away to his farm. He felt that life was a lot simpler in the 1930s and he wanted to capture that period and preserve it for others to enjoy.

The town includes a blacksmith shop where Lowell's great-grandfather once worked, a schoolhouse, general store, a cemetery, along with other businesses and homes of that period. Davis himself lives here in the house where lady-outlaw Belle Starr grew up. Plus there are several pieces of original art structures made by Davis himself. Stop for a stroll to get a glimpse of life during simpler times.

To reach Red Oak II, instead of bearing left on Esterly Drive, continue on Highway 66 another .2 miles, then turn right on County Road 120 to ride a mile, then left on Kafir Road about .2 miles and it will be on your left.

On your approach into Carthage, Kellogg Lake Park is a nice

place to stop for a break. There are restrooms and picnic tables. Esterly Drive will also route you past Spring River. As the name would suggest, this is a spring fed stream, and the cold water makes for a refreshing break from the Missouri heat in the summer.

This area is renowned its limestone mines. The rock is so hard that it can be polished into a beautiful finish called "Carthage Marble". You will see a lot of this impressive stone in many of the houses and businesses on your ride through Carthage. The Jasper County Courthouse is a great example. With its medieval castle features that include turrets, towers, and arches, this interesting 1894 structure is the 2nd most photographed building in Missouri. This is a must see.

Carthage was pretty much destroyed by guerilla warfare during the Civil War; however the period following the war was a very prosperous one for the city. Much of the fine Victorian architecture present today is the result of this opportunistic timing.

There is a lot to see here, either by foot or from the seat of your bike. Stop off at the Chamber of Commerce Visitor Center, located at 402 S. Garrison Street, for a visitor's guide to help you plan your tour. At the right turn onto Oak Street, just continue on Garrison Street another block and the center is on your left. While you are there, you should also get directions to reach the courthouse, which is only a couple blocks away. Also check out the

Rainbow Bridge is the sole surviving bridge of this type on entire Route 66.

Route 66 Section 8

Carthage Underground. The underground mines stretch all the way to Joplin.

As you are leaving Carthage be sure to stop to admire the still operating 66 Drive-In theater. This was built in 1949, closed in 1985, then reopened 1998. It brought back many fond memories for me of loading up in the family car as a kid to go to the movies.

In Carterville, with all the stone homes, you will once again be reminded that this is a major rock quarry mining district.

Webb City is also helping to preserve the Route 66 theme with a 30s movie theater, The Bradbury Bishop Deli, the King Jack Park, a gas station converted to visitor center, and great displays of murals, located both on exterior and interior walls throughout the city.

As you are riding through Joplin on 2nd Street, be sure to turn down Main Street for a look at the city's impressive downtown. If you are in need of a chocolate fix, turn left off Main Street onto 5th Street, then ride 3 blocks to 510 Kentucky Avenue to the Candy House Gourmet. You can watch them make the sweet concoctions right there in the shop. They also have a lot of Route 66 theme candies. My favorite souvenirs while touring are the ones I can eat.

You can stop at the tourist information center, located at 602 South Main Street, for more information about things to see in the area.

You enter the third state of your Route 66 Adventure on a bumpy county road. It feels like you're sneaking into Kansas.

Your first stop is going to be the really cool town of Galena. This place is all about Route 66. The "Cars on the Route" is an old service station that has been converted into a deli and Route 66 memorabilia. But their claim to fame is the "Tow Tater" truck parked outside the building that inspired the character "Tow Mater" from the movie Cars. Stop to grab a snack and visit with the owners. They are a wealth of information about the Cars movie and Route 66, and they seem to enjoy sharing this with visitors.

The entire town is a CRA with the murals, Route 66 Howard "Pappy" Litch Park (with restrooms and picnic tables), the Will Rogers Highway memorial, and an alleged former bordello.

Just after leaving the traffic circle onto Beasley Road you pass an interesting roadside kiosk. There are several displays telling the interesting history of the area that make it well worth a stop.

After this you have the privilege of bicycling across Rainbow Bridge. The bridge, built in 1923, is a single-span concrete Marsh arch bridge and the sole surviving bridge of this type on the entire length of the Route 66. Thank you to all the people who kept this historic treasure from ending with the fate of the other historic bridges. Definitely a CRA.

Route 66 only includes 13.2 miles in the state of Kansas. Baxter Springs is your last stop. There are several interesting attractions here, and we also get to bag another "-est", with Big Brutus, the world's biggest electric shovel, which even has its own museum. Plus there is the site of Baxter Springs Massacre (where Quantrill's raiders attacked Fort Blair), the heritage museum, heritage museum log cabin, the Little League museum, and many other attractions. Stop off at the Chamber of Commerce, at 1004 Military Avenue for more info.

I know I direct cyclists to the town visitor center a lot, but if I put all the attractions along Route 66 in this guidebook it would be several times bigger than it already is.

Warning, don't' get your hopes up for a classic malt or shake when you see the neon sign outside the Route 66 Soda Fountain. This is a classic restored 1930s era fountain, complete with glass block walls, stools at the soda fountain counter, and colorfully covered booths, however it does not serve the public. This is the Bill Abernathy Memorial Lifetime Learning Center. I guess they wanted to restore the building when making it a learning center, so why not use this décor and make something interesting at the same time.

However, I sure did want a shake. I settled for "The best frozen custard in Cherokee County" at Angels on the Route, just down the street.

Camping

Joplin KOA
4359 Dakota Lane
Joplin, MO 64804
417-623-2246

Zan's Creekside Campground
2480 Coyote Dr
Joplin, MO 64804
417-782-0441

Riverside CG
E 12th St about 1/2 mile
Baxter Springs, KS 66713
620-856-2112
(only $5 for bikes)

Lodging

*Boots Court Motel
107 S Garrison Ave
Carthage, MO 64836
417-310-2989
(Classic Art-Deco)

*Guest House Motel
417 E Central Ave
Carthage, MO 64836
417-358-4077

Budget Inn
1822 W 7th St
Joplin, MO 64801
417-623-6191

Plaza Motel
2612 E 7th St
Joplin, MO 6480
417-623-0610

Galena Motel
906 E 7th St
Galena, KS 66739
620-783-5428

* Baxter Inn
2451 Military Ave
Baxter Springs, KS 66713
620-856-21066

Route 66 Section 8

Bike Shops

Blues Bike Company
1825 S Main St
Joplin, MO 64804
417-553-0198

Bicycle Specialists
1202 S Range Line Rd
Joplin, MO 64801
417-553-0198

Halltown to Baxter Springs (85 Miles)

Miles E/W	Directions	Dist	R	Service	Miles W/E
	*Halltown (pop 173)				
0	S on SR266/R66	2.3	3		85
2	S on SR N (crossing SR96)	2.0	3		83
4	*Spencer				81
4	R on CR2062/R66	2.0	3		81
6	S at SS on CR2059 (crossing SR96)	1.1	3		79
7	R at SS on SR96	1.1	3		78
9	R on CR1155	2.3	2		76
11	L at SS on SR DD (unsigned)	4.1	3		74
15	*Miller (pop 699)			GQR	70
15	R at ss on SR39	1.3	3		70
16	BL on CR2030	2.3	2		69
19	R on CR1095	0.5	2		66
19	L on CR2020	1.1	2		66
20	R at SS on SR UU (unsigned)	2.9	3		65
23	L on SR NN	2.1	3		62
25	R at SS on SR97/SRNN	0.4	3		60
26	L on SR NN	4.3	3		59
30	L SR AA	2.5	3		55
32	R on SR C	4.9	3		53
37	S at SS on Nutmeg Rd	4.9	3		48
42	L at SS on CR90	0.5	3		43
43	L on CR95	0.5	2		42
43	BR on Maple Rd	1.5	2		42
45	L at SS on CR110	3.0	3		40
48	R at SS on SR96/R66 (unsigned)	0.7	3		37
48	L on CR118	1.3	2		37
50	BL on Esterly Dr/R66 thru Kellogg Lake Park	0.8	2	L	35
50	L at SS on SR96/R66	0.6	3		35
51	BR on Central Ave/SR96/R66	0.5	3		34
52	*Carthage (pop 14,378)			GLQR	33
52	L on Garrison Ave	0.1	3	R	33
52	R on Oak St/R66	1.6	3	R	33
53	BL at Y on Old 66 Blvd	2.8			32
56	BR on Old 66 BLvd to cross I-49	0.4	3		29

Route 66 Section 8

Miles E/W	Directions	Dist	R	Service	Miles W/E
56	L at SS on Old 66 Blvd	2.4	3		29
59	L at SS on Pine St	1.2	3		26
60	*Carterville (pop 1,891)			GR	25
60	R at SS on Main St/R66	0.6	3		25
61	BL on Carter St/R66	0.1	3		24
61	BR on CR HH/R66	0.5	3		24
61	BL on Broadway St/R66	0.4	3	R	24
62	*Webb City (pop 10,996)			QR	23
62	L at SS on Webb Ave then BR on Broadway St/R66	0.7	3		23
62	L at SS on Madison Ave/Range Line Rd	2.2	4	QR	23
65	R at SL on Zora St	0.4	4	Q	20
65	L at SL on Florida Ave	0.3	4		20
65	R on Utica St	0.1	4		20
65	L on Euclid Ave	0.6	4		20
66	L at SS on St Louis Ave	0.7	4		19
67	R at SL on Broadway St	1.0	P		18
68	BR at SS on 2nd St	1.0	3		17
	*Joplin (pop 50,150)			CGLQR	17
68	S on 2nd St at Main St	1.9	3	Q	17
70	L at SS on Schifferdecker Ave	0.4	3		15
70	R at SL on 7th St/SR 66	3.3	4		15
73	R on R66	0.6	3		12
74	Enter Kansas	1.2			11
75	L at SS on Main St/R66	0.4	2	R	10
	*Galena (pop 3,085)			L	
75	R at SL on 7th St/SR66	3.5	3	GR	10
79	*Riverton (pop 929)				6
79	S on SR66	1.0	3		6
80	R at circle on Beasley Rd	1.5	3		5
81	VL on 50th St/R66/Willon Ave	2.7	3		4
84	VL on 3rd St	0.4	3		1
85	R at SS on Military Ave/US 69A/R66	0.4	3	QGR	0
85	*Baxter Springs (pop 4,238)			CGLQR	

Route 66 Section 8

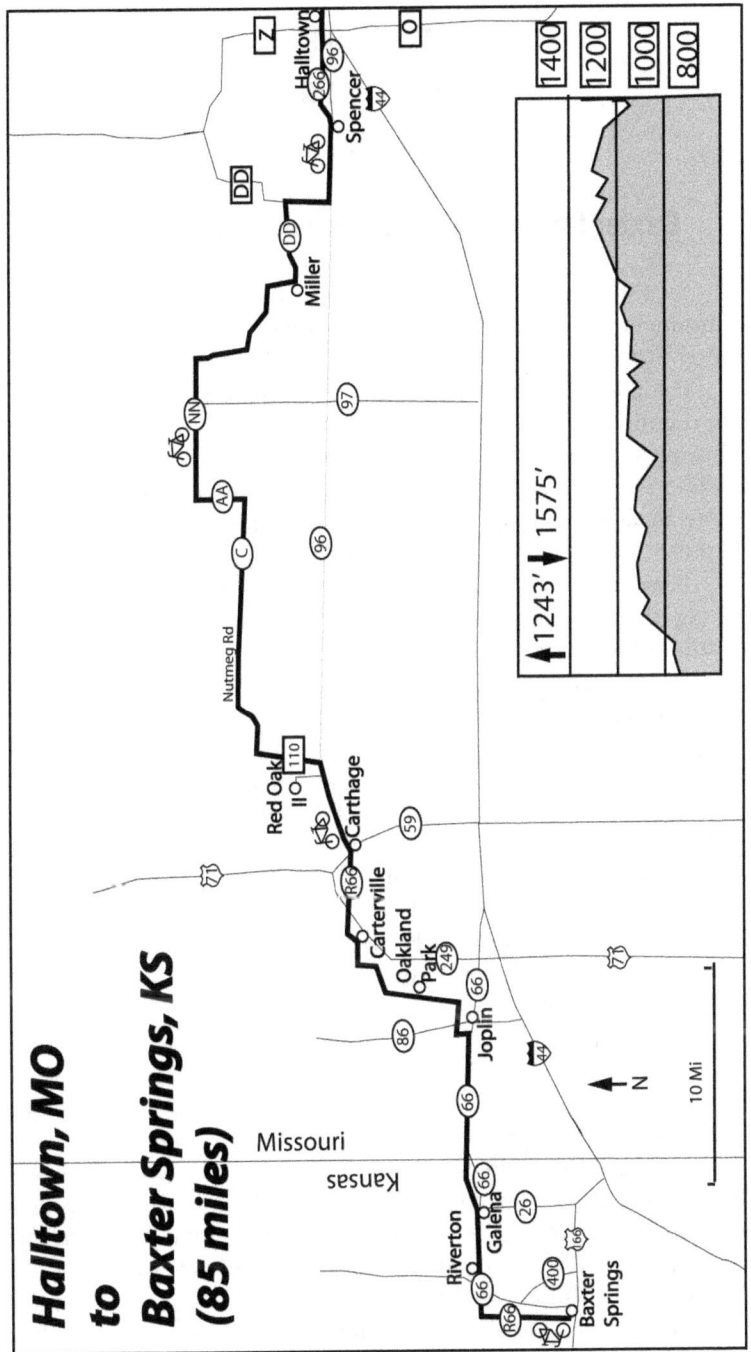

Route 66
SECTION 9

Baxter Springs, KS to Claremore, OK (80 miles)

    Just after beginning this section you pass a memorial announcing that you are Entering Indian Territory. This is the fourth state of your Route 66 Adventure, Oklahoma.

    If you look at a map of the U.S. you'll realize that Route 66 did not use the most direct route to connect Chicago and Los Angeles. This, plus given the fact that they used existing roads of that time in determining the route, it would have made more sense for the route to cross the top of Missouri, then through the middle of Kansas, avoiding Oklahoma entirely.

    It was the work of one man that was responsible for the route taking the sweeping swath south, Cyrus Avery, considered the "Father of Route 66".

    Early on, he had the foresight to realize how a major route across the country would benefit his adopted home state of Oklahoma. So Avery became involved in working with organizations related to highway improvement and interstate highway systems, such as the Good Roads Movement, Albert Pike Highway Association, the Ozark Trails, Associated Highway Association of America, and the Oklahoma Highway Commission.

    His work paid off when the U.S. Secretary of Agriculture appointed him to the Joint Board of Interstate Highways, which Congress had delegated responsibility for designing the new federal highway system.

    Originally Congress was favoring a cross country route that stretched from Virginia Beach, Virginia to Los Angeles, California via Kansas, Colorado, and Utah. Suggesting they should avoid the added expenses to build highways over the Rocky Mountains, Avery argued for an alternate route through Oklahoma, the Texas Panhandle, New Mexico, and Arizona. He must have been a convincing person, or else Kansas didn't have someone to champion their state, for Route 66 ended up running directly through Avery's home town of Tulsa, Oklahoma.

    Commerce, Oklahoma, is the boyhood home of Mickey Mantle. The route takes you past an impressive bronze statue of the baseball legend, appropriately positioned in front of Mickey Mantle Field. You can also go past the house where he grew up, 319 S. Quincy, to see a metal-sided barn full of dents where he practiced his hitting.

Also in Commerce you pass an original cottage style Marathon Service Station. You also bag another Route 66 "-est"; being built in 1929, it is the oldest standing Marathon Oil Company service station. Having been recently restored, it is now a Dairy King serving food. Stop by for a Route 66 cookie and wash it down with a Route 66 soft drink. The owners are a wealth of information about the history of the area, including a story about a shootout local authorities had with Bonny and Clyde.

In Miami be sure to stop to admire the Coleman Theater, 103 N. Main Street. Built in 1929, it was originally part of the Orpheum Vaudeville circuit, with entertainers such as Will Rogers, Tom Mix and the Three Stooges. Your ride will take you right past it and it would be difficult to miss the impressive Spanish Mission style building. They even offer free guided tours.

On your approach into Afton, you pass the site of one of the most popular tourist attractions on the Mother Road, the Buffalo Ranch. This was a classic tourist trap, with trained animals, curio shop, and other oddities to encourage travelers to stop. Unfortunately it is gone now, replaced by a convenience store.

However, Afton is still home of another CRA, the restored 1930s DX service station that has been converted into a visitor center and Packard Museum. This place is well worth a stop, with over 18 vintage cars and Route 66 memorabilia. They even have a 1917 Packard RV. They have a 58 Packard that I thought looked like a Studebaker. Turns out Packard sales were down and they asked Studebaker to help them design the car. Man, if they asked Studebaker for help they really were in trouble!

As you exit Afton you pass another remnant of better times, the Afton Motor Court ruins, complete with the neon sign and individual cottages.

Be sure to plan your ride for a meal at Clanton's Café, in Vivita, originally opened in 1927. They serve up traditional comfort food that will help cyclists keep those pedals churning.

On your approach into Chelsea watch for a left turn onto 1st Street. This isn't part of our Route 66 ride, but you can turn here to ride over the old Pryor Creek Bridge. This steel-truss bridge dates back to the original Route 66 route. You can continue on across the bridge and reconnect with the Route 66 documented in this book after less than a mile.

As you exit Chelsea, you can turn right on E. 10th Street and ride for a block, to see the first Sears Roebuck mail order house sold in Oklahoma, in 1913 for $1,663. It is impressive that the house is still owned by descendants of the original purchaser.

When you turn onto State Road 28A then make the quick right onto Poplar Avenue, if you continue straight on 28A another 4 miles you reach a true CRA, and bag another "-est", the World's Largest Totem Pole. This is a pretty cool place to visit, with a touristy gift shop, the totem pole, and ten other molded structures crafted by Ed Galloway. The highway to the totems is a little hilly, but if you don't mind that and have the time, it is an interesting place to visit. I asked the lady operating the gift shop why he built the business here, so far from Route 66, and she just replied, "This is where he owned the land."

At the end of Andy Payne Blvd there is a park with a picnic table and also a bronze statue of the park's namesake, Andrew Hartley Payne. Andy was of Cherokee ancestry, and won the Great Transcontinental Footrace of 1928, from Los Angeles, CA to New York, NY. It is a cool statue for someone who sounds like was a very cool person.

Camping

*Park Hills Motel & RV
438415 E. Hwy 60
Vinita, OK 74301
918-256-5511

Blue Creek Cove CG
13400 E 390 Rd
Foyil, OK 74017
918-341-4244
(4.8 miles off route from Foyil)

Lodging

Econo Lodge
900 E Steve Owens Blvd
Miami, OK 74354
918-542-6631

Deluxe Inn & Suites
1307 E Steve Owens Blvd
Miami, OK 74354
918-542-5600

Holiday Inn Express & Suites
232 South 7th St
Vinita, OK 74301
877-410-6681

Relax Inn Vinita
110 West Dwain Willis Ave
Vinita, OK 74301
918-256-6492

*Western Motel
437866 E Highway 60
Vinita, OK 74301
918-256-7542

Chelsea Motor Inn
325 E Layton St
Chelsea, OK 74016
918-789-3437

*Claremore Motor Inn
1709 North Lynn Riggs Blvd
Claremore, OK 74017
918-342-4545

*Elm's Motel
820 S Lynn Riggs Blvd,
Claremore, OK 74017
918-342-1778

*Will Rogers Magnuson Hotel
940 South Lynn Riggs Blvd
Claremore, OK 74017
918-341-4410

Bike Shops

N/A

World's Largest Totem Pole. Check out how small my bike is at bottom right in picture.

Baxter Springs, KS to Claremore, OK (80 Miles)

Miles E/W	Directions	Dist	R	Service	Miles W/E
0	*Baxter Springs (pop 4,238)			CGLQR	80
0	S on US69A/Military Rd	2.2	3		80
2	Enter Oklahoma	3.6	3		78
6	*Quapaw (pop 906)			QR	74
6	S on US69A	4.0	3		74
10	S on US 69/Mickey Mantle Blvd	2.2	3		70
12	*Commerce (pop 2,473)			QR	68
12	R at SL on Commerce Ave	0.5	3		68
13	L on Main St	0.8	4		67
13	*North Miami (pop 374)			GQR	67
13	S at SS on US69/R66	3.3	3		67
17	*Miami (pop 12,570)			GLQR	63
17	R on Steve Owens Blvd/SR10/US69	5.9	3	Q	63
23	*Narcissa (pop 100)				57
23	S on US69/US59	5.2	3		57
28	S on US60/US69 after I-44 underpass	4.2	4	QR	52
32	*Afton (pop 1,049)			QR	48
32	S on US60/69	15.1	3		48
47	*Vinita (pop 5,743)		3	GLQR	33
47	L at SL on Wilson St/US60/US69	3.7	3		33
51	S on US60	1.3	3		29
52	S on SR66	1.6	3		28
54	*White Oak (pop 263)			Q	26
54	S on SR66	9.6	4		26
63	*Chelsea (pop 1,964)			GLQR	17
63	S on SR66	7.8	4	R	17
71	*Foyil (pop 344)			C	9
71	L on unsigned SR28A then R on Poplar Ave	0.2	3		9
71	VL on Andy Payne Blvd	0.9	3		9
72	L on SR66/Lynn Riggs Blvd	7.7	3	GQ	8
80	*Claremore (pop 18,581)			GLQR	0

Route 66 Section 9

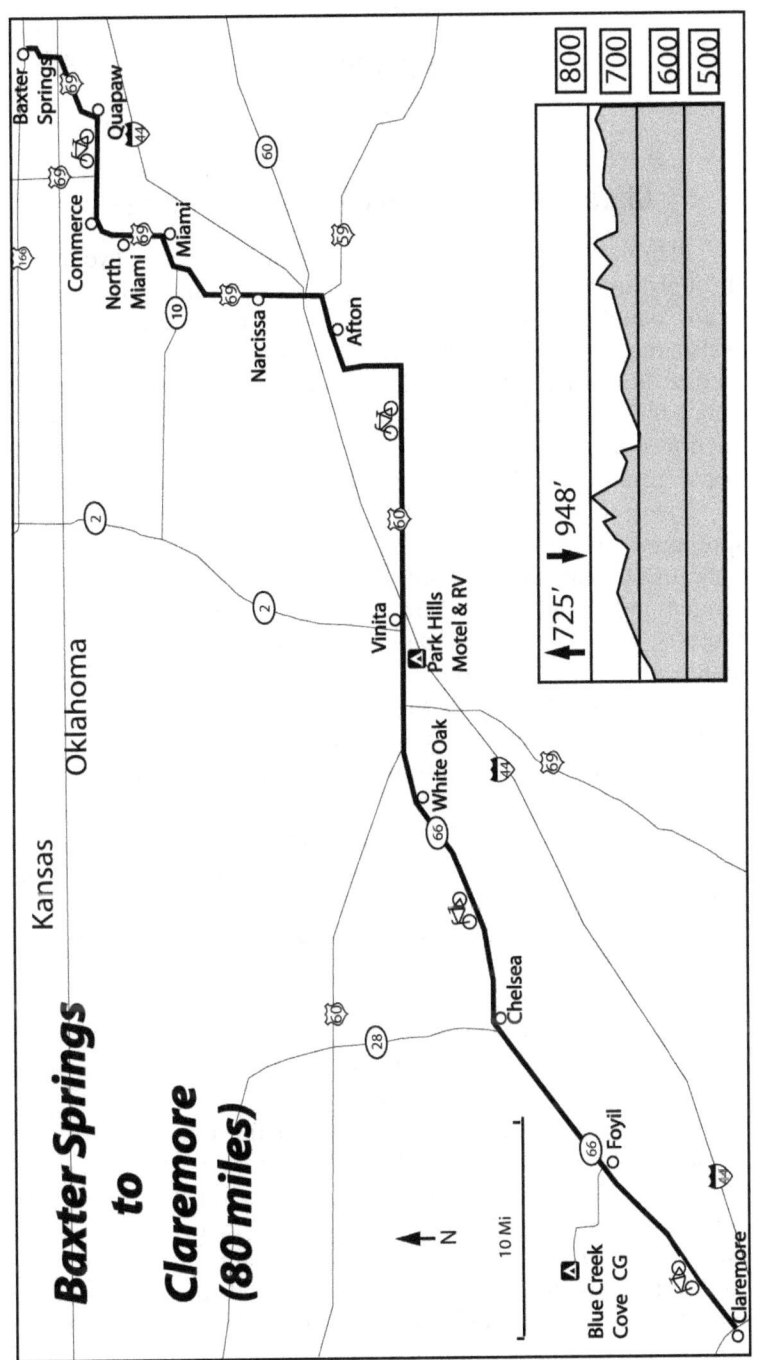

Route 66
SECTION 10

Claremore, OK to Davenport, OK (91 miles)

Plan to visit the Will Rogers Memorial Museums on your ride through his home town of Claremore, Oklahoma. I had always heard about Will Rogers and seen him in old movies, but I didn't realize the depth of this man. He was not only the top male motion picture box-office attraction 1933-1935, but he also wrote more than 4,000 daily and weekly newspaper columns, authored 6 books, anchored America's first coast-to-coast radio broadcast, and had a popular radio program that was heard across the country.

There was a lot more to Will Rogers than just an entertainer spouting countrified philosophies while twirling a lasso. Visit the museums to learn more about this intelligent, thought provoking, unique individual. There are also twelve galleries of priceless artifacts, a theater to watch one of his 21 feature films, and even a children's museum. There is also a beautiful statue of the man on his horse, along with the tomb where he and wife, Betty, along with three of their four children were laid to rest.

It is about a mile off-route on, appropriately named, Will Rogers Boulevard.

A few miles after leaving Claremore you get to cross what's known as the Twin Bridges over the Verdigris River, which is part of the McClellan-Kerr Arkansas River Navigation System. Well, they aren't actually twins, one was built in 1936 and the other in 1957. And the later one is wider to accommodate the increased traffic of the time. But they are both steel.

A little way up stream is the Port of Catoosa, which is the most inland ocean port in the United States. Ships can navigate from here all the way to the Gulf of Mexico.

Just past the Twin Bridges is one of the most recognizable attractions on Route 66, The Blue Whale, truly a CRA. This is an 80 foot long and 20 foot tall whale built with a steel frame and concrete sides, floating in the middle of a pond. Hugh S. Davis built this in 1972. Visitors used to love diving off the whale's tail. And just across the highway is the abandoned Arrowood Trading Post that was ran by Davis's brother-in-law, Chief Wolf-Robe Hunt.

As you are riding along busy 11th Street you will get your first glimpse of the Tulsa skyline. Tulsa, the home of Cyrus Avery, Father

Route 66 Section 10

of Route 66 as I stated earlier, routes cyclists past several Route 66 era attractions. There are several classic motels, such as the Oasis Motel, Desert Hills Motel, plus many eateries which have proven themselves through the test of time, like Rancho Grande Mexican Food, Coney I-Lander, and Tally's Café (claiming to serve the best chicken fried steak on Route 66). Plus 11th Street has several Route 66 related murals painted on many buildings.

At the stop light where South Mingo Road intersects with 11th Street, if you turn left there is a small park with several interesting plaques about Tulsa's interesting history with Route 66. Further along 11th Street there are several other plaques located under an enormous restored neon Meadow Gold sign with more history of the area and Route 66. I recommend stopping at both.

Tulsa is a great city to visit and you only see a small section of it from Route 66. At the turn onto Southwest Boulevard you can go off-route and ride a loop on separated bike paths that border both banks of the Arkansas River, crossing the river on a converted railroad bridge.

Also at the turn onto Southwest Boulevard, be sure to stop at the Cyrus Avery Centennial Plaza. There is a cool bronze statue of Avery and his family in a Model T Ford meeting a horse-drawn carriage, titled "East Meets West". The Cyrus Avery Memorial Bridge begins here also, crossing the Arkansas River; however it was closed the last time I came through. There are also plans for the construction of a museum.

After crossing the river, further along Southwest Boulevard, you pass Route 66 Village. This is a work-in-progress exhibition with a mission to preserve the history of all modes of transportation that contributed to the growth in the area, which includes Route 66. It will be easy to spot, just look for the 154-foot-tall oil derrick.

On your ride through Sapulpa, take the time to tour around some of the downtown district to view the reproductions of antique advertisement murals on many of the buildings. If you turn north off Dewey Ave. on Water St. and ride a block you can see one of the old unique corner service stations that were once popular. This is a beautifully restored Gulf station, complete with the old price stand in front advertising 19 cent-a-gallon gasoline.

Sapulpa is also home of Frankoma Pottery, however they no longer have a presence here, and their unique art deco style home is no longer open for tours.

Outside of Sapulpa you pass one of the oldest bridges on Route 66. This steel-truss Rock Creek Bridge, built in 1924, was originally built for the Ozark Trail and later incorporated into the Route 66 network. There will be more on the Ozark Trail later.

Route 66 Section 10

If you are planning to camp at Heyburn Campground, there are a couple different routes to reach it. The shortest route will be to turn north about 4 miles south of Kellyville onto S. 257 W. Avenue. After about 2.2 miles turn left on Heyburn Lake Rd. and ride another 1.8 miles.

As you approach Bristow you pass the Magnolia Memorial Cemetery with a beautiful rock monument. It is a nice place to pause on your journey to remember lost loved ones.

On your ride through downtown Bristow, if you turn east on 7th Ave. and ride a block you can visit their restored 1923 train depot, now hosting a museum and visitor center. There is also a courtyard in front of the depot that makes for a nice place to take a break. There are also some colorful murals on several of the buildings.

After Bristow, you'll be cycling through good old Oklahoma open countryside. When you reach Depew, you can take a short side trip and witness the fate of many small towns that were bypassed by Route 66. What appears to have once been a thriving town is now just a lot of empty deteriorating buildings.

On the western outskirts of Stroud keep an eye out for the Stable Ridge Vineyards and stop for a taste of their current stock and a visit of the winery. This is also where a friend and I were introduced to port wine and a piece of dark chocolate. Yummm!

Also, if you are a fan of the Pixar movie "Cars", you will want to stop at the Rock Café to meet owner Dawn Welch, whom the character Sally Carrera was based on. I'll let her tell the story behind this.

As you make the turn in front of the old restored Sinclair Service Station in Davenport, continue straight on Broadway Ave. to visit the downtown area. I had a nice talk with a local who shared a lot of the history of the area, and also explained the unique method they used when painting the beautiful murals throughout the city. They would project the image of historic photographs onto the walls, then art students would trace over them. This resulted in some very detailed paintings and proved to be a great method of preserving their history.

He also helped me bag a bonus "-est", the world's largest spherical oil storage tank. This was pretty cool looking. It was the first round steel oil storage tank in the world. To reach the tank, ride north of town on Route 66 about half-a-mile then turn on N. 3503 Rd., ride about half-a-mile, then turn right on E 0890 Rd to ride another tenth mile on a dirt road. The tank will be in a field on your left. You can still see the faint trademark red Flying Pegasus on the side.

Route 66 Section 10

Camping

Heyburn Lake CG
W, 27349 Heyburn Lake Rd
Kellyville, OK 74039
918-247-6601

*Evergreen Rv Park CG
37661 W Hwy 66
Bristow, Oklahoma 74010
918-367-2610

Lodging

* La Quinta Inn & Suites
2009 S. Cherokee
Catoosa, OK 74015
918-739-4600

Super 8
19250 Timbercrest Cir
Catoosa, OK 74015
918-266-7000

*Oasis Motel
9303 E 11th St
Tulsa, OK 74112
918-835-3240

*Desert Hills Motel
5220 E 11th St
Tulsa, OK 74112
918-834-3311

Super 8 Sapulpa
1505 New Sapulpa Rd
Sapulpa, OK 74066
918-227-3300

*Hummel HideAWay Homes
424 Roland St
Bristow, OK
918-519-3510

*Skyliner Motel
717 W Main St
Stroud, OK 74079
918-968-9556

Best Western Motor Lodge
200 N 8th Ave
Stroud, OK 74079
918-968-9515

Sooner Motel
412 N 8th Ave
Stroud, OK 74079
918-968-2595

Bike Shops

*Superleggera Cycling
506 E. 11th St
Tulsa OK 74120
918-585-5555

Lee's Bicycles
20 E 2nd St
Tulsa, OK 74120
918-743-4285

Tom's Bicycles
1506 East 15th
Tulsa OK 74120
918-592-2453

Tulsa greets Route 66 Adventurers.

Claremore to Davenport (91 miles)

Miles E/W	Directions	Dist	R	Service	Miles W/E
	*Claremore (pop 18,581)				
0	S on Lynn Riggs Blvd/R66	7.8	4	GLQR	91
8	*Verdigris (pop 3.993)			QR	
8	S on R66	2.2	3		83
	*Catoosa (pop 7,151)			GQR	
10	S on R66	2.4	3		81
12	VR on unsigned Ford St	0.3	3	GQR	79
13	L at SS on Cherokee St	1.6	4	LQR	78
14	L at SL on 193rd Ave/SR167	1.3	3	QR	77
16	R at SS on 11th St/R66	5.7	4	GQR	76
	*Tulsa (pop 391,906)			GLQR	
21	S at SL cont 11th/R66	6.6	4	LQR	70
28	Exit Traffic Circle on 10th St	0.4	3		63
28	BR on 11th St/R66	0.2	3		63
29	BL on 12th St/R66	0.5	3	Q	63
29	L on Southwest Blvd/R66 cross Arkansas	7.2	4	LQR	62
36	S on Frankoma Rd/R66	4.9	3		55
	*Sapulpa (pop 20,544)				
41	R at SL on Mission St/R66	0.9	4	QR	50
42	R at SL on Dewey Ave/R66	0.4	4		49
42	S at SL on Dewey Ave/R66/SR33	4.5	3	CQ	49
47	S on R66	3.4	3		44
	*Kellyville (pop 1,150)			CGQR	
50	S on R66	4.9	3		41
55	S over I-44 overpass	5.7	3	Q	36
61	SR48 joins route	3.9	3	LQR	30
	*Bristow (pop 4,222)			C	
65	R on 4th St/Roland St/R66	3.0	3	Q	26
	*Depew (pop 476)			Q	23
68	S on R66	16.1	3		23
	*Stroud (pop 2,690)			GLQR	
84	S on Main St/R66	7.2	3	GLQR	7
91	*Davenport (pop 814)				0

Route 66 Section 10

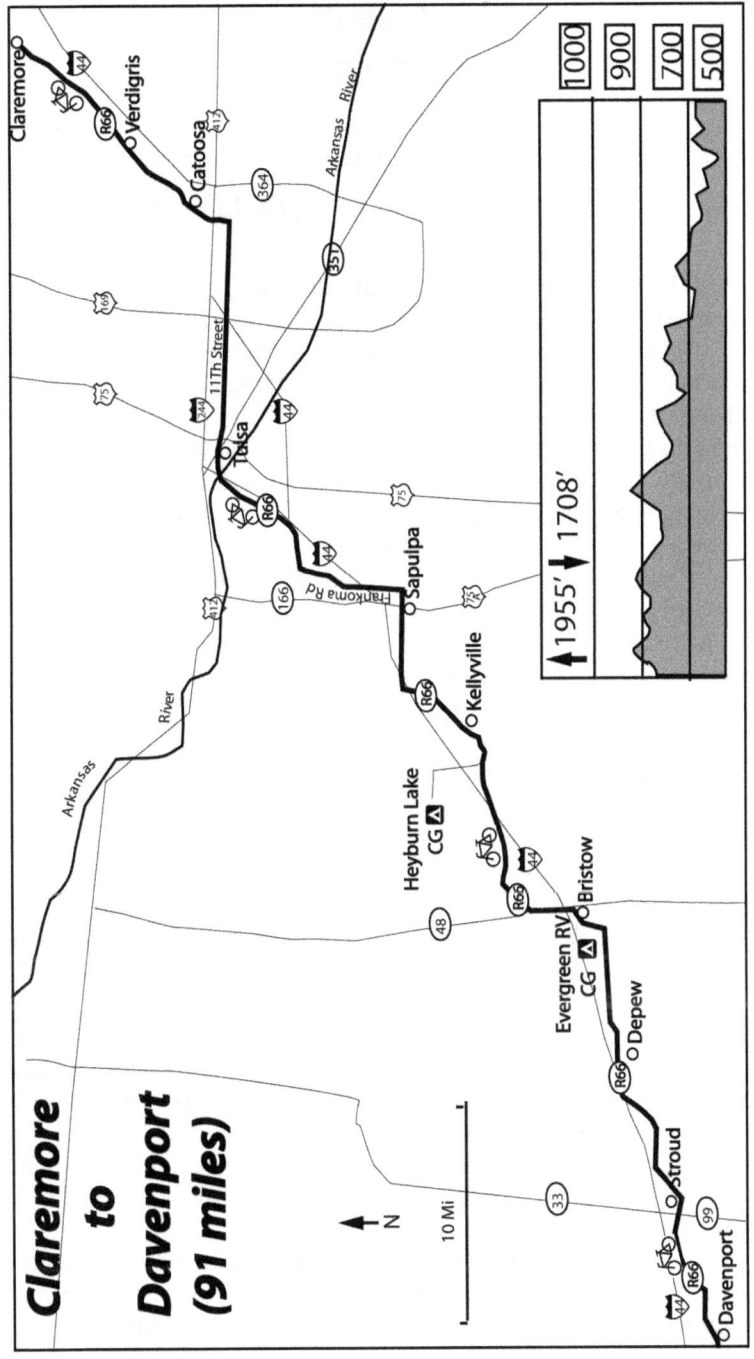

Route 66
SECTION 11

Davenport, OK to El Reno, OK (82 miles)

There are several traditional CRAs in this section, plus a relatively new one in the making.

In the town of Chandler you pass the 1936 armory building that has been converted into a state-of-the-art Route 66 Interpretative Center. Utilizing old video footage and interactive technology, the exhibits help visitors relive Route 66 from the bleak dust bowl years, through the happy days of the 60s, to experiencing the unique lodging enjoyed by early travelers via a virtual hotel room. They've done a great job creating these exhibits.

Chandler also has a restored 1930 Phillip 66 "B" cottage style service station. This was a popular design the oil company used from 1927-1938. Its great people are taking the trouble to restore these old gas stations, because they play a major role in preserving the Route 66 experience.

After Chandler, you'll soon pass another must see stop, the Seaba Station Motorcycle Museum. The building itself is worth a stop. It was a 1921 DX service station, built five years before Route 66 was even created. Since then the building has experienced several uses before arriving at its current incarnation.

If the classic building isn't enough reason for a stop, then the massive collection of vintage motorcycles will be more than enough. They have old race bikes, collector bikes, bikes that are still in the crate that have never been ridden, and other motorcycle memorabilia, like an Evil Knievel pinball machine.

And if that still isn't enough reason to stop, how about a phot op sitting on the toilet at what remains of the oldest plumbed outhouse west of the Mississippi River.

Riding across the open Oklahoma countryside after Luther, while pedaling up a short rise, you'll pass a roadside oddity on your right. A large metal storage building, with the front end of a VW beetle sticking out of the second floor, a pair of vintage gasoline pumps out front, and a menagerie of welded art structures scattered about. The fixtures on the inside of the building are just as unexpected, with a very detailed recreated 60s soda fountain,

Route 66 Section 11

Route 66 memorabilia, and automobiles in various stages of restoration. An interesting stop if you have the time.

In Arcadia you'll pass a CRA unlike any other on the route, the Round Barn. Built in 1898, this architectural wonder stands 48' tall and 60' in diameter. William H Odor's neighbors told him that it couldn't be done. But Odor developed special jigs to create the needed bend in the boards for the structure and proved them wrong. In 1988, with the decline of visitors from Route 66, the structure fell into disrepair and the roof collapsed. Thankfully people have since worked hard to restore it back to its original glory.

If you can wait, hold off on eating until you are a few miles west of Arcadia, so you can help support a CRA in the making, Pops Soda Ranch. This place has the true feel and originality of many of the popular early roadside attractions that came up with a unique ploy for luring travelers to stop. The 66 foot tall neon soda bottle positioned out front and the modern glass art deco building is classic Route 66 promotion. This place is really encouraging for the future of Route 66 because Pops was constructed in in 2007.

I love this place. The Mother Road Burger, with Round Barn Root Beer, and then a classic hand-dipped shake powered my pedal stroke the remainder of the day. And if Root Beer isn't your soft drink of choice, they have over 600 others to choose from.

Edmond is known for its public art - statues, murals, stained glass, and steel structures on display throughout the city and downtown district. It would be a good place to end your day early and spend time biking, or walking, around town to view these interesting original works of art. The Arcadia Inn, listed in this guidebook, would be a convenient location to stay for your city tour.

Stop at the Edmond Visitor Bureau, 1030 Bryant, to learn more about the exhibits and their locations.

Route 66 pretty much skirts OKC. As you ride along Shartel Avenue and the first part of 39th Street, you will be going through the historic Crown Heights Historic Preservation district. This was primarily a residential area built in the 1930s and 1940s. With several interesting architectural styles incorporated in the homes, it makes for an interesting spin through the neighborhood.

I know this doesn't relate to bicycling, or Route 66, but as you are riding on Kelley Avenue in OKC, you can turn east on 63rd St. and ride about half-a-mile to the National Cowboy Western Heritage Museum. I'll just say that, with the world's most extensive collection of art and artifacts related to the heritage of the American West; this is a very interesting place to visit.

If you are ready to layover for a couple days, and you plan to spend some time in OKC, be sure to check out the Centennial Land Run Monument, located in the historic Bricktown District. This structure is amazing! With its 45, one-and-a-half time's life size, figures competing in the big land rush, 365 feet in length, 36 feet wide and over 16 feet high; it is one of the largest freestanding bronze structures in the world. The structure includes 24 horses and riders, sun-bonneted women riding sidesaddle, a buckboard, two covered wagons, and other action characters frozen in time. It is several miles off-route, but if you have the time it is a very memorable structure.

After leaving OKC your route takes you across another classic bridge that, for its time, was a very impressive design. The 1925 Lake Overhosler Bridge not only utilizes, what was at that time, the new steel truss technology, it also combined a variety of other trusses, to make the 748-foot bridge not only an unusual structure, but what many architects consider, a balanced and elegant one. Even we non-engineering visitors can appreciate the unique features of this structure.

On my bike tours around the country, it seems to me that bridge architecture experienced a drought of creativity for a good many years following the Route 66 era. Their goal seemed to merely build functional structures. So I was pleased to see a new spirit of design and imagination in some of the recently constructed bridges across the Mississippi River while cycling the Mississippi River Trail.

At the entrance to the bridge, and also along the shores of the Lake Overhosler, you pass several roadside parks with portable toilets and tables for you to take a break.

If you didn't get your burger fix back at Pops, then you'll have another opportunity at one of the burger restaurants in El Reno, which is home of the famous "fried onion burger". In 2015, Sid's Burger version of the classic burger was good enough for it to be featured on the Food Network as one of its Top 5 Restaurants. If you are riding through on the first Saturday of May you can sample, and bag another "-est", the world's largest fried onion burger, weighing in at over 850 pounds.

Just outside of El Reno, Route 66 will take you past Historic Fort Reno. I'll have more on that in the next section.

Route 66 Section 11

Pops Soda Ranch with classic burgers, shakes, and over 600 sodas,

Camping

*Oak Glen RV Park
347203 E Hwy 66
Chandler, OK 74834
405-258-2994

Central State Park
9000 E. Second St.
Edmond, OK 73034
405-216-7470

Lake El Reno RV Park
1401 S. Babcock Dr.
El Reno, OK 73036
405-262-4070
(West, on next section map)

Lodging

*Lincoln Motel
740 East 1st Street
Chandler, OK 74834
405-258-0200

Econo Lodge
600 North Price
Chandler, OK 74834
405-258-2131

*La Quinta Inn And Suites
200 Meline Drive
Edmond, OK 73034
405-513-5353

Arcadian Inn
328 E 1st St,
Edmond, OK 73034
405-348-6347

Oxford Inn
5301 N Lincoln Blvd,
Oklahoma City, OK 73105
405-605-0206
(LT half mile off route)

Value Place
3800 Service Rd
Oklahoma City, OK 73112
405-917-6300
(LT half mile off route)

*Guest Inn Yukon
10 E Main St
Yukon, OK 73099
405-265-2700

Americas Best Value Inn
2820 S Hwy 81 Srv Rd
El Reno, OK 73036
405-262-8240

Budget Inn
1221 Sunset Dr
El Reno, OK 73036
405-262-0242

Bike Shops

Al's Bicycles - Edmond,
2624 S. Broadway Ct.
Edmond, OK 73013
405-341-4331

The Bicycle Store
336 NE 122nd St
Oklahoma City, OK 73114
405-752-8402
(half mile off Kelley Ave)

Wheeler Dealer Bicycle Shop
2729 NW 50th St,
Oklahoma City, OK 73112
405-947-6260

Route 66 Section 11

Davenport to El Reno (82 miles)

Miles E/W	Directions	Dist	R	Service	Miles W/E
	*Davenport (pop 814)			QR	
0	VR on R66	7.4	3	CGR	82
	*Chandler (pop 3,100)			GLQR	75
7	VR on 15th/R66B	9.8	4		75
17	VR on R66B	1.3	3	Q	65
19	*Wellston (pop 788)	0.0		QR	64
19	S on R66B/R66	7.7	3		64
26	*Luther (pop 1,221) 1/4 mile off-route			GQR	56
26	S on Danforth Rd/R66	7.4			56
34	*Arcadia (pop 247)			QR	49
34	S on 2nd St/R66	5.4	4	CQR	49
39	S on US77/R66 (I-35 overpass)	2.6	5	GLQR	43
42	*Edmond (pop 81,405)			GLQR	41
42	L at SL on Bryant Ave/US77	3.0	5	QR	41
45	R on Memorial Rd	2.0	5		38
47	L at SL on Kelley Ave/R66	5.8	5	QR	36
52	R at SL on 50th St	1.7	5	Q	30
54	L SL on Shartel Ave	0.8	L		28
55	R at SS on 39th St	2.1	4	GQR	27
57	L on Miller Ave	0.2	4		25
57	*Oklahoma City (pop 610, 613)				25
57	R at SS on 36th St	1.2	4		25
58	R at SL on Portland Ave	0.2	4	QR	24
59	L at SL on 39th St/39th Exp/R66	4.5	5	LQR	24
63	L on Overholser Dr/R66	2.0	3		19
65	R on unsigned 36th St to ride under turnpike/Lakeshore Dr	1.7	3		17
67	R Yukon Pky then L on Main St/SR66	1.3	5	GQR	15
68	*Yukon (pop 22,709)			GQR	14
68	S on Main St/SR66	11.8	3	LQR	14
80	VR at SL Rock Island Ave	2.0	3		2
82	L at SL on Wade St	0.1	3	Q	0
82	R at SS on Choctaw Ave	0.1	3	Q	0
82	*El Reno (pop 16,749)			CGLQR	0

Route 66 Section 11

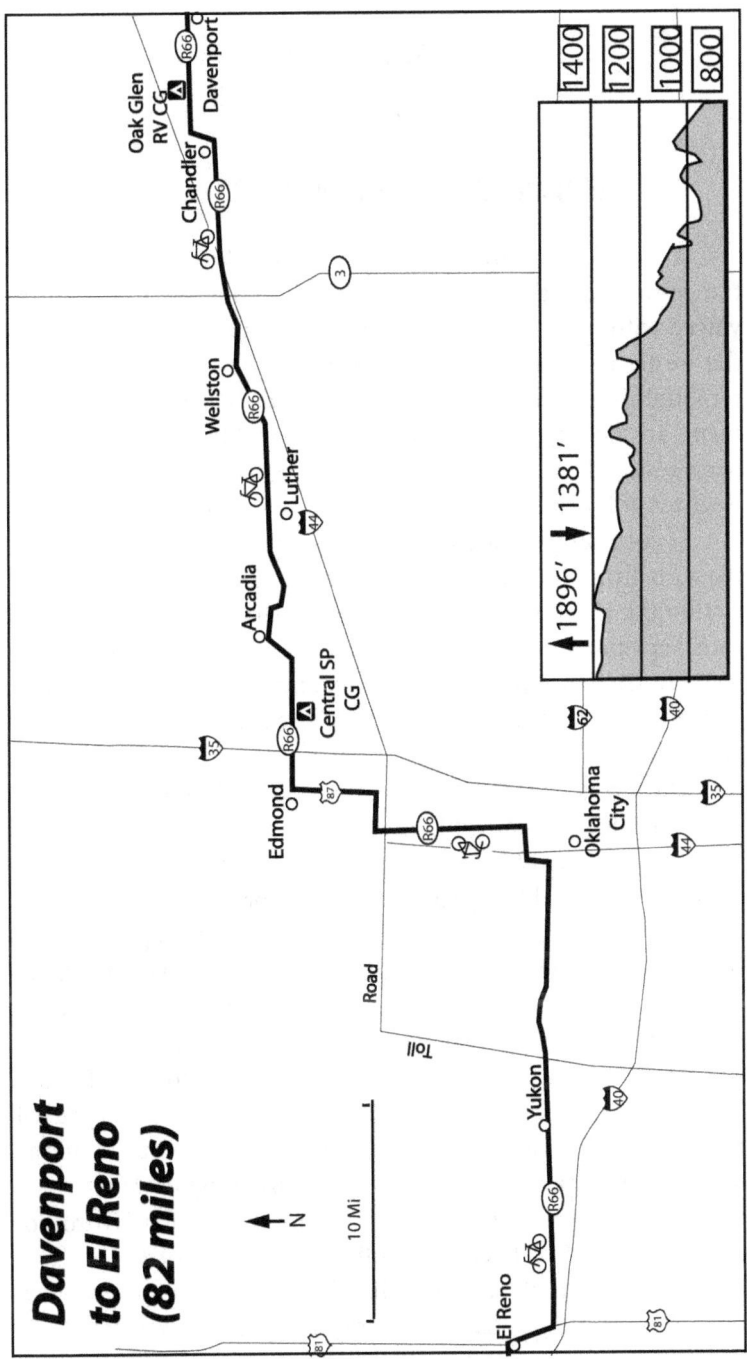

Route 66
SECTION 12

El Reno, OK to Elk City, OK (88 miles)

As you are leaving El Reno, Route 66 takes you past the entrance to Fort Reno. Established in 1874, the fort has been involved with many of the events that were associated with settling the western frontier, such as supervising the Land Run of 1889, remount depots for the U.S. Cavalry, and managing new settlements in the territory, just to name a few. Much of the fort has been restored, with 25 historic structures listed on the National Register of Historic Places.

Several activities are held at the fort that demonstrates life on the early frontier for the Calvary. The United States Cavalry Association (USCA) Bivouac & National Cavalry Competition is held each September. USCA members compete in events that demonstrate horsemanship, marksmanship, and mounted combat skills. USCA members and competitors include active duty soldiers and civilian re-enactors.

The fort is also the site of the U.S. Calvary Museum and a Fort Reno Visitor Museum, both open to the public.

After leaving El Reno the landscape begins to change, as you see fewer trees and foliage and more open prairieland. I enjoy riding among the trees and forest, however the western plains have a beauty all their own. Plus, it makes for safer cycling as the visibility improves for motorists. Be sure to carry plenty of water because even the farm houses are becoming few and far between.

At the intersection where US 281 turns south towards Hinton, leaving Route 66, if you remain on US 281 another 5 miles you will reach Red Rock Canyon State Park. The park has camping, hiking, and swimming, all bordered by the beautiful canyon walls.

On the stretch of highway past the turnoff for Hydro you pass another CRA, Lucille's Roadhouse. Built in 1929, this "over the drive" design filling station had living quarters for its owners built over the pumps. Lucille Hamons operated the business for 51 years, before passing away in 2000, and she never tired of sharing her stories about America's Main Street with visitors.

A few miles further along the route as you enter the town of Weatherford, you can stop at the new Lucille's Roadhouse. With the Travel Inn located within walking distance of the roadhouse, you can have an inexpensive place to stay, a good home style meal, and then wash it down with a cold beer.

If you do stay over at the Travel Inn, you can walk less than a mile the other direction to visit Stafford's Air and Space Museum. With over 3,000 artifacts on display, this is an interesting place to spend some time learning about the history of aviation and spaceflight.

You're going to begin seeing a lot of wind turbines in this part of the country. To help you appreciate just how big these things

Largest Route 66 logo on the route, located in Elk City, OK.

are, as you are heading out of Weatherford, turn south on South 6th Street then right on West Rainey Avenue to visit Heritage Park, where they have one of the turbine wings on display. There is also a kiosk telling about the wind turbine industry. Well worth the two block detour.

A lot of Route 66 utilizes interstate frontage roads. I really don't mind riding them because with most of the traffic using the interstate, the frontage roads pretty much become a separated bike path. And the vehicles that do drive them usually aren't driving very fast, because if they were in a hurry they would be on the interstate.

As you are riding on Route 66 after crossing the interstate on N2330 Road, if you want to visit the Cherokee Trading Post, you can use N2310 Road to reach it. This is a nice gift shop with Native American crafts. Plus there is a Love's Travel Shop on that side of I-40.

Watch for the hordes of swallows roosting under the interstate overpasses. My little bicycle caused a whirlwind of activity when I road through.

When you cross I-40 on N2290 Road you're going to see something you really wouldn't expect to see out in the middle of nowhere. That is what appears to be an old pickup truck, abandoned alongside of the frontage road, with a billboard mounted on the truck bed reading, "Come for the VIEW Stay for the FOOD". This is for the White Dog Hill Restaurant located another .2 mile further up the dirt road. The restaurant opened its doors in 2007; however the building housing it was built in 1926 as a clubhouse for the Clinton Country Club. It serves really good food and, perched atop a hill, offers a great view. If you plan to stop they advise you to make a reservation at 580-323-6922.

There are plenty of places to stay and eat in Clinton, but the Route 66 attractions are mostly on the west side of town. To reach these, you can remain on Gary Boulevard a couple miles further past the turn in the guidebook on 4th Street, but I recommend following the route I'll describe later.

As you turn off Opal Avenue onto 10th Street, if you turn right and ride a block you'll reach the entrance to McLain Rogers Park. The entrance sign into the park is true Route 66, with the park's name spelled out in classic neon lettering. Plus, while you're there, pop into the park to see the outdoor amphitheater built by the WPA. Maybe you'll luck out and there will be a performance scheduled during your visit. There are also restrooms and picnic tables within the park.

Now the route I recommend for a side trip to reach the attractions on the west side of Clinton: after riding about half-a-mile on 10th Street, turn right on Jaycee Lane to ride less than a mile to reach Gary Boulevard. Turn right on Gary Boulevard and ride another block to reach two CRAs.

On your left will be the largest Route 66 museum dedicated exclusively to the Mother Road and on the right is the place where The King slept.

The Oklahoma Route 66 Museum focuses primarily on that part of the route within Oklahoma, but it is still very much worth a stop. You can sit down and rest your legs while watching a movie they put together about the route, plus there are different displays telling about the history of transportation in the state.

Outside they have one of the original Valentine Diners on display. These portable diners were manufactured from 1938 and 1974 in Wichita, Kansas and sold for $5,000 each. The one on display here was originally located in Shamrock, Texas in 1956. Worth-a-see.

And across from the museum is the Trade Winds Inn, where Elvis Presley and his entourage used to stay. Big E decided the Inn was the best midway point place to stay on their trips from Memphis to Las Vegas. To preserve the memory the Inn has kept his room, 215, decorated the same way it was for him during the Swingin' Sixties.

Backtrack to return to 10th Street to resume Route 66.

As you are riding along Commercial Road, as with other similar situations, use caution when crossing the exit ramps. The traffic is travelling pretty fast and they probably aren't expecting to see a bicycle crossing in front of them.

Foss is only half-a-mile off route, however there are no services located there. You can cross I-40 at the turn for a convenience store on the other side.

If you look hard in the thickets across the intersection at the Foss turn, you will see the ruins of the old Kodel's Place gas station. When I last came through you could just barely make out the lettering on the exterior walls. Someone's dream gone bad.

You ride past some really nice bronze sculptures on your ride through Elk City. I had to stop to admire the one of two cowboys mounted on their horse, shaking hands, appropriately titled "Binding Contract". And of course there is also a beautiful sculpture of an elk later on the route.

You will also pass the Parker Drilling Companies Rig 114. When this was built in the 1960s it was the biggest rig in the world. It was built for the Atomic Energy Commission to drill deep shafts to test-detonate bombs underground.

The Elk City founders were quite industrious. They attempted to name the town Busch in an attempt to entice Adolphus Busch into building a brewery in the new town. When this failed they chose to name it after the local Elk Creek.

Also in Elk City you'll have the opportunity to bag two "-est" in one stop. The National Route 66 Museum is not only the largest museum on the route, it also has the largest Route 66 logo posted in front. What makes this the largest museum is that it includes the adjoining Old Town Museum, the Farm & Ranch Museum, and the Blacksmith Museum. Needless to say, there is a lot to see, so plan to spend some time here.

Camping

*El Reno West KOA
301 South Walbaun Road
Calumet, OK 73014
405-884-2595

*Hargus RV Park
1410 Neptune Dr
Clinton, OK 73601
580-323-1664

*Elk City/Clinton KOA
I-40 & N. 2110 Rd
Canute, OK 73626
580-592-4409

Lodging

*Travel Inn
3401 East Main Street
Weatherford, OK 73096
580-772-6238

*Scottish Inn
616 E Main St
Weatherford, OK 73096
580-772-3349

*Super 8 Clinton
1120 S 10th St
Clinton, OK 73601
580) 323-4979

Trade Winds Inn
2128 W Gary Blvd
Clinton, OK 73601
580-323-2610

*Econo Lodge Inn & Suites
1413 Neptune Drive
Clinton, OK 7360
580-323-6640

*Sunset Inn-Canute
119 N 9th St
Canute, OK 73626
580-472-3141

*Motel 6 Elk City
2604 E Hwy 66
Elk City, OK 73644
580-225-2541

*La Quinta Inn & Suites
2611 E Hwy 66
Elk City, OK 73644
580-303-4536

*Kings Inn
1918 W 3rd St
Elk City, OK 73644
580-225-1442

Bike Shops

N/A

Route 66 Section 12

Miles E/W	Directions	Dist	R	Service	Miles W/E
	*El Reno (pop 16,749)			CGLQR	
0	R at SS on Choctaw Ave/I40B	0.1	4		88
0	L at SL on Sunset Dr/I40B/R66	4.4	4	QR	88
5	R on E1020 Rd/R66 (unsigned)	11.4	3	C	84
16	R at SS on US281 spur	3.8	3	QR	72
20	L on US8/US281	4.3	3		68
24	S on R66 (unsigned)	12.4	3		64
36	*Hydro (pop 969) R on SR58 1 mile			GQR	52
36	S on R66/Main St	5.9	3	GLQR	52
42	L at SS on Lyle Rd then QR at SL on Main	1.3	4	LQR	46
44	L on Washington Ave then QR on Main St	1.1	4	LQR	45
45	*Weatherford (pop 10,833)			GLQR	43
45	L on 4th St/SR54	0.8	3		43
46	S on R66	6.3	3		43
52	L at SS on N2330 Rd to cross I40	0.2	3		36
52	R at SS on R66	4.3	3		36
56	R at SS on N2290 Rd	0.1	3		32
56	L on frontage road	1.1	3		32
58	R YS on Gary Blvd	2.3	4	LQR	31
60	*Clinton (pop 9,033)			GLQR	28
60	L at SL on 4th St/US183	0.5	4		28
60	R on Opal Ave	0.4	3	R	28
61	L at SS on 10th St/Neptune Dr	1.5	3	CGLQR	27
62	VR cont on Neptune Dr	0.4	3	C	26
63	VR on Commerce Rd/R66	7.5	3		26
70	R on N2170 Rd	0.1	3		18
70	L at SS on R66	3.7	3		18
74	*Foss (pop 151) R on Broadway .5 mile				14
74	S at SS on R66	3.0	3		14
77	L at SS on NS 2110	0.3	3	C	11
77	R at YS on R66	3.6	3		11
81	*Canute (pop 541)			CLQR	7
81	S at SS on R66	3.0	3	LQR	7
84	R at SS on N2050 Rd	0.3	3		4
84	L on R66	1.8	3		4
86	L on SR34 then R on I-40B	1.6	3		2
88	S on Van Buren Ave/R66	0.6	4		1
88	*Elk City (pop 11,693)			GLQR	

Route 66 Section 12

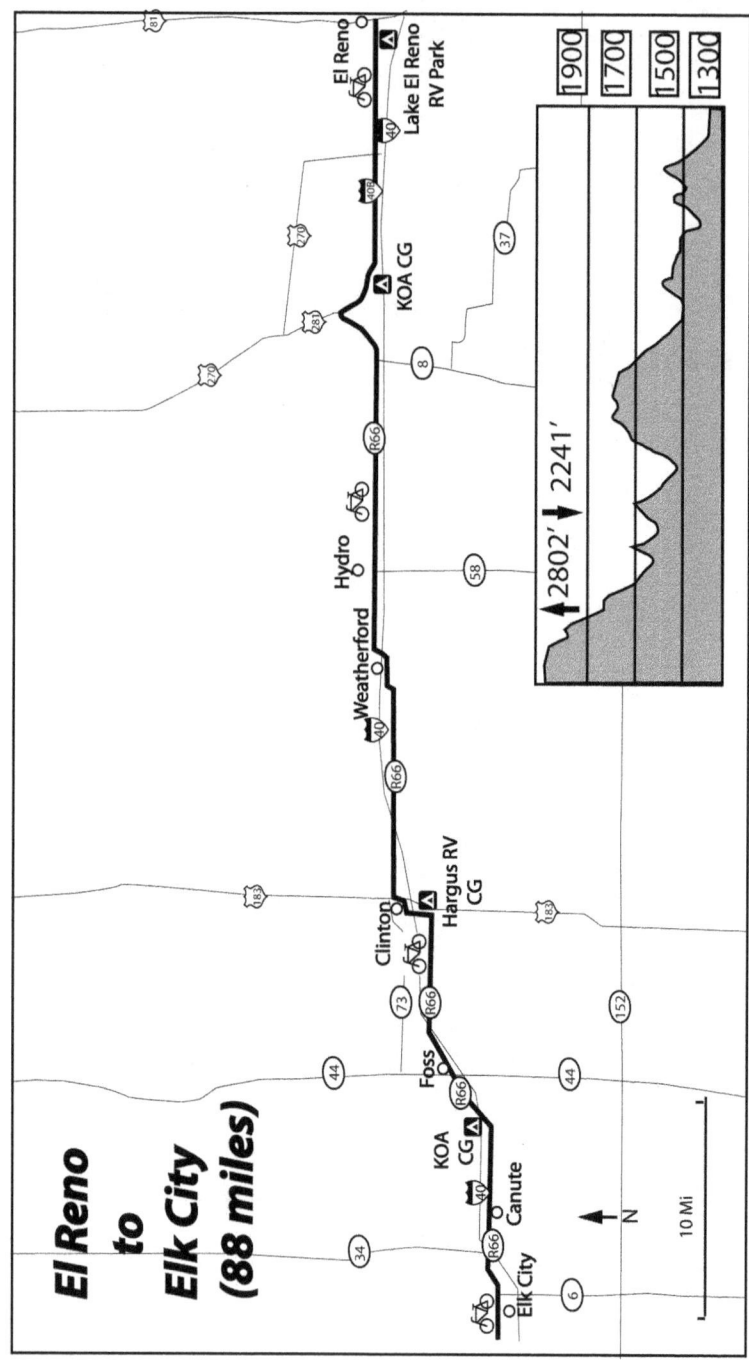

Route 66
SECTION 13

Elk City, OK to Alanreed, TX (86 miles)

As you are leaving Elk City stop at the 66 Sweet Shop, on West 3rd Street, for a one of their original Salty Frog snow cones. They are very refreshing on a hot day.

The turn for N1948 is easy to miss. But if you do pass it by you'll be routed onto I-40, so you'll know pretty quickly that you've missed it.

As I was riding through Sayre, they were working on renovation of the 1920s Rock Island Depot. It has a planned reopening in 2016, and will host the Shortgrass Museum, with a focus on displays showing early-day life on the shortgrass prairie.

Also, at the corner of 4th Street and Elm Avenue, stop to check out what looks like entrances to a storm cellar, and they are on both sides of the street. These are entrances to another of the underground tunnels under the highway we've seen in other towns along Route 66. It's really hard to imagine there was ever enough traffic here to justify a tunnel.

The Western Motel sign in Sayer is a classic Route 66 attention getter, with its neon lights and bright colors. It has also been well maintained.

The next time you're watching the movie *The Grapes of Wrath*, see if you recognize the Beckham County Courthouse. The large dome roof should make it easy to spot.

The town of Erick is proud of its favorite son, with Roger Miller Boulevard, Roger Miller Museum, and a Roger Miller Festival.

Erick also has the 100th Meridian Museum, located in a former old bank building. The museum is dedicated to the presentation of the 100th Meridian Line, which is very important for them because the location of the line has been an international and state dispute for over 166 years. I learned all about the dispute from a local while I was taking a break in front of the old bank. She also gave me the inside story on the Sand Hills Curiosity Shop, located down the street. It's nice the way people open up to a total stranger riding a bicycle.

About half-a-mile west of Texola you enter the 5th state on your Route 66 Adventure. Pause at the state line sign to capture the moment in a selfie.

Shamrock is home of one of the most iconic symbols of Route 66, the U-Drop Inn. Almost everyone has seen a picture of it at one time or another. The distinctive art deco architecture, the two flared towers, its unique geometric detailing, and the neon lighting sets it apart from any other structure on the route. Originally there were two separate business located in the building; the "Tower Station", which was a service station, and the "U-Drop Inn" café. Now, the recently renovated structure hosts the local chamber of commerce and tourist information center.

To reach downtown Shamrock, turn left on Main Street at the U-Drop Inn intersection, and ride less than a mile. The 1920s Reynolds Hotel now hosts the Pioneer West Museum. There are 20 rooms outfitted with displays, like a pioneer doctor's office, a general store, and schoolroom. There is also a city park nearby with kiosk telling about the water tower located there.

And don't forget to pay the Blarney Stone a visit. Located in Elmore Park, this is a fragment of the true Blarney Stone from Ireland. Legend has it that if you kiss the stone you will have everlasting good luck. I knelt way down to find a spot where I didn't think anyone else would have kissed it.

When I was eating lunch at a local Tex-Mex restaurant in Shamrock, I met at group of Europeans who had rented Harley Davison motorcycles and were touring Route 66. They talked like it is a very popular thing to do for Europeans. They told me there are businesses that cater specifically to this market. It appears Route 66 is quite popular across the pond.

Later, when I was riding along the route the group passed me and gave me the classic, hand down, two fingers salute.

The stretch of highway after leaving Shamrock is said to be one of the most authentic sections of the old road in existence. You'll know when you reach it because of the rhythmic thumpety-thump from the gaps in the concrete.

McLean claims to have "the first Route 66 museum ever". It's not a bad little stop for a small town, and they claim everything in it is authentic, with no replicas. If you're tired of Route 66 museums, try the nearby Devil's Rope Museum to learn more about barbed wire than you ever thought possible.

Just down the street from this is the first Phillips 66 station built in Texas. The local 66 preservation group did a great job restoring it to its original condition.

The origin of the name Phillips 66 came when one of the

Phillips petroleum company's officials was on a test drive using their new grade of gasoline. He was so excited that he said the car was going "like 60", then the driver replied back, "Sixty nothing ..... we're doing 66". At the time they also happened to be driving on Route 66, so it all made sense.

A few miles west of Alanreed you're going to be doing something I bet you didn't think you would be doing, you're going to be riding your bike on the interstate, or at least its shoulder. The traffic is fast and furious, so use caution. Also, whenever you reach an exit ramp, don't try to ride across it. You would be amazed how fast a vehicle going over 70 mph can cover distance when you're travelling slowly on a bike. Just take the exit and reenter the interstate on the vehicle entrance ramp.

Shortly after beginning your ride on the I-40 you pass the Texas Welcome Center. This is a really nice, well maintained, rest stop. There are also several interesting displays telling the history of the area, plus information on wind turbines. There are also several outdoor eating areas to take a break and enjoy the views from the relatively high vantage point.

Camping

Bobcat Creek RV Park
2005 NE Hwy 66
Sayre, OK 73662
580-210-9877
(.2 mile off route)

Sayre City Park CG
Hwy 283 S
Sayre, OK 73662
580-928-3660

Lake McCleelan CG
Farm to Market Rd
Alanreed, Texas
580-497-2143
(3 miles off route)

Lodging

*Western Motel
315 NE Highway 66
Sayre, OK 73662
580-928-3353

AmericInn
2405 South El Camino
Sayre, OK 73662
580-928-2700

Days Inn
1014 N Sheb Wooley Ave
Erick, OK 73645
580-526-3315

Premier inn and Suites
1001 N Shebwooley Drive
Erick, OK 73645
580-526-8124

*Shamrock Country Inn
711 E 12th St
Shamrock, TX 79079
806-256-3257

*Route 66 Inn
800 East 12th Street
Shamrock, TX 79079
806-256-3225

*Blarney Inn
402 E 12th St
Shamrock, TX 79079
806-256-2101

*Western Motel Restaurant
104 E 12th St
Shamrock, TX 79079
806-256-2342

Cactus Inn
101 Pine St
Mclean, TX 79057
806-779-2346

Bike Shops

N/A

The classic U-Drop Inn in Shamrock, Texas.

Route 66 Section 13

Miles E/W	Directions	Dist	R	Service	Miles W/E
	*Elk City (pop 11,693)			GLQR	
0	VR on 3rd St/I-40B/R66	6.5	3	GQR	86
7	R on N1948/E1149	4.5	3		80
11	L at SS on N1910	0.2	3		75
11	R at SS on frontage rd	1.4	3		75
13	R at SS on N1900 Rd to cross I-40	0.1	3	QR	74
13	L on frontage road	2.2	3		74
15	R at SS on R66/I-40B	1.4	3	CL	71
16	L at SS on 4th St/US283	1.2	3	GQ	70
18	*Sayre (pop 4,375)			CGLQR	69
18	S at SL on 4th St/US283	0.9	3	LQR	69
18	R on E1200 Rd	0.4	3		68
19	L at SS on US66	0.9	3	C	68
20	R at SS on El Camino/R66	8.5	3		67
28	S on R66/I-40B	4.5	3		58
33	*Erick (pop 1,052)			GQR	54
33	S on Roger Miller Blvd/R66/I-40B	2.5	3		54
35	S on R66/E1243	4.4	3		51
40	*Texola (pop 36)			Q	47
40	S US30 spur/R66/Frontage Rd/12th St	13.5	3		47
53	*Shamrock (pop 1,910)			GQR	33
53	S at SS on 12th St/I-40B/R66	1.6	3		33
55	Caution: At SS cross off-ramp then R on frontage rd/R66	15.0	3		32
70	R at SS on County Line Rd	0.3	3		17
70	L on R66/frontage rd	2.3	3		16
72	*Mclean (pop 778)			LQ	14
72	R on I-40B/R66	2.8	3		14
75	L on CR26 (unsigned)	0.1	3		11
75	L on service rd	0.3	3		11
76	R to ride under I-40 then R again to resume R66/3rd Ave	6.5	3		11
82	*Alanreed (pop 80)			CQ	4
82	S on 3rd Ave/SR271	0.3	3		4
82	L on unsigned frontage rd	2.8	3		4
85	R on Johnson Rd (unsigned) to go under I-40 then L	0.2	3		1
85	R to begin riding I-40	1.0	3		1
86	Rest area				

Route 66 Section 13

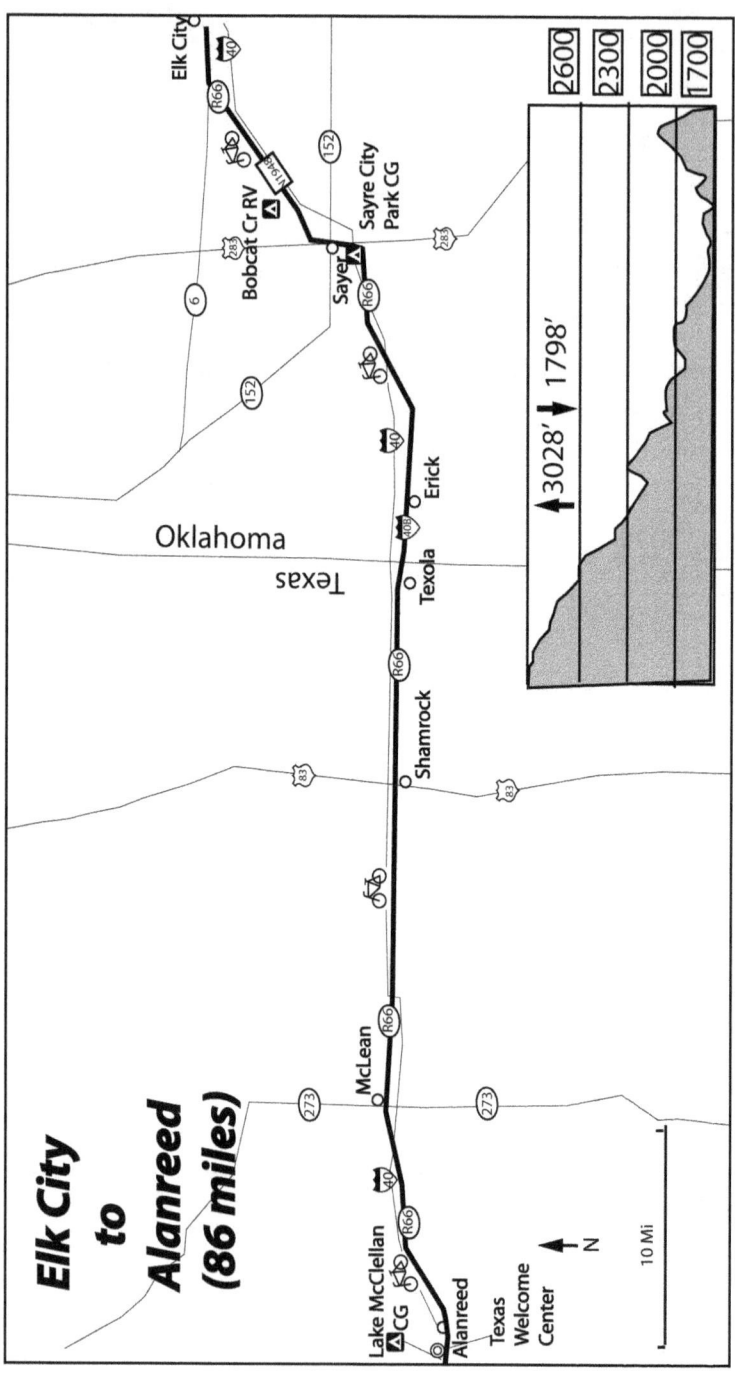

Route 66
SECTION 14

Alanreed, TX to Wildorado, TX (82 miles)

The exit for Lake McClellan Campground is a couple miles west of the Welcome Center, exit 128, on Farm to Market Road. The campground is about 3 miles off-route.

As you approach Groom, after passing the yield sign and crossing over the I-40 ramp (use caution), if you turn right to ride under the interstate, then turn right again, you'll see another CRA, The Leaning Tower of Texas.

In classic Route 66 marketing tradition, this was never a working water tower; it was built as a ploy to get people to stop. Ralph Britten, owner of the truck stop and restaurant located next to the tower, had it hauled in from a nearby town. He then pushed it upright with a bull dozer to an 80 degree angle and buried one side partway in the ground, leaving the other two legs dangling in midair. Even now, after the truck stop and restaurant are gone, the tower is still doing its job, because it got me to stop.

Shortly after resuming your ride, you can turn right on Eastern Avenue to reach the lodging listed in the guidebook. A Dairy Queen is conveniently located next door. There is also a restaurant in Groom, a little past this turn. The last I saw it was only open until 2:00 p.m.

As you are exiting Groom, turn right on Western Street to see The Cross. Even though, at 190-foot-tall, some claim that it is the largest cross in the Western Hemisphere, it actually falls short of several other structures. But this is none the less an interesting stop. In addition to the Cross, its base is surrounded by life-sized statues of the 14 Stations of the Cross. It is all a very moving solemn scene.

After leaving Groom you begin riding past some really large farm country. When I came through, there were fields of hay stretching to the horizon. I paused for a break alongside the highway to watch the wind whipping it around like waves in a stormy sea.

On the subject of wind, before beginning my ride I had heard that the predominant wind on the western end of Route 66 was from the west. I have encountered some strong head winds while cycling westward, however, talking to the eastbound cyclists I met, they said they had encountered their share of headwinds also. I prefer the idea of following the traditional westward migration of the earlier travelers by beginning my Route 66 Adventure in Chicago. However, you could consider breaking it down in halves, and riding eastward on the western half.

I noticed my first billboard for the Big Texan on this stretch. Maybe, just maybe, this will be the time I take on the 72 ounce steak challenge?

Not much remaining in Conway's downtown district. An abandoned service station and what appears to have been a school. Turn right on County Road N and ride half-a-mile to reach the Conway Inn/Restaurant and another CRA, the Slug Bug Ranch. What I am sure was meant as a tribute to the Cadillac Ranch further west, someone has taken 5 VW Beetles and buried them nose down, and given them creative psychedelic paint jobs. A must-see.

There is a Love's station just past the Bugs on the other side of I-40. There are also two five foot tall revolvers, guarding the driveway of a nearby house. At a closer look, the revolvers are BBQ grills. Just another reminder that this is the Wild West.

West of Conway the route gets you up close and personal with some of the big wind turbines. They were still installing some of these when I rode through. It was interesting watching these huge cranes assemble the gigantic parts, section by section, like it was a giant erector set.

Also in this section, watch out for the large cracks near the shoulder of the highway. It looks like they widened the road at one time, and now the added section is breaking away.

First the Leaning Tower, then the Cross, next the Slug Bug Ranch, and now a giant peace sign and numerous other metal art structures, in a field alongside the highway in the middle of nowhere. This section is quite unique, even by Route 66 standards. Keep an eye out for this Peace Park. It is well worth a look-see, and definitely a CRA.

The ride through Amarillo is a busy one, and this city does stretch on. However, the route we're riding avoids some of the busier sections. Once again use caution at the highway ramps.

While cycling along Interstate Drive, you'll pass another CRA, The Big Texan Steak House. In classic Route 66 marketing style, they advertise that if you can eat a 72 ounce steak, with all the trimmings which include shrimp cocktail, in one hour, your meal is free. What a promotional draw! Scanning through "The 72oz Hall of Fame", the smallest person I saw who completed the feast weighed only 136 pounds. So whenever one of you hungry cross-country cyclists get to add your name to the list, send me an email.

If you remain on the frontage road another block past the turn onto Quarter Horse Drive you can visit the American Quarter Horse Hall of Fame.

When you reach Polk Street, if you turn left and ride five blocks, you'll reach two blocks of what is considered the finest stretch of historical residential neighborhood in Amarillo. Think a minute, this is Texas. For these homes to stand out here, they have to be special. So check them out.

The stretch of Polk Street that the route does follow is lined with several buildings sporting some really classic neon signs that would make the early Route 66 business owners proud.

As you wind your way through Amarillo (I did warn you that this city stretches out) it is sometimes difficult to spot the street names. So, when in doubt, just follow the Route 66 signs. Also, watch out for the stretches of cobblestone surface.

When someone mentions Route 66, I think the first thing that comes to people mind for most would be this next CRA, The Cadillac Ranch. I know I've said this before, but this is classic Route 66, even though it wasn't constructed until 1974.

I didn't see anything at the site explaining the history behind the Ranch, so I'll provide a little info. This public art installation and sculpture was created by an alternative architecture group called "Ant Farm". They came up with the idea to plant 10 Cadillac automobiles nose-first in the ground, at an angle corresponding to that of the Great Pyramid of Giza. Each vehicle was meant to represent the birth and death of the defining feature of Cadillacs from the years 1949 to 1963: the tailfins.

Ant Farm artists approached Amarillo's local somewhat eccentric millionaire, Stanley Marsh 3 (I wish I had space to tell his story), about the idea. Legend has it, that he responded he would give them their answer by April Fool's Day, which obviously was "yes."

To reach this must-see work of art, shortly after beginning your ride on Indian Hill Road, turn left on Hope Road to ride .2 miles, then turn right on the frontage road and ride another .7 miles. Look to your left, and there, in all its glory, are the famous Caddies.

Another aspect that makes this is truly a unique piece of art is the tradition for visitors to make their own contribution to the structures. So dig a couple cans of partially filled spray paint cans out of the handy dumpster, walk across the field and add yet another layer of paint to the already thick skin coating the vehicles.

Don't make the mistake I later heard a group of women made. While I was eating at a restaurant further west, I overheard them talking to a local. They were saying how disappointed they were in the Cadillac Ranch. They had heard so much about it over the years; they thought it would be more than just a single restored pink Cadillac. After quizzing them about this, it turned out that the ladies had stopped at the Cadillac RV Park, located at the turn off Hope Road onto the frontage road, which does have a single pink Cadillac mounted on a pole. I felt so sorry for them.

A guy I met while making my mark on the Cadillacs told me about another Marsh 3 art piece to watch for while riding west, The Floating Mesa. This is the illusion of the top portion of a mesa being suspended in midair, created by a line of painted white plywood sheets installed just below the top of the mesa. Unfortunately, I was unable to locate this.

On the road between Bushland and Wildorado I passed the largest field of wind turbines I have ever seen. It stretched for as far as the eye can see. It was truly mesmerizing to watch that many blades slowly turning in disjointed synchronicity.

Camping

*Amarillo KOA
1100 Folsom Rd
Amarillo, TX 79108
806-335-1792

*Amarillo Ranch RV Park
1414 Sunrise Dr
Amarillo, TX 79104
806-373-4962

Lodging

Chalet Inn
610 Eastern Ave
Groom, TX 79039
806-248-7524

Conway Inn & Restaurant
9696 I-40
Conway, TX 79068
(806) 537-5127
(.5 mile off-route)

*Big Texan Motel
7701 I-40 East
Amarillo, Texas 79118
806-372-6000

*Motel 6 Amarillo
4301 E Interstate 40
Amarillo, TX 79104
806-373-3045

Comfort Inn & Suites
2300 Soncy Rd
Amarillo, TX 79121
806-457-9100
(1 block off-route to save $)

Royal Inn
711 I-40 Frontage Rd
Wildorado, TX 79098
806-426-3315

Bike Shops

Sun Adventure Sports
2826 Wolflin Ave
Amarillo, TX 79109
806-351-2453

Hill's Sport Shop
4021 Mockingbird Ln
Amarillo, TX 79109
806-355-7232

Outdoor Element Sports
3410 S Western St
Amarillo, TX 79109
806-353-2900

The famous Cadillac Ranch, documenting the evolution of the tailfin.

Route 66 Section 14
Alanreed to Wildorado (82 miles)

Miles E/W	Directions	Dist	R	Service	Miles W/E
	Rest area				
0	Exit Rest area on I-40 (caution)	4.5	5	C	82
5	Exit I-40 on exit 124	0.3	3		78
5	L at SS on SR70 to cross I-40	0.3	3		77
5	R on R66/frontage rd	3.7	3		77
9	L on frontage rd (unsigned) away from I-40	6.3	3		73
15	S at YS on I-40B to cross I-40 ramp then VL	0.8	3		67
16	*Groom (pop 574)			LQR	66
16	S on Front St/R66	2.5	3		66
18	S at SS to cross off-ramp then R on frontage rd/R66	12.2	3		64
31	S at SL on SR207/R66	0.9	2		52
32	*Conway (pop 20)				51
32	S on CR2161	7.0			51
39	R at YS to cross over I-40	0.3	2		44
39	L on frontage rd/R66	4.5	2		43
43	R at SS on I-40B/R66	4.0	4		39
47	L at SS on Amarillo Blvd/I-40B/SR60	5.8	4	C	35
53	L at SL on Lakeside Dr/Loop 335	2.1	5		29
55	R on Interstate Dr before crossing I-40(unsigned)	3.4	4	CLQR	27
59	R at SL on Quarter Horse Dr	0.3	4		24
59	L on Tee Anchor Blvd/Loop 395/10th Ave	2.0	4	GQ	23
61	*Amarillo (pop 190,695)				21
61	R on Polk St	0.4	3	R	21
61	L on 6th Ave/Loop 279/R66	2.5	3		21
64	VL on Bushland Blvd/9th Ave	1.2	4	QR	18
65	L at SL on Amarillo Blvd/R66	3.8	3	LQR	17
69	R on Indian Hill Rd	3.6	3		13
72	L at SS on S Hill Rd then R on frontage rd	2.0	3		10
74	*Bushland (pop 130)			QR	8
74	S on frontage rd/R66	7.7	3		8
82	*Wildorado (pop 423)			LR	0

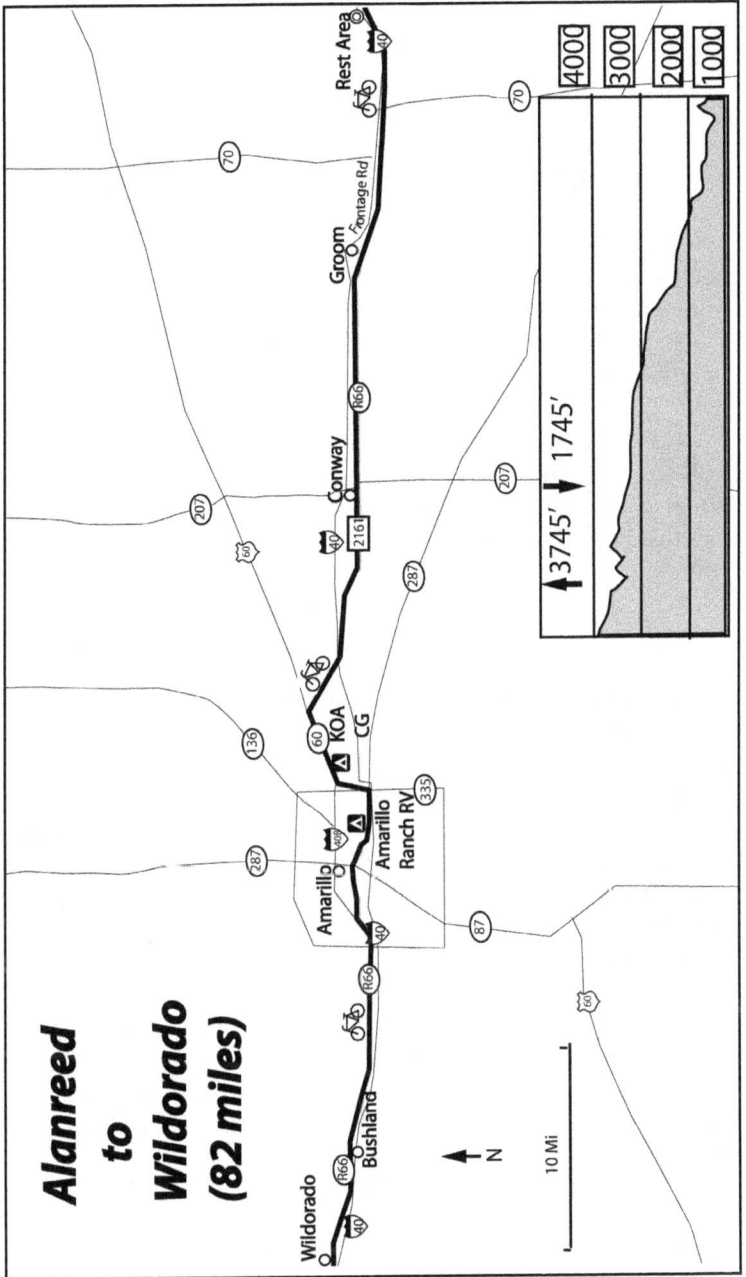

Route 66
SECTION 15

Wildorado, TX to Tucumcari, NM (89 miles)

If you check out the map for this section, you'll see there isn't much out there; be sure to carry lots of water because there are some long dry stretches.

To reach the motel in Wildorado turn left and go under I-40, then right on the frontage road. The Windy Cow Café is right next door

I spotted an entire herd of pronghorn on this stretch, peacefully grazing on the countryside. They can afford to feel safe and content on the open plains because they are the fastest mammal in the Northern Hemisphere. It's always nice to see them running free and wild.

When you reach Vega, if you are ready to do a little sightseeing, turn right on Main Street to check out the historic downtown. A few of the points of interest are the 1915 Oldham County Courthouse, several nice street murals, a historic kiosk telling about the town of Old Tascosa located a few miles to the north (which has a boot hill cemetery), and the restored Magnolia Service Station.

There is a story posted at the station, written by the original owners of the Magnolia Station, explaining what life was like living above the station. There is also information about the station being changed to a Mobil station and how at that time the highway was part of the Ozark Trail.

The Ozark Trail predates Route 66, and the federal highway system itself. It was built back in the days when citizens weren't always sitting around waiting for the government to run things. In 1913 a group of private citizens formed the Ozark Trails Association and set out to encourage local communities to build and maintain a connected network of highways across Missouri, Oklahoma, the Texas panhandle, and on into Mexico. They did such a great job that much of the highways they built were incorporated into Route 66.

By the way, Cyrus Avery, "The Father of Route 66", was first involved with the creation of the Ozark Trail.

When you reach Adrian it is time to break out the champagne, because as the town claims "when you're here, you're half way

Route 66 Section 15

there". You have reached the traditionally accepted halfway point of Route 66.

If you don't happen to have a bottle of champagne stuffed in your panniers, then stop at the Midpoint Café and celebrate this momentous occasion with a piece of their famous "ugly crust pie".

Starting out as a one-room, dirt-floor café in 1928, this establishment has seen a lot of changes over the years. In 2001, when a crew from Pixar Animation Studios came through, the café was the inspiration for the Flo's V-8 Café in their Cars film. Also, three of the characters in the film were inspired by the staff at the café.

Although the Midpoint Café is not as busy as it once was during Route 66's heyday, when it was open 24-hours, current owners Dennis and Donna say they stay pretty busy, and the route's popularity continues to grow each year. By mid-year, when I rode through, they had already had visitors from 37 countries dine at their restaurant.

As I had lunch at the Midpoint a tour bus load of Japanese tourists made it their lunch break also. So Route 66 is alive and well.

After leaving Adrian, when the route takes you on I-40 again, for once you may appreciate the highway rumble strips. With them between you and passing motorists maybe they will get the attention of a texting driver when they are veering off the interstate.

Just prior to crossing the Texas/New Mexico state line, you can take a side tour of Glenrio. There are several buildings listed on the National Register of Historic Places, but everything is closed and shutdown now. But it's just a short ride, and it will give you a break from I-40.

You enter the sixth state of your Route 66 Adventure while riding I-40. Yahoo! There is a really good welcome center shortly after entering New Mexico.

At exit 369, we aren't going to go to ride to the town of Endee that is listed for the exit, but we are going to exit I-40. Yay! The Russel's Travel Center at this exit has some nice Route 66 memorabilia, a sweet collection of vintage automobiles (with an obvious bias towards GM), and my favorite, a restaurant.

With the wide open plains you have a great opportunity to enjoy the views of the distant mesas. Here is something I use when determining if a formation is a mesa or a butte. A mesa is wider than tall and buttes are taller than they are wide. To remember, I take the m from mesa, turn it upside down to form a w, for wider.

Enjoyed seeing the iron work art at the entrances to some of the ranches.

There is a city park in San Jon with covered picnic tables, restrooms, and overnight parking. All the comforts of home and the best part is it's free.

After leaving San Jon I spotted my first butte. I bet the wind turbines mounted on top of these buttes get a lot of wind. It seems to me that wind turbines as a cash crop would require a lot less maintenance than growing traditional crops. Just one of the many thoughts that pass through my head while cycling across the plains.

Time for a celebration, "when you're here, you're halfway there".

Route 66 Section 15

This is really dry parched land. However, based on the deep arroyos they must get some rain. There is some farming taking place too, so that is another sign there is water somewhere. I felt sorry for the farmer I watched who was plowing his field. Each time he turned around he had to ride through the huge dust cloud he created.

You will pass the KOA listed in the guidebook just prior to reaching Tucumcari. There is also a cattle guard across the highway here that could pop a spoke.

There are a lot of options for lodging on the highway into Tucumcari. With the Tepee Curios Shop, the nostalgic signs, and other classic attractions, the ride along this strip is something of a throwback to an earlier Route 66 era. You can bag another "-est" here by stopping at the Convention Center to see the world's largest mural devoted to Route 66.

Tucumcari would be a nice place to spend a couple days to rest up. With all the older motels left over from the busy Route 66 days you can get a nice room for a good price. Plus there are a ton of interesting things to do, such as: Mesalands Community College and Dinosaur Museum, Tucumcari Historical Museum, New Mexico Route 66 Museum, and more. Stop at the Chamber of Commerce, at 404 West Route 66 to find out more.

If you do spend a night in Tucumcari be sure to get out after dark to see their colorful display of neon signs. I can only imagine what it must have looked like in the route's heyday.

As always, be sure to let businesses know you are touring on a bicycle. Maybe when they think of us a source of money maybe they will treat cyclists better when they see us on the highway.

Camping

*Walnut RV Park
1403 Vega Blvd
Vega, TX 79092
806-267-2310

*KOA Tucumcari
6299 Quay Rd A L,
Tucumcari, NM 88401
575-461-1841

Adrian City Park
7th St & Walnut Ave
Adrian, TX 79001
806-344-6535

Mountain Road RV Park
1700 S Mountain Rd
Tucumcari, NM 88401
575-461-96281

*San Jon City Park
4th St & Elm Ave
San Jon, NM

Route 66 Section 15

Lodging

*Bonanza Motel
607 Vega Blvd
Vega, TX 79092
806-267-2158

*Americas Best Value Inn
1800 West Vega Blvd
Vega, TX 79092
806-244-5637

San Jon Motel
715 E Main Ave
San Jon, NM 88434
575-576-2911

*Historic Route 66 Motel
1620 Rte 66
Tucumcari, NM 88401
575-461-1212

*Blue Swallow Motel
815 E Rte 66 Blvd,
Tucumcari, NM 88401
575-461-9849

*Americas Best Value Inn
3604 E Tucumcari Blvd
Tucumcari, NM 88401
575-461-9611

Bike Shops

N/A

Wildorado to Tucumcari (89 miles)

Miles E/W	Directions	Dist	R	Service	Miles W/E
	*Wildorado (pop 423)			LR	
0	S on frontage rd/R66/Vega Blvd	12.8	3		89
13	*Vega (pop 884)			CGLQR	77
13	S on frontage rd/R66	13.7	3	L	77
27	*Adrian (pop 166)			CGLQR	63
27	S on frontage rd (west)	4.9	3		63
31	L to enter I-40 (just past Gruhlkey Rd)	18.0	5		58
49	*Enter New Mexico)		5		40
49	S on I-40	3.3	5		40
53	Exit #369 then R on SR93 then L on frontage rd	13.8	3	Q	37
67	L at SS on SR469	0.5	3	CQR	23
67	*San Jon (pop 216)			CLQR	22
67	R on R66/frontage rd	19.3	3	C	22
86	R on R66/Tucumcari Blvd (unsigned)	3.1	3	GLQR	3
89	*Tucumcari (pop 5,363)			CGLQR	0

Route 66 Section 15

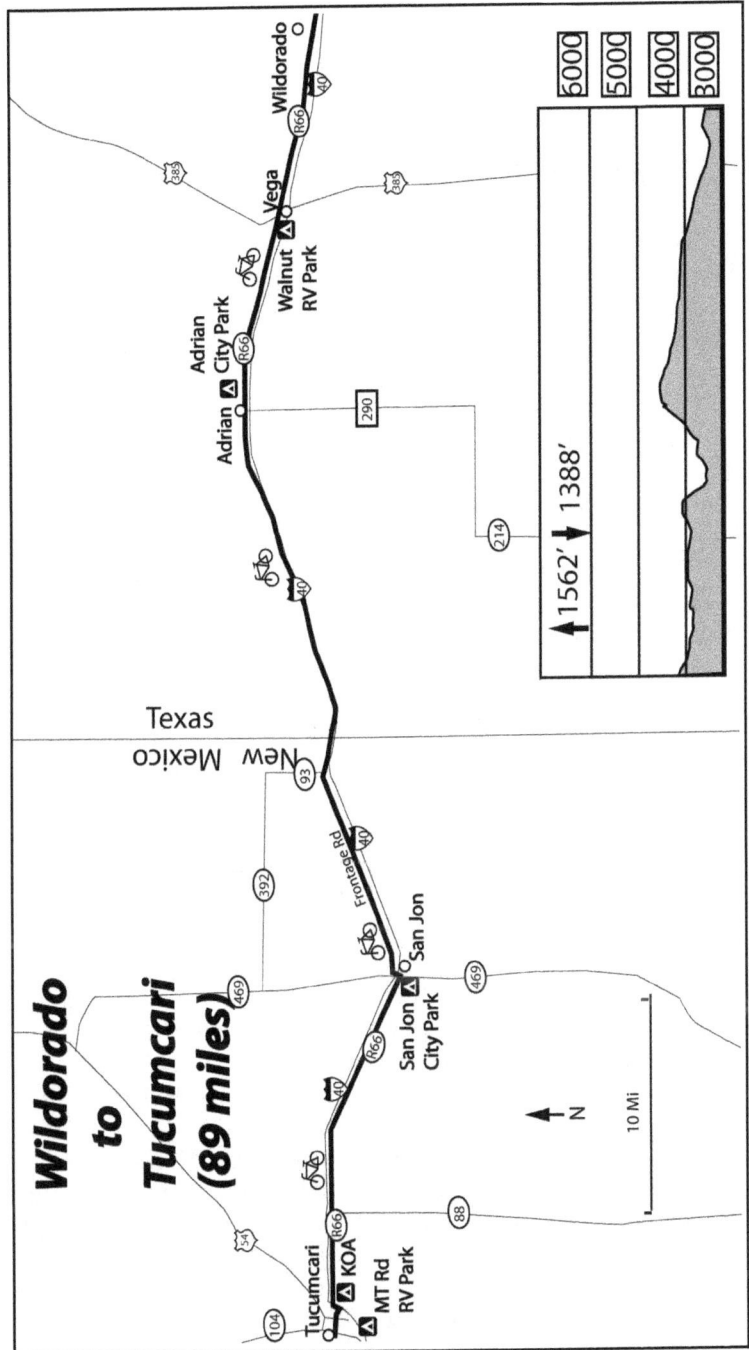

105

Route 66
SECTION 16

Tucumcari, NM to Romeroville, NM (117 miles)

Forget what I said about there not being much out there in the previous section. This section makes Section 15 look densely populated. You'll find yourself pretty isolated at times on this ride. Not only are the towns sparse through here but there are stretches where there aren't any houses. But hey, that's part of the cross-country cycling adventure.

With the layout of the highways of this section I was able to include more miles on the map than in previous sections, but the route is very obvious and there isn't much detail required on the map.

There is a large old abandoned Shell truck stop and restaurant on the outskirts of Tucumcari that looks like it was probably a pretty busy place at one time. I hope the owners had a lot of good years before it had to shut down.

You have a nice unobstructed view of Tucumcari Mountain off to the north after leaving Tucumcari. There was a cartoon version of the mountain in the Cars film. Pop quiz: Is it a mesa or a butte?

There is a convenience store when you leave I-40 at the 321 exit; however on my most recent trip through here it had burned down. I don't know if they will rebuild. Please email me if they rebuild and I will post it on the updates section of my website.

At this same exit watch out for the cattle guard across the highway. A large portion of this section must be passing through open range country because there are cattle guards across the start and end of many of the frontage roads. Some of them are pretty rough too, so keep an eye out for them.

You're going to get to flush out some more swallows again as you ride through the I-40 underpasses.

The route passes an old cemetery as you enter Montoya. Stretch your legs and check out some of the dates and names. There are also the ruins of an old gas station there. The façade has broken off in several sections, exposing the clay bricks and stones that makeup the walls. Sometimes you have to stop and take a closer look to find the forgotten stories of Route 66.

Leaving Montoya there is a particularly rough cattle guard.

Route 66 Section 16

You don't want to break down out here.

The red clay mountains just keep becoming a deeper even more beautiful color as we make our way across the foothills into the mountains. The canyon walls in the distance a growing taller also.

Leaving Cuervo, the route gives us a welcome break from I-40. There are a lot of potholes in the first miles of the route, however the second half of County Road 2C is smoother, and State Road 156 is much better. This is the straight stretch of highway where I took the picture for this section. I didn't see a single vehicle after Cuervo until returning to I-40.

I really enjoyed being away from I-40 for a while, however I was ready for a Mountain Dew and ice cream bar by the time I reached Santa Rosa.

Santa Rosa is doing a great job preserving the Route 66 theme, with a Route 66 Museum packed with classic vintage cars, the Silver Moon Café, and several classic neon signs. Be sure to support these and other Route 66 attractions, otherwise they won't be able to stay in business.

While you're in Santa Rosa, there is another attraction I recommend checking out, Blue Hole. This is an artesian well with a constant water temperature of 64 degrees, which even after a hot day in the saddle feels pretty chilly. The visible surface opening of the swimming hole is 80' in diameter; however it expands to 130' at the bottom, which is 80' down. This is one of the most popular dive destinations in the U.S. So if you happen to be a cyclist/diver you can rent equipment at a nearby dive shop.

Blue Hole is right in town, and only about half-a-mile off-route. You pass two other lakes on the ride to reach it.

After leaving Santa Rosa you're back on I-40 for about 14 miles. There's not much to see or do through here either. At exit #267 there is a convenience store, but the last time I came through here it was closed. If they reopen it would someone email me and I will post it on the updates section of my website.

The route chosen by Adventure Cycling Association (ACA) uses the pre-1937 route that takes you north, just short of Las Vegas, New Mexico (not Nevada). Both this route and the newer route take you to Albuquerque, however if you look at a map, the earlier route takes the long way around. You may ask yourself, why didn't the earlier route follow the most direct path? Politics!

During my layover in Santa Fe, which I highly recommend everyone should do, I was at a bar, making friends with some of

Route 66 Section 16

the locals, and they told me that at the time the earlier route was being laid out, New Mexico was pretty much ran by a group of businessmen, which just so happened to reside in Santa Fe. Realizing the boom Route 66 would have on the communities it passed through, they made sure Santa Fe did not miss out. Politics haven't changed much, have they?

However, I'd like to thank those politicians, because their route makes for a sweet bike ride. And, even though the post-1937 route is more direct, a lot of the old frontage roads on it are no longer available and we would have had to put in a lot more miles on I-40 if this had been our route. Also, I did have a favorable tailwind on most of this stretch on road.

You cross the Pecos River for the second time just south of Dilla. Your first crossing was leaving Santa Rosa. There was water in it at both crossing when I rode through, however it was pretty muddy.

About a mile after this second crossing you pass a historical marker alongside the highway. I'll not tell what it says so you will have a reason to stop and take a break.

The restaurant listed in the Mileage Log for Dilla is actually a lounge that serves snacks. I didn't want anyone to get their hopes up.

During the long stretch following Dilla you pass an occasional home where you might be able to get water or other assistance if needed, but it is still pretty barren. However, there isn't much traffic or other distractions, so you have a great environment to really appreciate the beauty of the area. I noticed the ruins of an old Spanish style villa, with a stone walled courtyard and stucco covered walls on what remains of the house. It looks like it was really special at one time.

There is some pretty serious climbing on this route, but the surroundings are worth it.

There are no services in Montoya, however, but once again there are a few houses.

North of Montoya you begin to have some trees along the roadside. It's a nice addition to the scenery.

When you reach Romeroville, you can go off-route and continue north another 10 miles on the frontage road to reach Las Vegas, NM, which has full services and camping.

Classic Route 66 mural in Tucumcari, New Mexico.

Camping

*Santa Rosa CG & RV Park
2136 Rte 66
Santa Rosa, NM 88435
575-472-3126

Santa Rosa Lake State Park
NM Hwy 91
Santa Rosa, NM 88435
575) 472-3110

KOA & Cabins
76 Romeroville Frontage Rd
Las Vegas, NM 87701
505-454-0180
(half-a-mile off route)

Lodging

*La Mesa Motel
2415 Rte 66
Santa Rosa, NM 88435
575-472-3021

*Motel 6
3400 Historic Route 66
Santa Rosa, NM 88435
505-200-3273

*La Quinta Inn
2277 Historic Rte 66
Santa Rosa, NM 88435
575-472-4800

*Best Western Inn
2491 Historic Route 66
Santa Rosa, NM 88435
575-472-5877

Holiday Inn Express & Suites
816 South Grand Avenue
Las Vegas, NM 87701
877-410-6681

El Fidel Motel
500 Douglas Ave
Las Vegas, NM 87701
505-425-6761

Bike Shops
N/A

Tucumcari to Romeroville (117 miles)

Miles E/W	Directions	Dist	R	Service	Miles W/E
	*Tucumcari (pop 5,363)			CGLQR	
0	S on R66/Tucumcari Blvd	0.8	3		117
1	VL on R66/US54/I-40B	2.3	3		116
3	VL then VR to enter I-40	7.3	5		114
10	Exit #321 then L to cross I-40	0.3			107
11	R at SS on frontage rd	1.1			106
12	S to cross CR AZ cont on frontage rd	3.0			105
15	R on dirt road to ride under I-40	0.1			102
15	L on frontage rd (pavement)	6.0			102
21	*Montoya				96
21	VL on frontage rd to cross over I-40 then VR to cont frontage rd	6.3	3		96
27	VR to cross over I-40 then L on frontage rd	4.9	3		90
32	*Newkirk (pop 7)			Q	85
32	S at SS on frontage rd	8.6			85
41	*Cuervo (pop 58)				76
41	L on Cuervo Ln/CR 2C (ride under I-40)	5.1	2		76
46	R at SS on SR156 (unsigned)	14.0	2		71
60	R at SS on SR84/Will Rogers Dr go under I-40 the VL	3.0	3	CLQR	57
63	*Santa Rosa (pop 2,848)			CGLQR	54
63	S then VR on US84/I-40B	1.2	3		54
64	S on US84 to ride over I-40 then enter I-40	16.0	5		53
80	Exit #256 R66/SR84	0.1	3		37
80	R at SS on R66/SR84	13.6	3		37
94	*Cross Pecos River				23
94	S on R66/SR84	1.7	2		23
95	*Dilla			R	22
95	S on R66/US84	21.7	2		22
117	*Romeroville			CQR	0

Route 66 Section 16

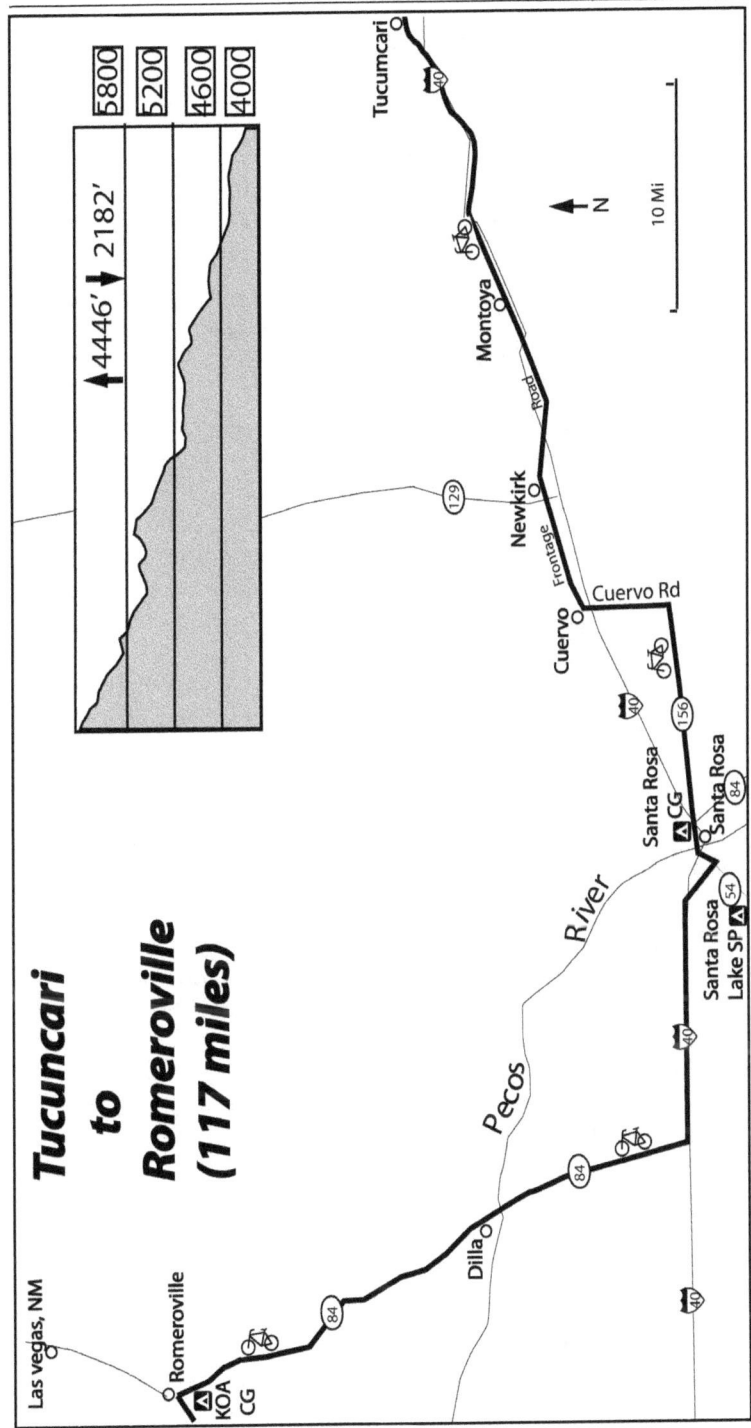

111

Route 66
SECTION 17

Romeroville, NM to Golden, NM (98 miles)

Even though the beginning and ending elevation for this section is about the same, you have over 5,000 feet of climbing and descending to overcome in between. And with the route at times cresting over 7,000 feet in elevation, which has about 25% less oxygen in the air than at sea level, you may experience difficulty breathing until you have become acclimated.

The best method for acclimating to this thin air is to drink plenty of water. With the towns being few and far between, this will probably require you to carry more water than normal. An easy way I found to prepare for carrying extra water along select sections of a tour is to use collapsible water bottles, because they are easy to store when not in use.

After passing Serafina keep watch to the south for an interesting pointed mesa. This is Starvation Peak. Legend has it that settlers were chased up the mesa by Indian warriors, where they stayed until they starved to death.

When researching this section, I found something that mentioned a convenience store at the exit for State Highway 3. FYI, I didn't see one when I came through.

The convenience store listed just after crossing the Pecos River was open the last time I came through, however it was listed for sale. So you might not rely too much on it being open.

After passing Rowe our route is going to start heading north, following the pre-1937 Historical Route 66 towards Santa Fe. Early into this stretch you pass a Historical Marker for Pecos National Historical Park. A little further after that you pass the park itself. The Pecos Indians inhabited this location for over 1200 years.

Be sure to stop at the park's picturesque visitor center to watch a 15 minute movie on the history of the park and stretch the kinks out of your legs on a mile and a half self-guided walking tour around the remains of an old pueblo and mission. It makes for a pleasant break from your ride.

On your approach into Glorieta, be sure to stop to read the interesting Historical Marker about "The Gettysburg of the West".

Route 66 is following the old Santa Fe Trail in this section.

Route 66 Section 17

This was an important transportation route pioneered in 1821 that was part of a network of trails which linked Europe, New York, St. Louis, Santa Fe, and Mexico City.

After the exit off I-25, as you turn onto the Old Las Vegas Highway there is another Historical Marker on your left. If you turn right, you can take a short ride off-route to visit a quaint Old Catholic church. It's pretty small, and not especially ornate, but they are keeping it up nicely and it's good to visit it so they will see their labor is being appreciated.

On this first road after exiting the interstate you pass the KOA, the Rancheros de Sante Fe campground, the SpinDoc Bike Shop, and Café Fina. The café is a converted Fina Station and the food really hit the spot for me after a long day in the saddle. However, you might want to wait a few more miles to eat at the trendy Harry's Roadhouse. If having numerous cars parked outside a restaurant is a testimony to the food, their food must be something special because the parking lot was packed.

There are several more interesting Historical Markers along this stretch of highway on your approach into Santa Fe.

Our route does not take you through the historic district in Santa Fe; however it does come within a mile. So with a dozen or more museums and cultural centers, plus more than 250 galleries located within this cultural Mecca, I highly recommend that you ride that extra mile and take some of it in. Or maybe even layover for a couple of days and try to experience it all.

To reach the International Hostel, instead of turning onto the Arroyo de Los Chamois Trail, continue straight on Alta Vista Road another .2 miles, then turn left on Cerrillos Road to ride another .3 miles, and the hostel is on your left. The Broken Spoke Bike Shop is conveniently located next door. Plus, Pantry Restaurant, a favorite dining place for the locals, is just a couple blocks further south. You will also find several reasonably priced motels that are listed in the guidebook located in this area. So your layover wouldn't be an expensive stay.

If you look at a city map there are a variety of routes to reach downtown historic Santa Fe, however to keep it simple, you can turn right on Cerrillos and ride about a mile to reach it.

There is so much to see that it will probably be best to begin you Santa Fe adventure with a stop at the Visitors Bureau, located at 201 West Marcy Street, in the heart of the historic district. This will also put you within walking distance to bag a couple more "-est", being the oldest house and oldest church in the U.S. While visiting the church be sure to ring the 780 pound San Jose Bell, located inside the church, to experience its deep rich tone.

Njoy!

The Arroyo de Los Chamois Trail starts out paralleling a set of railroad tracks then veers off to follow the banks of the arroyo. It was dry when I came through, but even if it had water it looks like it would be pretty shallow. There are several kiosks alongside the trail telling about the environment and area wildlife. It is an easy route to follow but it would be easy to miss your exit because the trail continues on beyond the turn. Shortly after riding under Rodeo Road watch your exit on your left. There are actually two exits, and they are not very far .apart. You want to take the second one. However, if you do take the first one it will still take you to Big Sky Drive, and you will just be a little further up on the road.

The trail drops you out into a maze of identical looking stucco homes on Big Sky Drive. Just follow the directions in the Mileage Log to find your way out.

When Governor Miles Road reaches Cerrillos Road, if you need to pick up some supplies before heading out of town, there is a Walmart to the right, plus some restaurants.

Almost immediately after leaving the big city you are back riding through some beautiful scenery once again. You will also pass a correctional facility and a penitentiary, so don't pick up any hitch hikers.

The listed convenience store on the long stretch after leaving Santa Fe is located about ten miles into the ride.

Around the turn for Los Cerrillos you will begin to pass some really impressive art work in front of many of the homes. Not to be outdone, Mother Nature has created a lot of interesting art-like rock formations in this area for you to enjoy also.

The Cerrillos State Park that you pass is only a day use area that does not offer camping. However, it does have restrooms and water.

When you reach Madrid, with the studios and shops, the artistic tone that began back in Santa Fe continues. You can see from the piles of rock tailings on the mountainsides that this was once a working community; however this is pretty much an art community now. I think that if I were an artist, this is where I would want to live.

On the ride between Madrid and Golden you have a beautiful view across an expansive wide basin with the mountain range in the distance.

Sweet!

Some of the local art alongside Turquoise Road near Cerrillos, New Mexico.

Camping
*US Forestry Dept
32 S Main St
Pecos, NM 87552
505-757-6121

The Lotus
12 Waldo Mesa Rd
Madrid, NM 87010
505-473-1464
(1/2 mile off-route)

*Santa Fe KOA
934 Old Las Vegas Highway
Santa Fe, NM 87505
505-466-1419

*Rancheros De Santa Fe CG
736 Old Las Vegas Hwy
Santa Fe, NM 87505
505-466-3482

Lodging
Pecos River Cabins
20 Cabin Rd
Pecos, NM
505-757-8752

Santa Fe Sage Inn
725 Cerrillos Road
Santa Fe, NM
505-982-5952

*Bobcat Inn
442 Old Las Vegas Hwy
Santa Fe, NM 87505
505-988-9239

King's Rest Court Inn
1452 Cerrillos Rd
Santa Fe, NM 87505
505-983-8879

The Broken Spoke
1426 Cerrillos Rd
Santa Fe, NM 87505
505-992-3102

Motel 6 Santa Fe
646 Cerrillos Rd
Santa Fe, NM 87505
505-982-3551

*Java Junction B&B
2855 NM-14
Madrid, NM 87010
505-438-2772

Bike Shops
SpinDoc Bicycle Shop
628 Old Las Vegas Hwy,
Santa Fe, NM 87505
505-466-4181

Rob & Charlie's Bike Shop
1632 St. Michael's Drive
Santa Fe, NM 87505
505-471-9119

Miles E/W	Directions	Dist	R	Service	Miles W/E
	*Romeroville			CQR	
0	S under I-40 then L at SS on FR2116/Old Las Vegas Hwy (OLVH)	4.5	3		98
5	*Tecolote (pop 298)				93
5	S at SS on FR2116/OLVH	5.0	3		93
10	*Serafina				88
10	S on FR2116/OLVH	8.6	3		88
18	*Cross Pecos River				80
18	VL on FR2116 over I-25	0.9	3	Q	80
19	VR on FR2116/OLVH	11.4	3		79
30	*Rowe (pop 415)				67
30	R to ride under I-25 then L at SS on R66/SR63	3.6	3		67
34	*Peco Natil Historical Park				64
34	S on R66/SR63	2.0	3	C	64
36	*Pecos (pop 1,392)			GQR	62
36	L at SS on SR50	5.7	3	Q	62
42	*Glorieta (pop 430)				56
42	L at SS then R to enter I-25	5.0	5		56
47	*Canoncito				51
47	Exit #294 R at SS then L on OLVH/FR2108	3.4	4	C	51
50	*Café Fina across from US285				48
50	S on OLVH/SR300	6.5	3	QR	48
57	R at SL on Old Pecos Tr/SR466	1.1	3	R	41
58	*Santa Fe (pop 67,947)			CGLQR	40
58	R at SL cont Old Pecos Tr	0.7	4		40
58	L at SL on San Mateo Rd	0.3	4		39
59	R on Don Gasper Rd	0.3	4		39
59	L on Malaga Rd	0.2	4		39
59	L at SS on Galisteo St then R on Alta Vista	0.7	4		38
60	L on Arroyo de los Chamisos Tr	4.3	P		38
64	Ride under Rodeo Rd	0.3	P		33
65	L on path then R on Big Sky Dr	0.2	P		33
65	L on Dancing Ground Rd	0.3	2		33
65	R at SS on Governor Miles Rd	0.7	4		33
66	L at SL on Cerrillos Rd/SR14	17.5	4	Q	32
83	*Los Cerrillos (offroute .3)			R	14
83	S on SR14/Turquoise Tr	2.8	3		14
86	*Madrid (pop 204)			CGLR	12
86	S on SR14/Turquoise Tr	11.6	3		12
98	*Golden				0

Route 66 Section 17

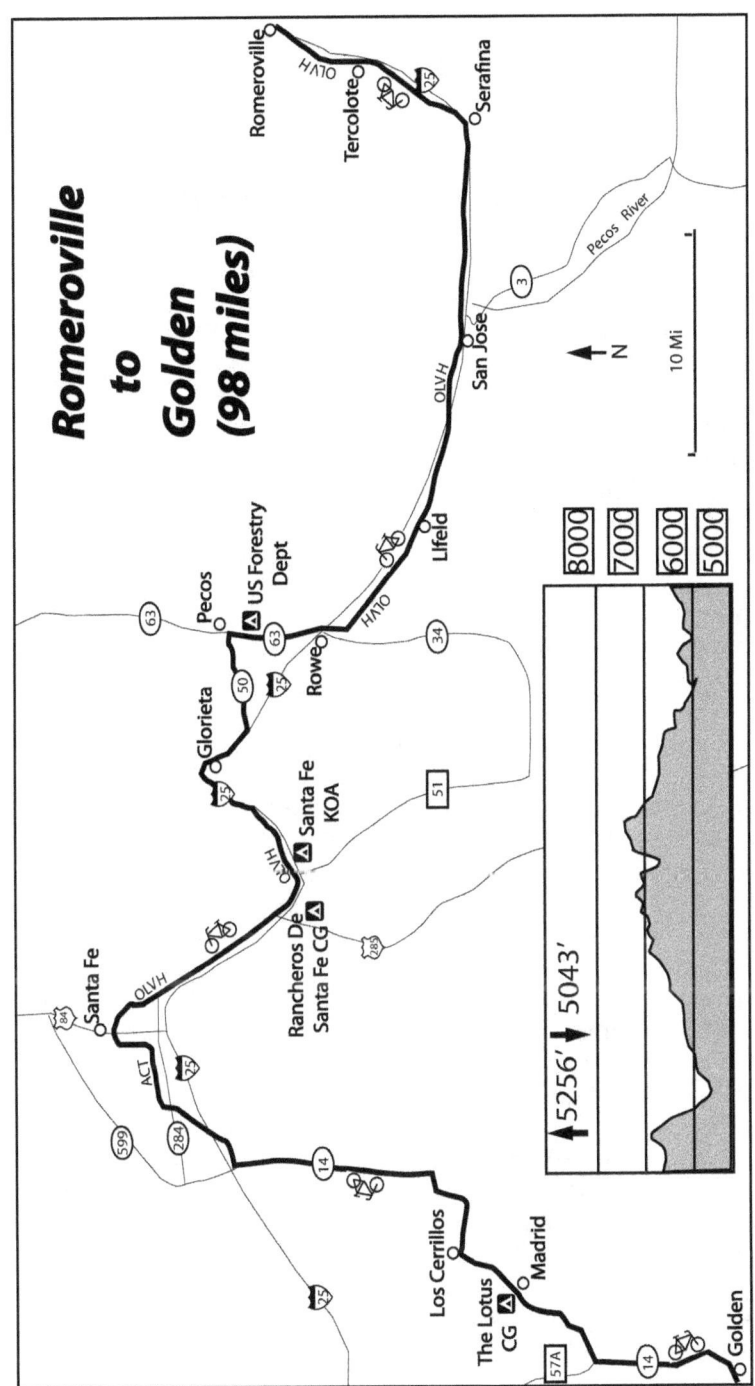

Route 66
SECTION 18

Golden, NM to Paraje, NM (102 miles)

This section begins in the town of Golden. During the mid-1800s this was a typical gold rush town that sprang up virtually overnight. However, due to limited gold finds the boom had fizzled out by 1880.

About the only thing remaining in Golden is the San Francisco Catholic Church. This adobe building was originally built in 1830. With its restoration in 1960 it is still an attractive structure, perched on a small hill beside the road. Mass continues to be held there each Saturday.

The beginning of this section of Route 66 follows State Road 14. Also known as the Turquoise Trail, named after the blue-green turquoise first mined here by the Pueblo people as early as 900 AD. It is on rides through scenic areas like this that you see where New Mexico gets its nickname, "Land of Enchantment". There are not many man-made attractions along this stretch, but the vast openness and natural beauty is overwhelming.

However, if you want an attraction to visit, turn north on State Road 536 in the town of San Antonio and ride for a little over a mile to reach Tinkertown Museum. This place is truly a one-of-a-kind attraction that's difficult to describe.

It took artist Ross Ward 40 years to carve, and collect the exhibits housed in this 22 room museum, which is surrounded by a wall constructed of over 50,000 glass bottles. With elaborate handmade dioramas of Old West scenes, antique toys, and a massive display of other collectibles, it's quite an interesting place.

Keep an eye out for the memorial for James N. Quinn on the left side of the highway in Tijeras. He was killed in 2007 while riding his bike in the area. Judging by the great condition of the bicycle positioned beside the highway in his memory, he is still remembered. RIP brother.

There are a few bike lanes and sharrows painted on some of the streets in Albuquerque.

There are also a lot of Route 66-era motels and newer businesses keeping the spirit of Route 66 alive with their neon sign décor. To reach the KOA, rather than turning on Tramway Boulevard, continue straight on Central Avenue another .6 miles, then turn

Route 66 Section 18

right on Figueroa Street to ride another .2 miles.

If you continue on Tramway Boulevard a little over seven miles past the turn in the Mileage Log you can bag yourself a fun "-est", a ride on the longest aerial tram in the U.S. When you reach Sandia Crest, at the end of the tram ride, at 10,678 feet elevation you have a great view of Albuquerque and the surrounding plains.

Just off Constitution Avenue on Wyoming Boulevard is a cool little Mediterranean Deli and Grocery called Café Istanbul, where you can pick up some interesting prepared foods and tasty treats for the road.

If you don't stop at Café Istanbul then you might try DJ's Deli on MLK Avenue. They have a nice retro theme décor and their sandwiches are prepared to order. I recommend the Italian Grinder.

You can turn left on Hermosa Drive, just before the Campus Boulevard turn off Copper Avenue, and ride a block to reach the Historic Nob Hill District. This is a popular trendy stretch with historic buildings and retro styling.

Route 66 is well represented in Albuquerque. If you turn right off Marquette Avenue on 4th Street and ride about .3 miles to Maple Avenue you get to see one of the famous Madonna of the Trail monuments. This is one of twelve such statues that the Daughters of the American Revolution (DAR) installed in each state the National Old Trails Road (NOTR) passed through. Established in 1912, the NOTR was somewhat the father of Route 66. It was a coast-to-coast highway system that followed the Cumberland Road and Santa Fe Trail. Future president of the U.S., Harry S. Truman, was the president of the NOTR.

What a small world. Also, while researching Bicycling Guide to the Mississippi River Trail, I read about navigation work performed by a Corps of Engineer supervisor, and it turned out to be non-other than Robert E. Lee. It just to to show that all great people had a prior life.

The 18-foot high DAR monument, featuring an 11-foot tall pioneer woman, with baby in her left arm, a musket in her right arm, and a small boy clinging to her skirt demonstrates the toughness of our early travelers.

If you do visit the monument, which I encourage, you can turn west on Maple Avenue to ride 3 blocks to rejoin the route on 7th Street.

BTW, Marquette Avenue is a one-way street; eastbound cyclists will follow Tijeras Avenue.

We are riding the original Route 66 through Albuquerque.

Route 66 Section 18

There is a stretch of the 1937 version that still has a lot of restored and maintained businesses, such as the El Rey Theatre that makes for a nice side trip. To reach this just turn south off Marquette Avenue on 3rd Street (passing the visitor center), and ride .2 miles to Central Avenue and turn right.

You will enjoy the impressive retro look of the area and also the selection of eating places, such as Sushi Hana. If you want to spend the night in Albuquerque, the Hotel Blue is located on this stretch. It is reasonably priced and a great location for checking out the strip.

There are a lot more interesting places to visit in Albuquerque. If you want more info to plan your stay, stop off at the visitor center you passed on 3rd Street to help you plan your visit.

As you come off Paseo del Bosque Trail bike path you can take a left on Central Avenue to ride a couple tenths of a mile to see what historian David Kammer calls "one of the best examples of largely unaltered pre-World War II tourist courts remaining along Route 66 in New Mexico", the El Vado. It is currently closed, however there are plans approved for its restoration in 2016.

When you resume your ride at the intersection of the bike path and Central Avenue, after crossing over the Rio Grande River, several of the motels listed in the guidebook are on this stretch.

After leaving Albuquerque, when you exit the roundabout to enter I-40, you may notice the Frontage Road you were just riding continuing on and wondering why you aren't still riding on it. Well, the frontage road will eventually end, so just go ahead and get on the Interstate. I found the shoulder on this section of the interstate to be very clean and rideable. I was wondering if they sweep it for the bicyclists.

Ignore the Route 66 exit sign at the State Highway 6 junction. This uses dirt roads and takes you way off course.

There is a nice service center when you transition from Old Route 66 to Route 66 in Laguna. Just past this, if you turn left on Indian Service Road 502 and ride about a tenth of a mile you can reach Indian Arts Center. They have a lot of locally made jewelry, and pottery, but I was there for the fresh made flatbread.

Shortly after passing New Laguna, State Road 279 veers off to the right. Do not follow it. Continue straight on State Road 124.

At Paraje you have an option for a side trip to Sky Center Cultural Center and Haak'u Museum. This is a pretty cool place to visit and the roads to/from make for a nice ride among the picturesque mesas, but just be aware that you have about 600 feet of climbing going in and over 400 feet coming out.

The Acoma Pueblo is a Native American village built on top of

Route 66 Section 18

a mesa that has been occupied for over 800 years, making it one of the oldest continuously inhabited communities in the U.S. Oh, a bonus "-est". You can buy a ticket at the Visitor Center to ride a bus to visit the pueblo. It makes for an interesting tour walking among the adobe structures.

The museum and cultural center are both modern facility, with films and exhibits on the history of the area. There is also has a café that serves traditional foods. It is an interesting place to visit if you don't mind the extra miles and climbing.

If you remain on Route 66, and do not take the alternate route, you pass Villa De Cubero Trading Post. It was built in 1936 and is a welcome stop out in the middle of nowhere. They have snacks and cold beer. The worker at the trading post allowed me to pitch my tent on the property.

A couple miles past the trading post you can turn left on Pueblo Road and ride a half-a-mile to the Sky City Casino Hotel. You might get lucky at the casino and win enough to pay for your trip.

Camping

Turquoise Trail CG
22 Calvary Rd, Cedar
Crest, NM 87008
505-281-2005
(.3 mile off-route)

Hidden Valley Mnt Park
844-B State Highway 333
Tijeras, NM 87059
505-281-3363
(3 miles off-route)

KOA
12400 Skyline Rd NE
Albuquerque, NM 87123
505-296-2729
(LT 1 mile off-route)

Dancing Eagle RV Park
Casa Blanca, New Mexico
505-552-7730

Lodging

*Cedar Crest Inn & Hostel
12231 Hwy 14 N.
Cedar Crest, NM 87008
505-281-4117

Elaine's B&B
P.O. Box 444
Cedar Crest, NM 87008
505-281-2467

Univeristy Lodge
3711 Central Ave NE
Albuquerque, NM 87108
505-266-7663
(Nob Hill area)

Hotel Andaluz
125 2nd St NW
Albuquerque, NM 87102
505-242-9090
(downtown area)

The Hotel Blue
717 Central Ave NW
Albuquerque, NM 87102
505-924-2400
(downtown area)

Sky City Casino Hotel
Acoma, NM 87034
(505) 552-6123

Bike Shops

*Two Wheel Drive
1706 Central Ave. SE
Albuquerque, N.M. 87106
505-243-8443

Trek Bicycle Superstore
5000 Menaul Blvd, NE
Suite A
Albuquerque, NM
505-312-7243

The Bike Coop Ltd.
120 Yale blvd SE
Albuquerque, NM 87106
505-265-5170
(LT 1 mile off-route)

Route 66 Section 18

Golden to Paraje (102 miles)

Miles E/W	Directions	Dist	R	Service	Miles W/E
	*Golden				
0	S on SR14/Turquoise Tr	9.2	3		102
9	*San Antonito (pop 985)			QR	93
9	S on SR14/Turquoise Tr	3.8	3	C	93
13	*Cedar Crest (pop 958)			CLQR	89
13	S on SR14/Turquoise Tr	2.1	4	QR	89
15	VR at SL on R66/SR333	0.6	4		87
16	*Tijeras (pop 541)				86
16	S on R66/SR333	4.8	3		86
21	VL over I-40 then VR on R66/Central Ave	1.9	3		81
22	R at SL on Tramway Blvd/SR556	1.8	4	Q	79
24	L at SL on Indian School Rd	0.2	3	Q	78
24	L on Constitution Ave	3.3	3	QR	77
28	R at SL on Pennsylvania St	0.2	3	Q	74
28	L at SL on Paseo de las Mountanas Tr (cross I-40)	0.9	P		74
29	R on Constitution Ave to cross Louisiana Blvd at SL	1.5	3		73
30	*Albuquerque (pop 545,852)				72
30	L at SS on Washington St	1.0	3		72
31	R at SL on Copper Ave	0.5	3		71
32	VR on Campus Blvd	0.9	3	Q	70
33	VL at SS on Los Lamas Ave	0.4	3	Q	69
33	L on Redondo Dr	0.2	3		69
33	R at SS on MLK Jr Ave	1.0	4	R	69
34	VR on Marquette Ave (one way, use Tijeras Ave east bound)	0.7	4		68
35	R on 7th St	0.5	3	R	67
36	L at SS on Mountain Rd	2.3	3		66
38	VR on Paseo del Bosque Tr	1.2	P		64
39	VR on ramp then R on Central Ave/R66 to cross Rio Grande	6.3	4	GLQR	63
45	R on Atrisco Vista Blvd to cross I-40	0.3	4		57
46	L on frontage rd	9.3	3		56
55	L on Rio Laguna Rd to enter I-40W	13.0	5	Q	47
68	*SR6 junction				34
68	Cont on I-40W	8.9	5		34
77	Exit #117 then R on Mesita Rd	0.4	3		25

Route 66 Section 18

Miles E/W	Directions	Dist	R	Service	Miles W/E
77	L on Old R66 Rd	4.7	3		25
82	L then R on R66				20
82	*Laguna (pop 1,241)				20
82	S on R66/SR279	2.6		Q	20
85	*New Laguna				17
85	S on R66/SR124	3.9			17
88	*Paraje (pop 777) see below for alternate route				13
88	S on R66/SR124	13.4		GLQR	13
102	*ISR30 return road for Alternate				0
	Alternate Route Begin				
0	L on Casa Blanca Rd/ISR23	0.5			27
1	*Casa Blanca				26
1	S on Casa Blanca Rd/ISR23/CR22	12.6			26
13	*Sky City				14
13	R on Haak'u Rd/ISR38/ISR30	12.6			14
26	*McCartys				1
26	S on ISR30	1.0			1
27	Alternate Route End				0

One of twelve Madonna of the Trail monuments erected by Daughters of the American Revolution.

Route 66 Section 18

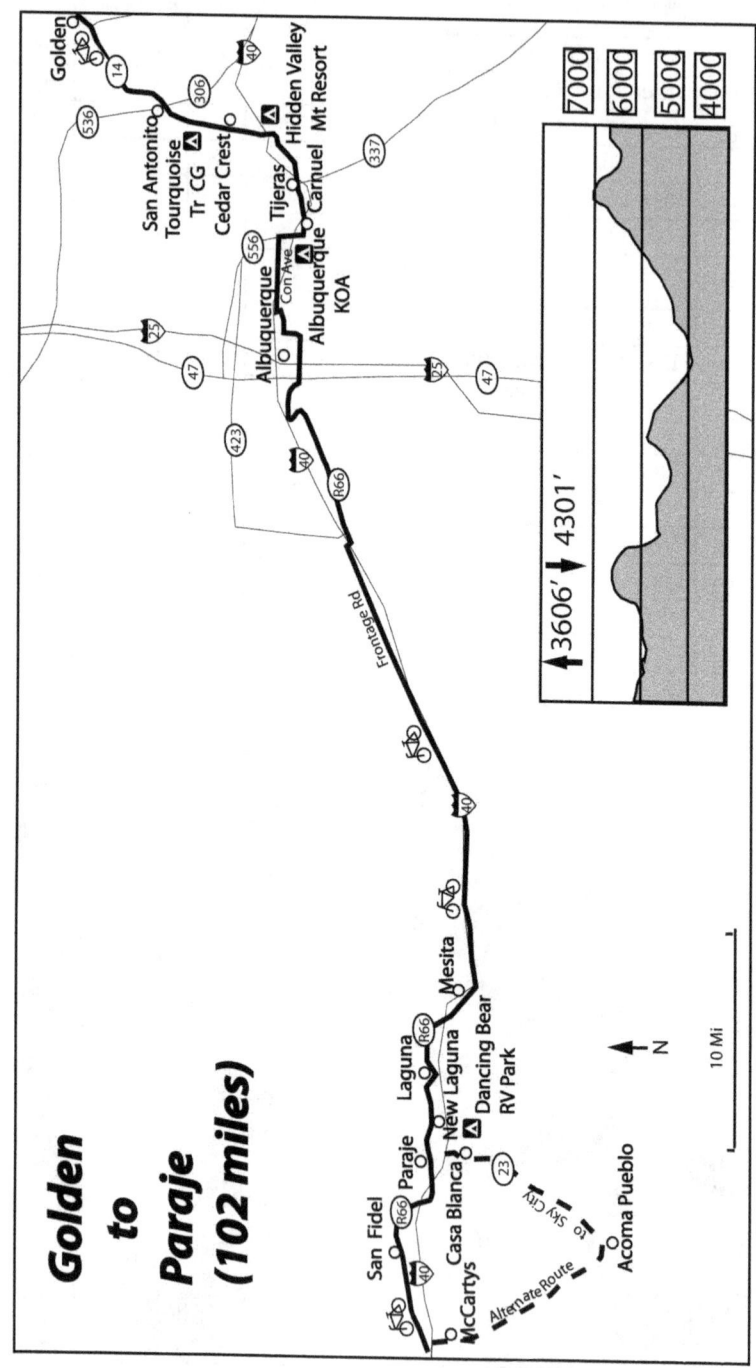

Route 66
SECTION 19

Paraje, NM to Gallup, NM (106 miles)

This is a really nice section for cycling. Not much traffic, a least some shoulder on a lot of the roads, no major cities, and plenty of natural wonders to check out. Some of my favorite places to ride are through parks and national monuments, and this section has a really good one with El Malpais National Monument.

The fun begins even before El Malpais when the highway routes you through a lava field at the very start. If you look off to the north while you're riding here, that beautiful tall 11,305 foot peak, seemingly levitating on the horizon, is Mount Taylor. And the dark black molten rock you are riding through is from its eruption over 1.1 million years ago.

Be sure to stock up on supplies in Grants, because one of the drawbacks of this section is there aren't many places to shop, unless you're wanting to buy Native American jewelry, rugs, or art.

It would also be a good idea to stop off at the Northwest New Mexico Visitor Center while you are in Grants, so you will have your information on El Malpais to plan your visit before entering. There are three different visitor centers for the park but this one is the most convenient for the route we will be riding.

To reach this visitor center, on your approach into Grants, turn left, rather than right as the Mileage Log directs you, on State Road 117 towards I-4, then ride to the other side of I-40 then and turn left on Cliflear Boulevard.

There are also some franchise motels and eateries in the area of this I-40 exit. But I prefer continuing into town, after collecting all my brochures on El Malpais, to stay in one of the older motels. They are less expensive and some of them are in really good condition. I also like to support the old Route 66 businesses. Plus, these motels will put you within walking distance to check out downtown Grants.

Some of the attractions in the downtown area are the New Mexico Mining Museum (with a replica of the uranium mine shaft), the still operating Old West Theater, and a nice city park. The park has a large metal art structure that is a collage of events that traces the history of the town. Also, be sure to venture out after dark to see all the bright neon lights of the vintage motels.

When you are in your room, going over the literature you picked up to plan your El Malpais adventure, you might consider a side trip down the east side of the park, on State Road 117. There are some nice formations in that area. Even if you just ride down to the Narrows formations area I believe you will be glad you did. There is also a camping area on this road, so you could camp out, explore around, then return to town to continue your Route 66 Adventure.

You could continue through El Malpais on 117 and loop around to rejoin the route, but it would be a long way out of your way, and then you would miss some of the CRAs on the west park border.

The two campgrounds listed in the guidebook for Grants are both located on State Road 53, after leaving Grants. There is also free camping on this highway just prior to the El Morro National Monument visitor center. It's a nice campground with water, picnic tables, pit toilets, and great views.

It is nice riding past the interesting rock formations in this area. I recommend hiking the La Ventana Trail that you pass. It takes you to the one of New Mexico's largest natural arches. Most of the trailheads for the hiking trails on State Road 53 have restrooms.

State Road 53 will weave in and out of the National Monument and a conservation area. You will also pass another visitor information center, but if you wait until you reach this one to collect information you might miss some of the attractions.

Be sure to stop at The Land of Fire and Ice. This dramatic name came from Bandera Volcano and an ice cave that formed within a lava tube when the volcano erupted. This CRA has been operated by the same family for four generations. Nestled in the pine trees, this is one of those old time stops with a gift store and cottages. The cottages are no longer operating, but you can tell this was a busy place at one time. The hike to the rim of the caldera of the volcano and among the lava flow formations is pretty interesting.

Shortly after exiting the Ice Caves you get to ride over the Continental Divide, always a momentous occasion. The Cimarron B&B is also along this stretch. When I rode through here I was lucky enough to come across a roadside stand (actually just a pickup with a table out front) that was selling made fresh flat bread with taco meat and sauces on it. Boy, a couple of those hit the spot.

When you're riding through El Morro, stop off at the Ancient Way Café to get something to eat, and then if it's a hot day stop at

Inscription Rock Trading Post next door to wash it down with a refreshing smoothie. Ahhh, I can still taste it.

Inscription Rock is a sandstone bluff that borders an ancient watering hole that has been serving weary travelers for centuries. The etchings on the stone walls document the visits of many of those travelers in both text and pictographs. I highly recommend the hike that routes you among these historic and unique inscriptions.

As I mentioned earlier, there is free camping located near the El Morro National Monument visitor center, which is next to Inscription Rock.

Also in this area you will pass a sign for the New Mexico Historic Women Marker Initiative. This is a statewide forum to recognize women's contribution to the state's history. I am glad to see there are organizations like this, because I for one know the contribution women play. Both my mother and my late wife were strong women who achieved great accomplishments on their own, in addition to partnering with my dad and myself on joint endeavors.

The grocery store listed in the Mileage Log following Ramah is actually a Family Dollar Store. You can get supplies there; I just didn't want anyone to get their hopes up for something special.

The Winfield Trading Company is a nice place on State Road 602 to stop for a break. They are one of the largest authentic wholesalers of Native American arts and crafts in the world. There are also several more arts and crafts shops as you approach Gallup, but I think Winfield has the largest selection of authentic products.

The surroundings are becoming more barren and dry towards the end of this section.

See the next section for information pertaining to Gallup.

Camping

Lavaland R.V. Park
1901 E. Santa Ave
Grants, NM 87020
505-287-8665
(by visitor NW visitor center)

*Blue Spruce RV Park
1708 Zuni Canyon Rd
Grants, NM 87020
505-287-2560
(on SR53)

*Grants / Cibola Sands KOA
26 Cibola Sands Loop
Grants, NM 87020
505-287-4376
(on SR53)

*El Morro RV Park & Cabins
HC 61 Box 44
Ramah, NM 87321
505-783-4612

*El Morro Natl Monument
HC 61 Box 43
Ramah, NM 87321
505-783-4226
(next to Inscription Roc

*Kamp Kiwanis
20 Cousins Rd,
Vanderwagen, NM 87326
505-778-5764
(reservatoins only)

Lodging

*Southwest Motel
1000 E Santa Fe Ave
Grants, NM 87020
505-287-2935

*Sands Motel
112 McArthur
Grants, NM 87020
505-287-2996

*Leisure Lodge
1204 E Santa Fe Ave
Grants, NM 87020
505-287-2991

*Cimarron Rose B&B
689 Oso Ridge Rt.
Grants, NM 87020
800-856-5776

*El Morro RV Park & Cabins
HC 61 Box 44
Ramah, NM 87321
505-783-4612

La Tinaja Cafe & RV
3658 Ice Caves Road,
Ramah, NM 87321
505-783-4349

Bike Shops

N/A

Metal art structure tracing events in the history of the town of Grants.

Route 66 Section 19

Paraje to Gallup (106 miles)

Miles E/W	Directions	Dist	R	Service	Miles W/E
	*IR30 return road for Alternate				
0	S on R66/SR124	4.1	3		106
4	R to ride under I-40 then L on SR124	1.2	3		102
5	R on R66/SR117	5.1	3	QR	101
10	*Grants (pop 9,182)			CGLQR	96
10	VR on Santa Fe Ave/R66	2.7	3		96
13	L at SL on SR53 (cross I-40)	3.5	3	C	93
17	*San Rafael (933)				90
17	S on SR53/Ice Caves Rd	18.5	3		90
35	*Information Center				71
35	S on SR53/Ice Caves Rd	2.7	3		71
38	*Ice Caves				69
38	S on SR53/Ice Caves Rd	0.4	3		69
38	*Continental Divide	0.0			68
38	S on SR53	14.0	3		68
52	*El Morro			QR	54
52	S on SR53	1.1	3		54
53	*El Morro Natl Monument/Inscription Rock	0.0		C	53
53	S on SR53	10.5	3	Q	53
64	*Ramah (pop 370)			QR	43
64	S on SR53	5.9	3	G	43
70	*Pescado				37
70	S on SR53	6.7	3		37
76	R on SR602	12.4	3	C	30
89	*Vanderwagen				18
89	S on SR602	16.0	3	Q	18
105	S at SL on 2nd St/SR610	1.6	3	GQ	2
106	*Gallup (pop 20,178)			CGLQR	0

Route 66 Section 19

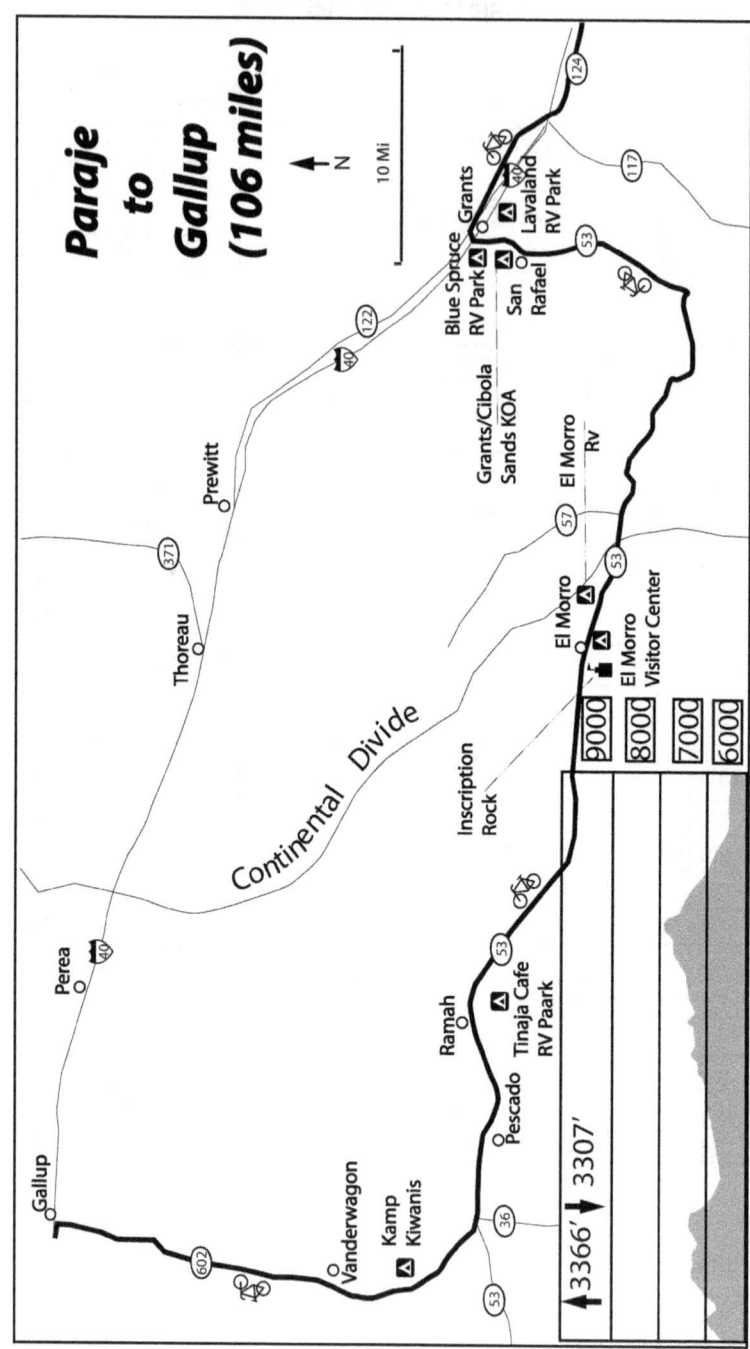

Route 66
SECTION 20

Gallup, NM to Petrified Forest NP, AZ (103 miles)

Gallup reminds me a lot of Santa Fe, with the use of adobe style architecture, street art, and outdoor murals. You ride past a good example of the adobe architecture at the 1938 McKinley County Courthouse on Second Street. The building was sponsored by President Roosevelt's Federal New Deal Arts project.

In 2005 the city of Gallup commissioned a mural project to beautify and capture the area's heritage and history. This resulted in nine colorful murals painted on buildings in the downtown area, with each relating to the area's culture and heritage.

On your ride on Second Street you pass two of these murals. The mural across the street from the courthouse colorfully depicts early life of the Zuni people. The second mural you pass honors the Navajos who served in the military as Code Talkers during World War II. The code talkers actually trained at an abandoned fort located just 12 miles east of Gallup. There is also a museum dedicated to them at the Gallup-McKinley County Chamber of Commerce building.

For a tour of Historic Downtown Gallup, at the intersection of Second Street and Route 66 you'll need to go off-route and turn right. On this one mile side trip you will pass the Rex Museum (which traces the presence of the area's earliest human inhabitants), the Gallup Cultural Center (housed in the historic Santa Fe Depot), the legendary El Rancho Hotel, and other attractions. The El Rancho Hotel hosted many of the early actors who were in the area filming western movies in nearby Monument Valley, including John Wayne, Kirk Douglas, Betty Grable, and Ronald Reagan.

There are a ton of trading posts in Gallup. They are part of what Gallup is known for so you should check out a couple of them. I liked Richardson's Trading Post the best. It is packed with authentic Native American pottery, hand woven rugs, painted dolls, and jewelry. Opened in 1913, this is the real deal. Plus I liked their classic sign on the front of the building.

To help you plan your tour of the city, your first stop should be the Chamber of Commerce Visitor Center, located at 106 West Highway 66, which you pass near the beginning of your side trip.

If you can't fit your visit into a single day, there is a good selection of lodging to choose from in Gallup. Another option would be to camp at the USA RV Park, which is only a few miles away.

State Road 118 gets you up close and personal with some really beautiful and interesting massive rock formations and bluffs, so close in fact some of the rocks have rolled onto the highway. The rock scree is especially bad at the edges of the pavement, where you will be cycling, so keep an eye out for it. The highway is also your pathway to the seventh state on your Route 66 Adventure, Arizona. Or, if you are riding west to east your third state, New Mexico.

Shortly after crossing into Arizona you will ride past Chief Yellowhorse Trading Post, which they promote as straddling the state line, complete with a painted line on the floor of the building. It was closed the last time I was through here. However, no need to fret, because you will pass a string of other trading posts through here, including another Yellowhorse Trading Post, owned by a different Yellowhorse. And you also get to bag another "-est" at the Tomahawk Indian Store by visiting the largest teepee in the southwest.

These trading posts don't see much activity these days; however you can tell they were abuzz with activity at one time. If any of the posts are open when you come through be sure to pick up some of the unique dried jerky flavors, such as buffalo, elk, and deer. The tough jerky provided a contented chew while riding through these beautiful red tinted bluffs. Also, check out the fake animals and teepees perched high on the rock walls behind the trading posts.

You have probably noticed how a lot of the vintage billboards were into promoting their "Clean Restrooms". This was a really big deal for travelers in the early days of Route 66. Some of the franchise service stations even hired teams of women to travel across the country to inspect the restrooms for cleanliness before certifying them as being officially clean.

After crossing the state line and passing the string of trading posts, if you continue straight another half-a-mile, rather than turning left and riding under I-40, you will reach a really nice Arizona Welcome Center.

After passing under I-40 to resume your ride on the Frontage Road on the south side of the interstate you pass another genuine CRA, Ortega's Indian Market. This place is classic Route 66 promotion at its best, with the attention grabbing geodesic-domed building with a Mohawk down the middle, brightly colored signs advertising Native American jewelry, jerky, trinkets, and "over 1,000 handmade items". It would have been the perfect place to get that rubber tomahawk you've been wanting. Sadly this souvenir shop is closed now, but not before it, in addition to several other such stores, had made its owner Gilbert Ortega a multi-millionaire, according to what a local told me.

Watch the cattle guards on the frontage roads through here. Also use caution where some of the culverts running under I-40 have washed dirt and mud across this frontage road. Once you cross back over to the north side of the interstate you will be on the high side and it won't be a problem.

Did I mention how beautiful the bluffs are along this section? Well, even if I have it's worth repeating.

Once you cross back over to the north side of I-40 there is another CRA, Indian City, however this tourist trap is alive and well, plus they have ice cream. There is also a small shed bordering the parking lot that sells fresh fry bread.

Our next stop is Fort Courage. This is another tourist attraction that has seen better days, much better days because it is closed now.

Old 1932 Studebaker road warrior in the Petrified Forest National Park.

Route 66 Section 20

But, with its authentic replica of the fort from the 1960s television series called "F Troop," at one time I'm sure it was a must stop for any family travelling along Route 66 who had a child. With the adjoining Pancake House Restaurant, and "clean restrooms", it had everything a family needed to take a break on their long trek across the plains.

You'll find another of the historic Valentine Diners in Sanders. However, this one isn't in as good condition as the one you saw in Clinton, Oklahoma. This diner was originally located in Holbrook, Arizona and was moved here in 1980. It is for sale in case anyone has ever wanted to own a piece of Route 66 history.

The convenience store that used to be in Chambers is now a trading post. You can never have enough trading posts I guess. However, after crossing I-40 you will find another convenience store, plus lodging and a restaurant.

After leaving Chambers you are in for another jaunt on I-40, and this one is a long boring ride. You can see forever, however there still isn't anything to see. This is a good time to enter a cycling Zen, and reconnect with your inner self, and pray for a tailwind. After about eight miles there is a convenience store on exit #325.

Once you finish the section on the interstate you are rewarded with a ride through one of my favorite sections of highway on the tour, the Petrified Forest and Painted Desert. This place is magical. With the distinct varying lines of color coursing through the mountains, Mother Nature has made it her canvas for displaying some of her most beautiful work.

Try to plan your ride through the park during the morning or evening hours because the bright sunlight of midday bleaches out her brush strokes of colors on the surrounding mountainsides.

You reach the visitor center about a mile after riding past the park entrance. Stop to check out the exhibits and learn as much as you can about the park and it will make your visit even more enjoyable.

There is also a Fred Harvey Restaurant at the center. The origin of Fred Harvey's restaurants can be traced back to 1875, and is credited to being the first "restaurant chain" in the U.S. And the "Harvey Girls," as the women who served the customers were known, became so famous they made a movie about them starring Judy Garland. The food is good, and the price is fair, but the best part is they serve hungry cyclist sized portions.

After reading about all the interesting features within the park, pick up a map of the park so you won't miss anything, and begin your ride, checking off the attractions as you go. The Painted

Desert Inn (which is only used as a museum now), all the vistas that offer fantastic views of the colorful hillsides, Rainbow Forest Museum, Puerco Pueblo (with a short hike leading you to the ruins of a 100+ room pueblo site), Newspaper Rock, Jasper Forest (bag another "-est", this is one of the largest accumulations of petrified wood in the world), Blue Mesa, the Agate Bridge, the Agate House, and many more attractions along the route that are well worth the time to stop and explore.

If you decide you need more than one day to see everything, which I believe you will, the park does allow free backcountry camping a minimum of one mile from two designated parking spots. Permits are required and may be picked up at the Painted Desert Visitor Center, Painted Desert Inn, or Rainbow Forest Museum. The Crystal Forest Gift Shop also allows free camping, but there is no water or restroom. However, you will find water, restrooms, and snacks at the nearby Rainbow Forest Museum.

Oh yes, did I mention the gift shop has cold beer?

Camping

*USA Rv Park
2925 W Historic Hwy, 66
Gallup, NM 87301
505-863-5021

Petrified Forest NP
Backcountry camping
1 mile from parking lot
Permits at visitor centers
928-524-6228

*Crystal Forest Gift CG
US 180
Holbrook, Arizona
928-524-3500
(at south park entrance)

Lodging

El Rancho Hotel
1000 East 66
Gallup, NM 87301
505-863-9311

*Golden Desert Motel
1205 Rte 66
Gallup, NM 87301
505-722-6606

*Days Inn & Suites
3010 Rte 66
Gallup, NM 87301
505-722-7600

*Howard Johnson Inn
3404 W Historic Hwy, 66
Gallup, NM
505-863-6801

*Microtel Inn by Wyndham
3270 West Highway 66
Gallup, NM 87301
505-722-2600

*Days Inn
Hwy 191
Chambers, AZ 86502
928-688-6880

Bike Shops

N/A

Gallup to Petrified Forest Natl Park (103 miles)

Miles E/W	Directions	Dist	R	Service	Miles W/E
	*Gallup (pop 20,178)			CGLQR	
0	S on 2nd St/SR610 (eastbound will turn on 3rd St)	1.8	4	L	103
2	L on R66	5.1	3	CGLQR	101
7	*Ride under I-40				96
7	S on SR66	3.5	3		96
10	*Defiance				92
10	L on SR118 to ride under I-40	0.3	3		92
11	R on Rocky Point Rd/SR118 after riding under I-40	4.2	3		92
15	VR on SR118 to ride under I-40	3.3	3		88
18	*Manuello				84
18	S on SR118	5.1	3		84
23	*Enter Arizona				79
23	S on SR118	0.5	3	Q	79
24	L at SS on Grants Rd to ride under I-40	0.1	3		79
24	R at SS on frontage rd	0.3	3		79
24	*Lupton				78
24	S on frontage rd	7.4	3		78
32	R at SS to cross I-40	0.1	3		71
32	L on frontage rd	5.0	3		71
37	L on Pine Springs Rd	0.1	3		66
37	R on I-40	6.8	5	Q	66
44	Exit I-40 on exit 339	0.2	4		59
44	R at SS on CR 7080 (unsigned)	0.1	3		59
44	*Sanders (pop 630, 1/2 mile off-route)			GQR	59
44	L on frontage rd	6.0	3	Q	59
50	*Chambers			LQR	53
50	L at SS on US191	0.1	3		53
50	R on I-40	21.8	5	Q	53
72	Exit I-40 on exit 311	0.1	4		31
72	R at SS on Petrified Forest Rd (PFR)	16.5	2	C	31
88	S on Blue Mesa Scenic Rd (BMSD)	12.2	2		14
101	S on Petrified Forest Rd	1.9	2		2
103	*Petrified Natl Forest south entrance			CR	0

Route 66 Section 20

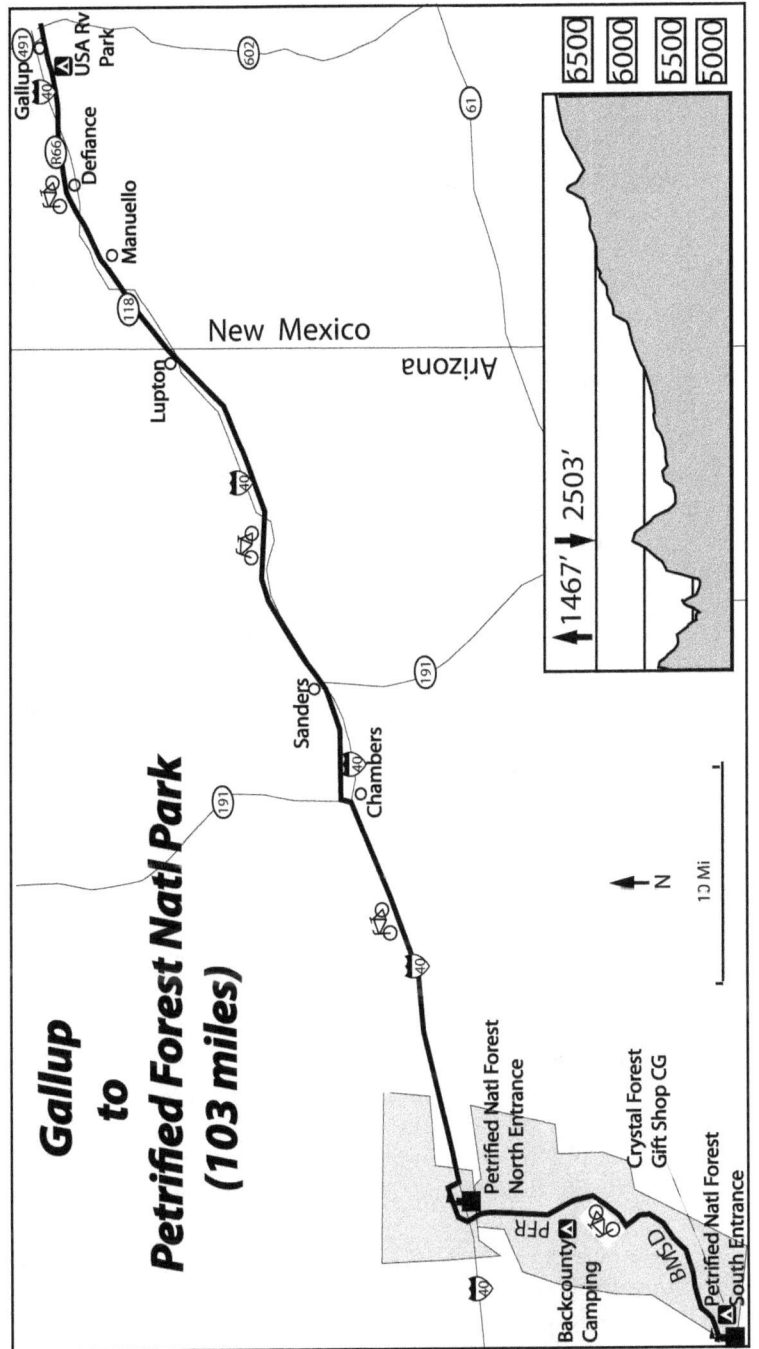

Route 66
SECTION 21

Petrified Forest NP, AZ to Winona, AZ (97 miles)

You should top off your water bottles before leaving the Rainbow Forest Museum, because the road to Holbrook is pretty desolate. But it's a wide open stretch of highway and the pavement is in pretty good shape. There is also a shoulder, but they have one of those stupid rumble strips in the middle, so you don't have much room to ride on either side of it. (I think the President needs to appoint someone from Adventure Cycling Association to the highway commission to remind this country bicycles are a means of transportation.)

On the approach into Holbrook you cross the Little Colorado River. This is the first of several crossings in this section. Shortly after this, at the intersection with State Road 77, you pass another CRA on your left, Jim Gray's Petrified Wood Company.

Check out the life-sized dinosaur statues skulking around the parking lot, with old T-Rex himself ready to pounce on some unsuspecting tourist. There is also a free museum that is loaded with interesting products they have carved and chiseled out of petrified wood.

Jim and wife Cathy started the business over 40 years ago out of the back of a pickup truck. It remains a family operated business, with them digging, cutting, and polishing their merchandise from Arizona Rainbow Petrified Wood mined on land they own that borders the park.

Oh yes, as for "Wild Bill", the 2.9 million year old alligator you'll see advertised on numerous billboards, Jim bought it in Florida and brought it here to attract tourists.

If you are in need of supplies, turn right at this crossing on State Road 77, and ride less than a mile to reach downtown Holbrook, a full service stop. Plus, you can bag another "-est", World's Longest Map of Route 66, at the corner of West 5th Avenue and West Hopi Drive.

The Route 66 theme is alive and well in Holbrook, with everything from steak houses to lodging associating themselves with the Mother Road. You can even spend the night in a teepee at the Wigwam Motel.

Route 66 Section 21

With its fifteen teepees circling the main office, and antique automobiles permanently parked at the door of several teepees, it is a classic Route 66 attention-getter. The rooms feature the original hand-made hickory furniture, along with a sink, toilet, and shower, to make for a cozy and original place to spend the night. Before crawling into your teepee for the night, I recommend eating at Joe & Aggies Café. The food is tasty and the people are friendly.

At the turn for Obed Road, you have an option of remaining on the primary Route 66 route or going cross-country to reach Winslow by riding the Territorial Road (TR). The distance is about the same, although the TR has more climbing, and this alternate does avoid riding a stretch of I-40. But it involves about eighteen miles of gravel road. I really wanted to ride the alternate, because I thought it would be an adventure. I started out riding it, but the road surface had excessive wash boarding, and it had been raining so it was also muddy. I just couldn't talk myself into it.

For those adventurous souls who do follow the alternate route, it's a straight shot. You just follow the gravel road about eighteen miles, then turn right on State Road 99, which is paved, to ride another six miles, then turn right on State Road 87 and follow it a little over a mile. You will be in to downtown Winslow at that point, to rejoin the primary route.

For those who choose the primary route, there is a very narrow bridge on Obed Road as you cross the Little Colorado River again. Be sure to yield to oncoming vehicles.

Joseph City is the oldest Mormon community in Arizona, founded in 1876. On your approach into the city you pass a memorial sponsored by the Daughters of Utah Pioneers commemorating the original fort constructed here by the colonists.

About five miles west of Joseph City you pass another CRA, Jackrabbit Trading Post. Route 66 historians claim that the silhouetted jackrabbit promoted on the numerous billboards across the country is the most recognized image associated with the Mother Road. Miles away from the trading post you will see smaller jackrabbit silhouette signs along the highway, counting down the number of miles remaining before finally arriving at the famous "HERE IT IS" version.

The Jackrabbit Trading Post has been there for over sixty-six years and the building even longer than that. So stop off to sip on a cold drink and eat a couple snacks as you wander among the collection of Route 66 memorabilia and other interesting items. Before leaving, be sure to climb on the back of the famous giant jackrabbit for the obligatory photo op'.

Route 66 Section 21

The stretch of I-40 you have to ride following the Jackrabbit is the shorter of the two stretches in this section. Just focus on the picturesque white-capped mountain in the distance straight ahead, and watch it grow closer and closer with each mile.

Once you do escape I-40, at the left turn on State Road 87, you can turn right and ride less than two miles to reach the Homolovi Ruins State Park, and less than two more miles following that to reach the campgrounds.

This is a really interesting park, with two of the seven Homolovi ruins open to visitors. There are ongoing studies and archeological digs active at the remaining sites. One of the ruins open to visitors was occupied between 1330 and 1400 A.D. and has about 1200 rooms. There is also a visitor center with exhibits and other information on the history of the area.

The main streets in Winslow are one-way; we will be coming in on Third Street. I recommend that you cruise down Third and then double back up Second Street, because most of the attractions are on Second. But if you just want to get on down the road, at least turn left on Kinsley Avenue and ride a block to the corner of Second and Kinsley to visit the intersection made famous in the Eagles' 1972 pop hit, Take It Easy.

It is really creative the way the town has decked out the corner to fit the song. They have a bronze statue of a man standing next to a lamp post with a guitar in hand. Above his head on the lamp post is a sign, resembling a Route 66 sign, with the words "Standing on the Corner". On a window sill in the background is a stuffed eagle, also in the background is a wall mural with the painted reflection of a flatbed Ford and a blond headed female driver. I mean, the entire verse of the song is represented there.

The corner, along with an old style Route 66 Dinner and other attractions make Winslow a nice place to lay over for a night or two.

Note: One day prior to writing this section I heard the announcement that Glenn Frey, of The Eagles band, had passed away. Frey co-wrote Take It Easy with Jackson Browne. The photo included in this section is a tribute to Glenn Frey. Thank you for brightening up the lives of so many. RIP brother.

After leaving Winslow you are back on I-40, and this time it is for 39 miles, ugh! But there are several interesting distractions to help break up your ride, in addition to the distant white capped mountain that is growing larger all the time.

Distraction #1: Meteor City at exit #239. It's hard to believe looking at what's here now, but at one time you could have bagged

Route 66 Section 21

two "-est" at this one stop. The "World's Longest Map of Route 66", (at that time) and the "World's Largest Dream Catcher". But the 100' foot wall that hosted the map has collapsed and the dream catcher must have blown away in the brutally strong winds that sweep across these barren plains. But it's still an interesting place to stop and stretch your legs. Check out the remains of a gift shop with geodome building like the one back at Lupton, also several of the murals are still visible, and there are still a few teepees standing guard.

Distraction #2: at exit #233, you can visit the world's best preserved meteorite impact, Meteor Crater, located only 5 miles off-route. Nearly one mile wide, 2.4 miles in circumference and more than 550 feet deep, this place is impressive. With the rim trails, viewing deck and the Interactive Discovery Center it is setup for maximum enjoyment. There is also a Subway restaurant and a campground.

Distraction #3: exit number 230 you can stop to snoop around the remains of an old ghost town named Two Guns. It's just right off the interstate on the south side. This was a pretty popular tourist attraction during the Route 66 heyday, with camping, lodging, café, souvenir shop, and a Zoo. The only things remaining now are the partial walls of a few buildings, and the pool for the campground. There is also a cool silo with a larger than life cowboy painted on its side, with a revolver in each hand, as in Two Guns. An old Route 66 bridge across Canyon Diablo still remains, also.

If you feel like riding three miles on a rough road to see the ruins of another ghost town, Canyon Diablo, then turn right after coming off Exit 230. There is even less remaining of this town than Two Guns, but it's there if you want to see it. It's too bad there aren't more remnants here, because the town had a lively history. It was a railroad town that sprang up around the bridge constructed across the wide arroyo located here. It was a wild lawless community, and it looks like the locals wanted to keep it that way. The first marshal arrived in town at 3:00 p.m. and was buried at 8:00 p.m. Five more marshals followed with the longest tenure lasting only a month.

You finish this section in the town of Winona, whose claim to fame is it was mentioned in the lyrics in the popular tune, "Get You Kicks on Route 66", recorded by Nat King Cole in 1946. Bobby Troup composed the tune while he and his wife Cynthia were traveling across country in a '41 Buick. What a fitting story behind creation the song.

The song provides a mini-travelogue of the major stops along the route, listing several cities it passes through. All of these cities follow a geographical order across the country except Winona, "Don't forget Winona". Some believe the only reason the town was included was to rhyme with "Flagstaff, Arizona."

Camping

KOA
102 Hermosa Dr
Holbrook, AZ 86025
928-524-6689

Homolovi State Park CG
SR-87 Exit #257
Winslow, AZ 86047
928-289-4106
(1.3 miles off-route)

Meteor Crater RV Park
Meteor Crator Rd
Winslow, AZ 8604741
928-289-4002
(5 miles off-route, exit 233)

Lodging

Wigwam Motel
811 W Hopi Dr
Holbrook, AZ 86025
928-524-3048

Holbrook Inn
235 W Hopi Dr
Holbrook, AZ 86025
928-524-3809

Super 8 Holbrook
1989 Navajo Blvd
Holbrook, AZ 86025
800-536-0738

*Desert Sun Motel
1000 E 3rd St
Winslow, AZ 86047
928-289-1007

*Motel 10
725 West 3rd Street
Winslow, AZ 86047
928-289-3211

Twin Arrows Navajo Casino
22181 Resort Boulevard
Angell, AZ 86004I
928-856-7200

Bike Shops

N/A

 Standing on a corner in Winslow, Arizona.

Petrified Forest NP to Winona (97 miles)

Miles E/W	Directions	Dist	R	Service	Miles W/E
	South Entrance Petrified Forest NP				
0	R on US180	17.2	3		97
17	*Holbrook (pop 5,053)			CGLQR	79
17	S at SS then VR on Apache Dr after crossing SR77	0.2	3		79
17	L on Romero St	1.0	3		79
18	L on Whitting Ave	0.5	3		78
19	VR on McClaws Rd	7.9	3		78
27	R on Obed Rd	3.6	3		70
30	L on Richards Ave	0.7	3		66
31	R at SS on 3rd Ave/Frontage Rd	0.2	3		66
31	L at SS on Westover Ave	0.3	3		65
32	*Joseph City (pop 1,386)			QR	65
32	L at SS on Main St	1.0	3	R	65
33	L to cross I-40		3		64
33	R at SS on frontage rd (ignore no outlet sign)	4.7	3		64
37	R on Jackrabbit Rd	0.1	3		59
37	L to enter I-40	12.8	5		59
50	Exit I-40 on exit 257	0.3	3		46
51	L at SS on SR87	0.4	3		46
51	R at YS on SR87/R66	2.9	3		46
54	*Winslow (pop 9,655)			GLQR	43
54	S a SS on SR87/3rd St (east bound on 2nd St)	3.0	3	QR	43
57	R at SS on Hipoke Dr	0.1	3		40
57	L to enter I-40	39.6	5	CQR	40
97	Exit I-40 on exit 211	0.1	3		0
97	*Winona (pop 116)			Q	

Route 66 Section 21

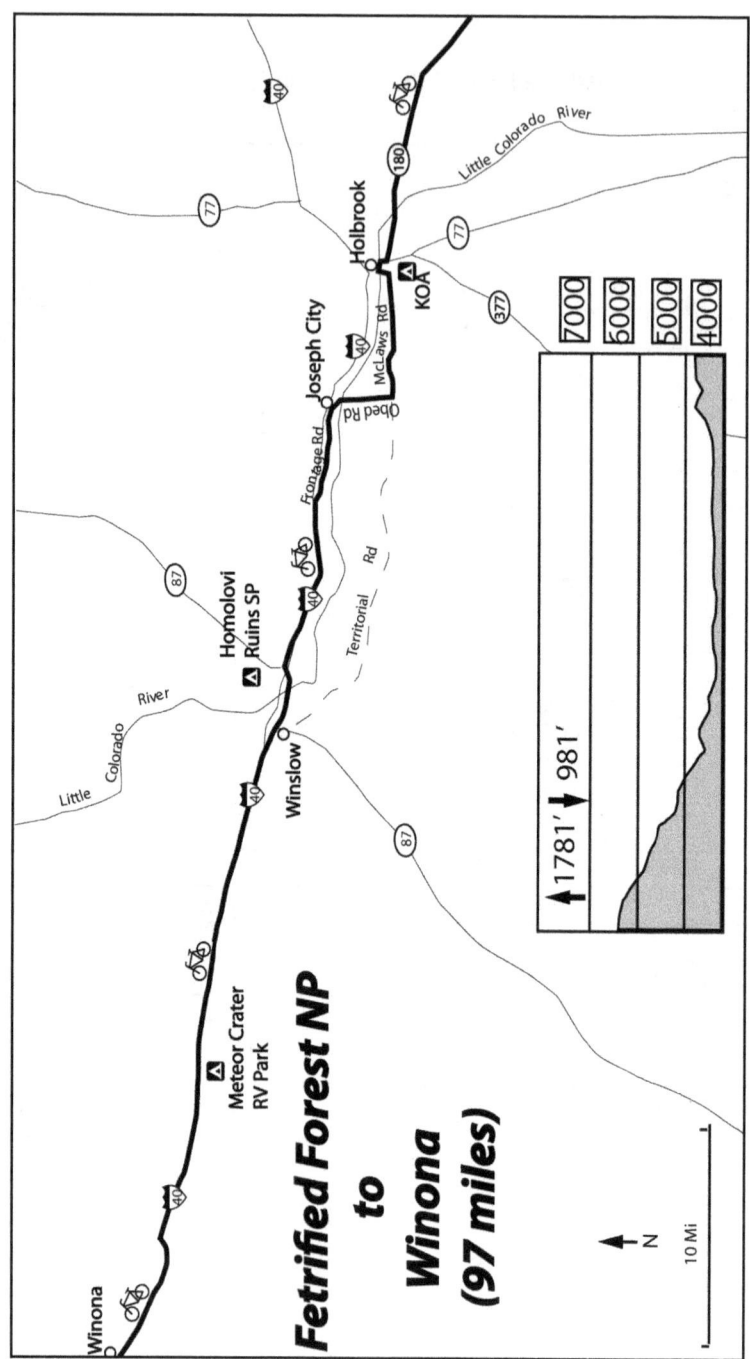

Route 66
SECTION 22

Winona, AZ to Seligman, AZ (85 miles)

Great news. Following this section there are only a couple of really short stretches remaining of riding on I-40. Yahoo!

As I mentioned in the previous section, Winona doesn't have a lot going on. You will ride past an old abandoned bridge that was used by the original Route 66. These old steel bridges are always interesting to stop and have a looksee as you munch on a snack.

Now Flagstaff, that's a different story. This is another city where Route 66 is alive and doing well. They even renamed their main street, which had been changed to Santa Fe Avenue, back to Route 66.

You'll see the neon sign for the 1926 Hotel Monte Vista, perched high above the four story building, before you even enter the outskirts of the city. If you are into haunted hotels, then this is your place. Even John Wayne reported encounters with a ghost while staying there, so if the Duke says it happened it must be true.

There are enough interesting attractions in Flagstaff to justify laying over for a day or two. There is the Riordan Mansion State Park, which is basically a museum of the historic house itself (which was built by Charles Whittlesey, who also built the El Tovar Hotel at the Grand Canyon), with emphasis on architectural style and furnishings of the times, and the life of the family, which in itself is pretty interesting. Two rich brothers married two sisters and both families lived in the mansion. That's the ingredients for a hit reality show. The mansion also includes exhibits of Arts & Crafts, Native American pottery & baskets, etc.

You could also visit Lowell Observatory, located only a couple miles out of town. In 2011 Time magazine named it one of the "World's 100 most Important Places". Pluto was discovered here. They open their 24-inch telescope, and others, to the public for viewing the various wonders of the night sky.

Also be sure to plan a meal at the '50's décor Galaxy Diner. If not a meal, then at least climb up on one of the bar stools at the counter to enjoy a delicious shake at their classic soda fountain.

Stop off at the Visitor Center, housed in the historic downtown

Santa Fe passenger train depot, to find out about other attractions in the area and plan your visit.

Also, if you plan to do a side trip to the Grand Canyon National Park, which I totally advise you to do; you can save yourself a few miles by cutting across on US Highway 180 to reach the park, and then coming back down State Highway 64 to Williams. However, if you wait until you reach Williams you can take the historic train ride to the canyon.

Even though you are back on I-40 once again after leaving Flagstaff, it's not too bad because you are at least riding through trees again. The plains are picturesque and the rock formations are impressive, but I'll take riding among the trees any day. You will also find many opportunities for stealth camping in this section, not that I am advocating anyone doing this.

After leaving Parks you will ride on a short section of Route 66 that has preserved the original concrete slabs so travelers can experience the notorious "thumpety-thump" of the road joints firsthand to see what it was like. You'll know when you reach it, believe me.

The section of I-40 west of Parks crosses a beautiful open meadow.

On your approach into Williams, you pass a very unique lodging opportunity at Canyon Motel and RV Park. They have cottages and camping, plus you can sleep in a 1950s Pullman railway car suite. Pretty cool!

Williams advertises itself as the last town bypassed by I-40. The story behind this is that the six mile section of US 66 leading to Williams, was the final section of I-40 to be constructed in 1984.

It is also known as "The Gateway to the Grand Canyon", because this is the home of the Grand Canyon Railroad, which in earlier times was the method of transportation used by most of the canyon visitors.

Williams' main streets are one-way, so you'll need to ride both East and West Railroad Avenue to see everything. West will route you past the information center, and also where you purchase your Grand Canyon Railroad tickets for the historic trip to the Grand Canyon South Rim, more on this later.

The East Railroad Avenue takes you past several more interesting places to visit. Like Twister's Eat & Drink, Cruisers 66 Café, Sultana Bar (the longest operating liquor license in the state of Arizona), the Red Garter Inn (a beautifully restored 1897 saloon and bordello) and several other sites of interest. The building the Sultana is housed in operated as a saloon as far back as 1912.

Route 66 Section 22

During prohibition, a web of tunnels underneath the building dug by Chinese railroad workers in 1882, were used for running and storing booze.

There are plenty of lodging options to choose from in Williams to use as your basecamp for a couple days while you explore around. You can pick up a walking tour map from the visitor center.

Now, as for the Grand Canyon, this is one of the Seven Wonders of the World, it is definitely a must-see. Treat yourself to the train ride. For only an additional $5 you can also haul your bike. And if you don't want to use the train, ride the 60 miles each way to visit this truly one of a kind place. You've heard about it all your life, and you will kick your butt if you don't go see it while you're so close. They have bicycle camping at the South Rim for only $6. If you are travelling west to east you can ride up State Highway 64, then on the way back, fork off on US Highway 180 to Flagstaff to save some miles and avoid backtracking as much.

When you get back on I-40, after leaving Williams, be sure all your gear is strapped down good, because most of this stretch is downhill, and at times you will reach some pretty fast speeds. Use caution.

Once you reach the bottom of the hill you will be in an open meadow surrounded be beautiful mountain peaks. Even on the Interstate, this isn't a bad ride.

Ash Fork is another town with one-way main streets. They also have a museum, with antique farm equipment on the outside and period exhibits on the inside. There are also a few interesting historic plaques in town along the west bound one-way street, telling about the history of the town.

There isn't much remaining now, but at one time this was a busy mining and railroad town. At the turn of the century they even had one of the famous Harvey Hotel and Restaurants in town. However, in the '50's the Santa Fe Railroad realigned their tracks away from Ash Fork, and then when Route 66 bypassed them the town really suffered an economic setback.

On your ride out of town you'll see tons of stacks of rocks. That's because Ash Fork is still the Flagstone Capital of the World.

After the short ride on I-40, you will be riding through open grazing land, so watch for livestock on the highway. It is a nice ride through here with a mix of grassland and forest.

Route 66 Section 22

Camping

*KOA CG & Cabins
5803 North US Highway 89
Flagstaff, AZ 86004
928-526-9926

*Woody Mountain CG & RV
2727 Historic Rte 66
Flagstaff, AZ 86001
928-774-7727

*Kit Carson RV Park
2101 Historic Rte 66,
Flagstaff, AZ 86001
928-774-6993

*Circle Pines KOA
1000 Circle Pines Rd
Williams, AZ 86046
928-635-2626

*Canyon Motel & RV Park
1900 Historic Rte 66
Williams, AZ 86046
800-482-3955

Cataract Lake CG
N on 7th Ave then W 1 mile
Williams, AZ 86046
928-635-5600

*Hillside RV Park/Texaco
925 Frontage Rd
Ash Fork, AZ 86320
928-637-2300

Grand Canyon RV Park & CG
783 W.Old Route 66
Ash Fork, Arizona 86320
928-220-8993

*Seligman/Route 66 KOA
801 E Highway 66
Seligman, AZ 86337
928-422-3358

Lodging

*Best Western Inn & Suites
3030 Historic Rte 66
Flagstaff, AZ 86004
928-526-2388

*Americas Best Value Inn
1990 Historic Rte 66,
Flagstaff, AZ 86004
928-774-2779

*Hotel Monte Vista
100 N San Francisco St
Flagstaff, AZ 86001
928-779-6971

Grand Canyon Intl Hostel
19 S San Francisco St,
Flagstaff, AZ 86001
928-779-9421

Debeau International Hostel
19 W Phoenix Ave
Flagstaff, AZ 86001
928-774-6731

*Days Inn Bellemont
12380 W I-40, Exit 185
Bellemont, AZ 86015
928-556-9599

*Lodge On Route 66
200 E Route 66
Williams, AZ 86046
928-635-4534

*Red Garter Inn
137 W Railroad Ave
Williams, AZ 86046
928-635-1484

*Grand Canyon Gateway Inn
334 East Route 66
Williams, AZ 86046
928-635-8888

*Ash Fork Inn
859 U.S. Highway 66
Ash Fork, AZ 86320
928-637-2514

*Stagecoach 66 Motel
21455 W I-40B
Seligman, AZ 86337
928-422-3470

*Deluxe Inn
22295 Old Highway 66
Seligman, AZ 86337
928-422-3244

Bike Shops

*Absolute Bikes
202 Historic Rte 66
Flagstaff, AZ 86001
928-779-5969

REI
323 South Windsor Lane
Flagstaff, AZ 86001
928-213-1914

Flag Bike Revolution
3 Mikes Pike
Flagstaff AZ 86001
928-774-3042

Welcome to Williams, Arizona, Gateway to the Grand Canyon.

Route 66 Section 22

Winona to Seligman (85 miles)

Miles E/W	Directions	Dist	R	Service	Miles W/E
	*Winona (pop 116)				
0	R on Townsend-Winona Rd	10.0	3	Q	85
10	L at SL on US89/US180/R66	6.7	4	CGQ	75
17	S at SL on Santa Fe Ave/R66	0.1	4	GLQR	68
17	*Flagstaff (pop 68,667)			CGLQR	68
17	VL on Milton Rd/HR66	0.5	4	Q	68
17	R at SL on R66/I-40B		4	CL	68
17	S on R66/I-40B		4		68
17	Enter I-40	12.8	5	LQR	68
30	Exit I-40 on exit 178	0.2	3		55
30	R at SS on Parks Rd	0.2	3	Q	55
31	L at SS on R66		3		54
31	*Parks (pop 1,188)			CQ	54
31	S on R66	6.2	3	Q	54
37	L on Cool Pines Rd				48
37	R to enter I-40	5.3	5	C	48
42	Exit I-40 on exit 165	0.1	3		43
42	L at SS on I-40B	2.2	3	LQ	43
44	*Williams (pop 3,023)			GLQR	41
44	S on I-40B/Bill Williams Ave (EB use Railroad Ave)	1.7	3		41
46	R to enter I-40	14.6	5		39
61	Exit I-40 on exit 146	0.3	3		24
61	R on Lewis Ave/I-40B/HR66	0.6	3		24
62	*Ash Fork (pop 396)			LQR	23
62	S on Lewis Ave (EB Park Ave)	0.8	3		23
62	R to enter I-40	4.7	5		23
67	Exit I-40 on exit 139	0.2	3		18
67	R at SS on Crookton Rd/SR66	17.1	3		18
84	L at SS on R66/SR66	0.6		CL	1
85	*Seligman (pop 445)			CGLQR	0

Route 66 Section 22

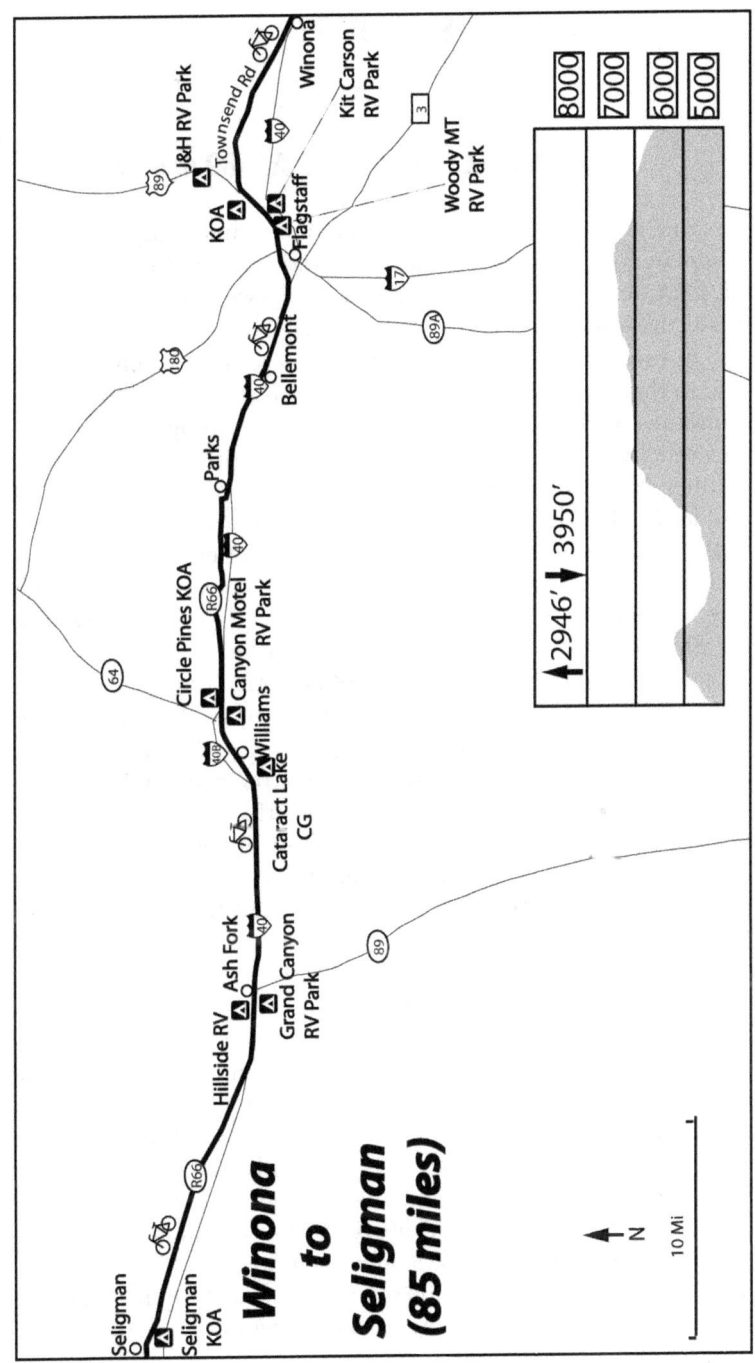

Route 66
SECTION 23

Seligman, AZ to Kingman, AZ (89 miles)

You really should plan to spend some time hanging out in Seligman. This is a cool, one of a kind town. The entire town is one big CRA, and this is by the design of the town's residents, seeing this as the town's only means of survival.

At the turn of the century Seligman was a major railroad hub. Due to the open flat terrain it became a large switching yard with numerous tracks. It was also an active livestock shipping center for area ranchers. However, when the mainline junction was moved to another town, like many other towns abandoned by the railroads, it was destined to become a ghost town. That is, if not for the actions of the local residents. When Route 66 was plotted to run through their city they set a goal to make it a popular destination along The Mother Road. And their plan worked. They even convinced the State of Arizona to make Route 66 an historic highway, with Seligman being named "Birthplace of Historic Route 66".

Seligman demonstrates why Route 66 became known as "Main Street of America." The route runs right through the heart of town, as it did in many other communities along the route. When Route 66 was initially developed the planners tried to take advantage of existing highways and at that time most highways ran through downtown. It wasn't until its popularity grew, and towns had to dig tunnels under the highway for pedestrians to be able to cross, that they began altering the route to bypass the busier sections of towns.

Seligman's entire down town is only about half-a-mile long, and both sides are lined with interesting shops and restaurants to browse through. However, you discover your first CRA on the outskirts of town. At the stop sign .6 miles out of town, if you turn right and ride off-route half-a-mile, you will reach the Norwegian owned, Stagecoach 66 Motel. This is a cool place, with an adjoining Pizza Bar & Grill and ice cream soda fountain. They've painted pictures of celebrities from the 50s on the outside walls, like Marilyn Monroe, Betty Boop, and Elvis (complete with his pink Cadillac). The restaurant also has outside seating. I met a group from France here who were riding Harleys across the USA on Route 66.

It is a nice clean place, and I really wanted to stay there to support these nice people, but it is located a mile out of town. I don't know reasoning behind this location, because I'd rather stay in town, so I can park my bike and walk to everything.

You won't need a walking tour map for Seligman, just park your bike and walk up one side of the highway and back down the other. There's the famous 1953 Sno Cap Drive-In (you will enjoy the owner's flair for showmanship beginning with his sign "Sorry, we're open"), Angel & Vilma's Route 66 Gift Shop, Copper Cart Motoporium , The Black Cat Bar, and the Roadkill Café (with daily specials like Splatter Plater, Highway Hash and other catchy menu items that play of the café's theme).

Leaving Seligman you get to bag another "-est" just by riding your bike, as you begin the longest unbroken remaining stretch of Old Route 66. The next 158 mile stretch was completely bypassed by I-40 and remains unspoiled all the way to the Colorado River on the California border. No I-40 in your peripheral vision or frontage roads, just Route 66 as the early travelers experienced it. And, at least in this section, there is a pretty good road shoulder through a lot of it.

The tall bluffs along the top of Red Mesa Mountain to the north give the mountain the appearance of a walled fortress. It is very scenic to ride through these wide open desert valleys surrounded by tall peaks.

To contribute to the feel of the Route 66 era, they've even added some of Berma Shave's rhyming words of wisdom signs. In 1925 Allan Odell, son of the company's owner Clinton Odell, erected the first of these signs which followed the concept of using sequential signboards to sell the product. By posting five or more consecutive signs it compelled people to read the whole series and it would hold the travelers' attention longer than conventional billboards.

It's ironic that Arizona, where you now see the signs, was one of only four of the lower 48 states that did not have the signs posted during the company's popularity between 1925 and 1963.

About 19 miles into your ride you'll reach Grand Canyon Caverns, the largest dry caverns in the U.S. This is a welcome oasis with a motel, restaurant, gift shop, camping, cavern tours, horseback riding, rafting, and just about anything else you can think of to do in the great outdoors. This would make a good home base to hang out and let your body rest while you indulge in some of these fun activities. And for just $800 a night you can bag a whole bunch of "-est", by renting the Underground Cave Suite, which is the largest, deepest, darkest, oldest, quietest motel in the world.

If you look at the contour map for this section, you'll notice a lot more downhill than uphill. On the approach into Peach Springs you'll experience a good deal of this descent. Enjoy!

Peach Springs has survived the economic effects of I-40 better than many of the other towns along this stretch of Route 66 because it is the Hualapai tribal headquarters. You will find full services here.

Truxton did not fare as well, as the boarded up Orlando Motel will confirm.

Just before reaching Valentine you have an opportunity to visit, and contribute to, a very worthy cause, Keepers of the Wild. This is a nonprofit organization that is currently home to over 130 exotic and indigenous animals that were rescued or placed in their care. It's not a zoo, but a sanctuary that provides a life-long home to the animals they rescue. They offer guided safari tours to view the animals living in the wild. Just so you won't be expecting a big commercial Disney World style production, like most of the attractions along this stretch, it is a small operation. But their hearts are in the right place.

Oh yes, one of the locals told me that Valentine was also the location where they filmed the scene that Peter Fonda was fixing a flat on his chopper in Easy Rider.

Be sure to stop at the Hackberry General Store, often referred to as "the mother lode of mother road memorabilia". Although it's original purpose was to fulfill the needs of the Hackberry community, its primary function now is to act as a museum of Route 66 memorabilia. You can tour the outside area to see the old gas pumps, vehicles (including a 1957 red Corvette), and tons of vintage signs, and then venture inside to sip on a Route 66 root beer as you check out the re-created '50's dinner, complete with manikins, jukebox, and Elvis cutout. Definitely a CRA.

A little further down the highway you come across a classic roadside oddity, the Cozy Corner Trailer Park. But the former gas station turned mobile home park isn't what provides the oddness, it's the 14' tall Tiki sculpture named "Giganticus Headicus" and the other assorted yard art on display, which would seem out of place anywhere other than in the desert on Route 66, that is.

This is also near the turn for an off-route trip to Grand Canyon Skywalk, a glass bottom, horse-shoe shaped bridge that extends beyond the rim of the canyon, 4,000 feet above the canyon floor. It is a 60-mile ride on a dirt road from here. If you are interested in visiting you might prefer riding north, out of Kingman, on US

Highway 93 which provides a paved route. The tickets are pricey, at about $80, but it does provide an impressive, unique view of the Grand Canyon.

You'll need to ride to the west side of Kingman to find the Route 66- oriented attractions. Just as the Hotel Monte Vista's neon sign towers over Flagstaff, the Hotel Beale neon sign promotes its "Air Cooled" rooms.

Some of the highlights in Kingman are the 1907 Powerhouse building (which houses the Route 66 Museum), the 1907 Railroad Depot (which houses the Kingman Railroad Museum), the Mohave Museum of History & Arts, Mr D'z Route 66 Diner, and many more attractions. Pick up a walking tour map at the museums just so you don't miss anything.

Camping

*KOA Seligman
801 AZ-66
Seligman, AZ 86337
928-422-3358

*Route 66 General Store
22940 W. Hwy. 66
Seligman, AZ 86337
928-422-3549

*Grand Canyon Caverns CG/Motel
115 Mile Marker Arizona 66
Peach Springs, AZ 86434
928-422-3223

*Mike's Outpost Bar & CG
9321 E Highway 66
Kingman, AZ 86401
928-692-2166

Circle S Campground
2360 Airway Ave
Kingman, AZ 86409
928-757-3235

Kingman KOA
3820 N Roosevelt St
Kingman, AZ 86409
928-757-4397

Lodging

Stagecoach 66 Motel
21455 West I-40B
Seligman, AZ 86337
928-526-2388

*Deluxe Inn
22295 Old Highway 66
Seligman, AZ 86337
928-422-3244

*Hualapai Lodge
900 Route 66
Peach Springs, AZ 86434
928-769-2230

Frontier Motel & Cafe
16118 E Highway 66
Truxton, AZ 86434
928-769-1206

*Hill Top Motel
1901 E Andy Devine Ave
Kingman, AZ 86401
928-753-2198

*El Trovatore Motel
1440 E Andy Devine Ave
Kingman, AZ 86401
928-753-   6520

Bike Shops

Bicycle World
1825 Northern Ave
Kingman, AZ 86401
928-757-5730

Bicycle Outfitters
3001 N Stockton Hill Rd
Kingman, AZ 86401
928-753-7538

Route 66 in the Wild Wild West.

Route 66 Section 23

Seligman to Kingman (89 miles)

Miles E/W	Directions	Dist	R	Service	Miles W/E
	*Seligman (pop 456)			CGLQR	
0	L at SS on R66	19.1	3	LQR	89
19	*Turn for Grand Canyon Caverns			CLR	69
19	S on R66	19.9			69
39	*Peach Springs (pop 1,090)			GLQR	50
39	S on R66	7.3	3		50
46	*Truxton (pop 134)			LQR	42
46	S on R66	10.3	3		42
57	*Valentine (pop 16)				32
57	S on R66	4.8			32
61	*Hackberry				27
61	S on R66	5.7	3		27
67	*Antares (pop 126)				21
67	S on R66	4.8	3	C	21
72	*Valle Vista			Q	17
72	S on R66	9.5	3		17
81	S at SL on R66/Andy Devine Ave	7.1	3	GQ	7
89	*Kingman (pop 20,068)			CGLQR	0

Route 66 Section 23

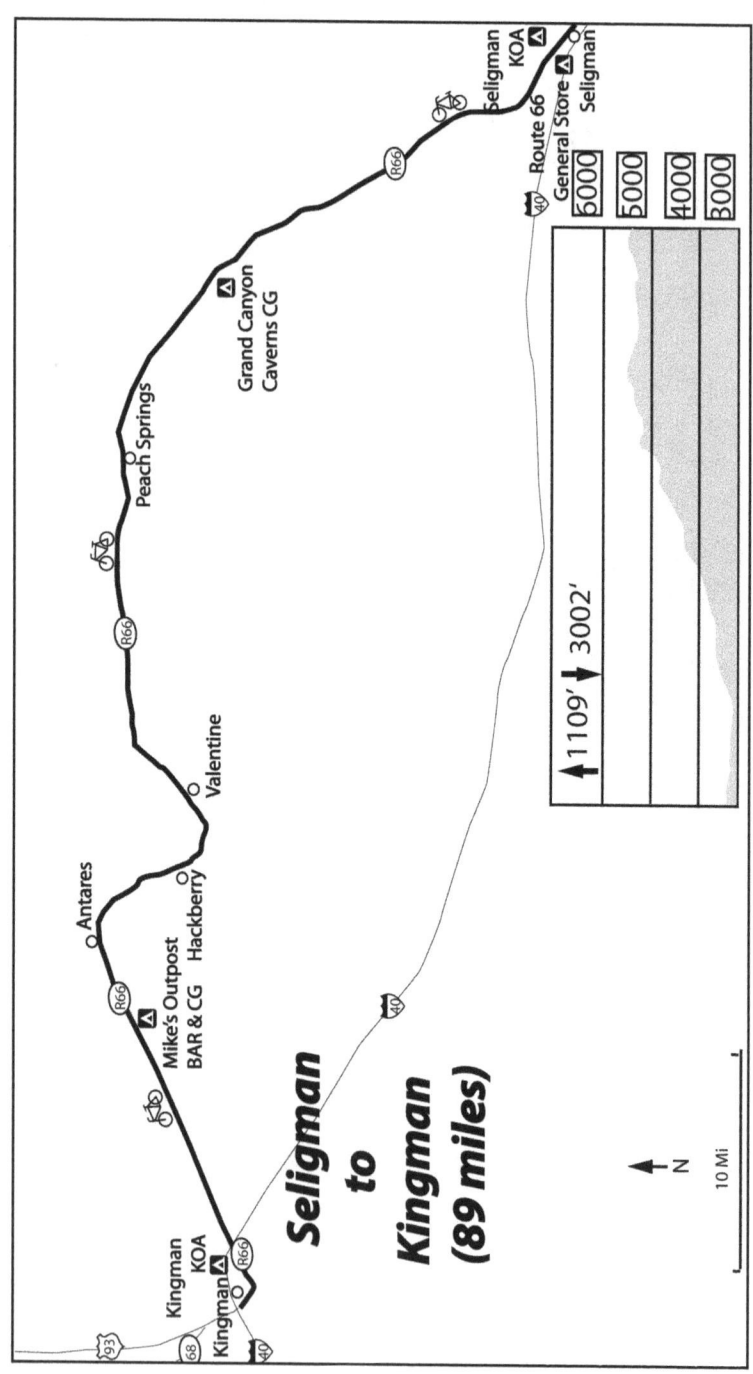

Route 66
SECTION 24

Kingman, AZ to Goffs, CA (98 miles)

Put on your big boy, or girl, britches for this section, there is a major climb, Sitgreaves Pass, 3550' elevation. However, after conquering the pass you are rewarded with an awesome downhill descent. That is unless you are eastbound, where you begin your climb at a lot lower elevation than coming from the west.

Be sure to top off your water bottles at every opportunity because services are limited through the early portion of the section and you are riding on the outskirts of the Mojave Desert, which often report the highest recorded temperatures in the nation.

Watch for the rough cattle guard at the end of Andy Devine Drive. As you may have already guessed, Andy Devine was Kingman's "favorite son". Although Devine was born in Flagstaff, he was raised in Kingman.

Shortly into your ride on Oatman Road you'll pass an information kiosk with several signs about the history of the area. Be sure to pause to read these interesting signs, you will appreciate the tour more.

This designated official Scenic Route is part of the national Back Country Byways program, by the Bureau of Land Management, in an effort to open up less travelled corridors to the public.

A word of warning, the ride over the pass can have strong crosswinds and rough cattle guards. On some stretches the highway lacks a shoulder and is bordered by steep drop-offs, so don't let the vehicles force you off the road because there is no place to go. But the speed limit is only 20 MPH on the steeper stretches, so it really shouldn't be a problem. Njoy!

There is an oasis for cyclists just before beginning the switchbacks that take you up to Sitgreaves Pass, Cool Springs Camp. Stop for a cold soda and snack, as you listen to the owner share this rare Route 66 success story of how he rescued the store from a pile of rubble.

Sitgreaves Pass was one of the most intimidating portions of Route 66 for many early motorists. The vehicles just weren't made to handle this steep grade. Shortly after leaving Cool Springs Camp you pass the remains of Ed's Camp, an early automobile service station. Ed probably made a good living off of these motorists, hauling their underpowered automobiles over the pass. Rather than pay him, many of the drivers chose to climb over the pass in reverse, taking advantage of the lower gearing in reverse, plus utilizing gravity to keep the fuel shifted towards the front of the vehicle for the gravity-fed fuel delivery system.

Once you top the pass it is free sailing down the long descent, with something exciting to see around each corner of the switchbacks: such as abandoned highway/mining equipment, interesting rock formations, and the battered automobile down in the ravine whose driver must have missed a turn.

There is a sign painted on the side of a block building advertising "Goldroad Mine", and the arrow seemingly directing tourists how to get there, but then there are words within the arrow warning, "Do Not Enter". Quite a contradiction, I thought.

Following several hundred feet of descent you enter a true Old West gold mining town, Oatman. Founded in 1908 the mine produced over 1.8 million ounces of gold by the mid 1930's, but the boom was over by 1942 when the government shut down the operation classifying it nonessential to the war effort.

Even though Oatman can at times become overrun by tourists, the small village has retained a frontier character. With the aged wooden boardwalks running along in front of the businesses, old abandoned mining equipment still waiting to be called back into service, and wild burros ruling main street, it would be difficult to find a more authentic western frontier mining town than this.

The Oatman Hotel is definitely a must-see CRA! Belly up to the bar and ask Dallas, the cute bartender, to tell you the story about when Clark Gable and Carole Lombard spent the night there on their honeymoon. The celebrated couple was wed in Kingman but the paparazzi harassed them so much they fled to Oatman. The hotel has the room they stayed in roped off, but you can peer in through the door. Gable liked the town so much that he would return to play poker even after the honeymoon ended.

Make your mark on a denomination of currency and staple it to the wall, along with the thousands of other bills, so future customers will know you were there.

The Oatman Hotel no longer offers overnight accommodations, but in addition to the cool bar they have a full service restaurant. But don't get caught in town too late, because when the last burro leaves town for the day they shut everything down.

There is a park with restrooms at the south end of the town of Golden Shores. You will also pass the turn for an alternate county

Route 66 Section 24

road on your right just after leaving town. I did not ride this route because I wanted to see Needles, and it didn't sound to appealing from what I had heard about it, but I included directions for it at the end of the Mileage Log of this section.

Between Golden Shores and Topock you ride through several low lying arroyos, which would indicate this area is subject to flooding. But I wasn't worried too much about flooding after talking to a local in Golden Shores, who told me they had had a lot more rain that year than normal through the month of May, "Yeah, we've had darn nearly an inch and a half of rain already."

Just before you enter California, the eighth and final state in your Route 66 Adventure, stop at the Topock 66 Marina & Bar for a cold one to celebrate this momentous occasion. What a great place to do it, too. The outdoor bar overlooks the Colorado River and it has a swimming pool right in the middle of the bar. And coming soon is the new Topock 66 Hotel, so you won't have to drink and ride.

As you are about to enter I-40 in Topock, take a short side trip and cross over I-40 to admire the impressive Old Trails Bridge that spans the Colorado River. The method of construction for this steel cantilever bridge was a daring move for its time. The engineers used a unique method of constructing the bridge in halves on the ground and then hoisting them into place with ball-and-socket center hinge, thus creating the longest arched bridge in America of its time (bagged another "-est"). In 1948 the paved deck was removed to accommodate a natural gas pipeline, which it continues to carry today.

Shortly after crossing the Colorado River on I-40, at the Park Moabi Road exit, ignore the sign that says "Exit Route 66", that road is closed. But this is the exit for Pirate's Cove Resort, which has cabins and a restaurant.

After taking exit 148, then turning onto Five Mile Road and crossing over I-40, be sure to stop to read the Historic Route 66 sign. I truly believe the more you know about the area the more you will enjoy it.

Those large mountains you are seeing in the distance to the west along this stretch are the San Bernardino Mountains. You will be getting up close and personal with them before long.

If you plan to get a room overnight in Needles, wait until you reach Needles Highway, there are several clean older motels along the road that are priced right. For those who rode the Alternate County Road, this intersection with Broadway Street is where you will rejoin the main route.

On your ride through Needles, prior to the Needles Highway turn, be sure to turn right off of West Broadway Street onto G Street, to see the former El Garces Hotel. With its Neoclassical and Beaux-Arts style, the 1908 hotel was considered "the Crown Jewel" of the entire Fred Harvey chain. The elegant structure underwent a complete renovation in 2014 and it is now the El Garces Intermodal transportation facility.

As I was having a beer in a bar the evening I stayed in Needles, a guy told me the interesting story behind the El Garces. It seemed that the renovation was initiated by an investor who had this grand plan to restore the hotel to its glory days. Deep into the restoration project he failed an audit of his books. At that time the Federal Transit Administration decided that since they had provided the funding for the renovation through a public funded grant, ownership of the building belonged to the city of Needles. So they took over the building.

After leaving Needles keep an eye out for the rock memorials people have constructed alongside the highway. They are makeshift piles of rocks that don't appear to have any theme for the project as a whole, but some people devoted a lot of time to these memorials.

I spotted my first palm tree on this stretch next to a roadside vendor selling honey.

I didn't meet a single vehicle on my ride on Goffs Road, just a lot of jack rabbits with the longest ears I have ever seen on a rabbit. As I could ride right past them and it didn't faze them at all.

There are no services in Goffs, but they do have an outdoor museum of sorts, with a couple historic markers, a restored schoolhouse, and a short walking path. I enjoyed it and was glad I stopped.

Camping

*Black Mountain RV Park
6600 W Oatman Hwy
Golden Valley, AZ 86413
928-565-5191

Fender's River Road Resort
3396 Needles Hwy
Needles, CA 92363
760-326-3423

Golden Shores RV Park
13021 Water Reed Dr
Topock, AZ 86436
928-788-1001
(LT 1 mile off-route)

Needles KOA & Cabins
5400 National Old Trails Rd
Needles, CA 92363
760-326-4207

Needles Marina Park
100 Marina Dr
Needles, CA 92363
760-326-2197

Lodging

*Imperial 400 Motor Inn
644 West Broadway Street
Needles, CA 92363
760-326-0133

Days Inn And Suites
1215 Hospitality Lane
Needles, CA 92363
760-326-5836

*Best Western CO River Inn
2371 W Broadway
Needles, CA 92363
760-326-4552

*Knights Inn
2306 Needles Hwy
Needles, CA 92363
760-326-0300

*Budget Inn
2104 Needles Highway
Needles, CA 92363
760-326-2212

*River Valley Inn
1707 Needles Highway
Needles, CA 92363
760-326-3839

Bike Shops

N/A

I left my mark at the Oatman Hotel Bar, how about you?

Route 66 Section 24

Miles E/W	Directions	Dist	R	Service	Miles W/E
	*Kingman (pop 28,068)				
0	L on Andy Devine Dr/Frontage Rd/R66	5.0	3	QR	98
5	R at SS on R66/Shinarump Rd to cross I-40	0.3	3		93
5	L on Oatman Rd/R66	15.1	3	C	93
20	*Cold Springs Camp				78
20	S on Oatman Rd/R66	5.0	3		78
25	*Sitgreaves Pass elevation 3550'				73
25	S on Oatman Rd/R66	4.2	3		73
30	*Oatman (pop 135)				69
30	S on Oatman Rd/R66	2.6	3		69
32	VL on Oatman Rd/R66	17.2	3		66
49	*Golden Shores (pop 2,047)			CGQR	49
49	S at SS on Oatman Rd/R66	4.4	3		49
54	*Topock (pop 10)			R	45
54	S on Oatman Rd/R66	0.5	3		45
54	R to enter I-40	0.6	5		44
55	*Enter California				44
55	S on I-40	6.2	5	CR	44
61	Exit I-40 on exit 148	0.3			37
61	L at SS on Five Mile Rd/US95/R66 to ride over I-40	1.9	3		37
63	BR at SS on US95	3.8	3	L	35
67	*Needles (pop 4,844)			GLQR	31
67	VL on Broadway St/R66	2.3	4		31
69	L at SS on Needles Hwy/R66	1.6	4	CLR	29
71	VL to cont on R66	1.2	4	C	27
72	L at SS on Park Rd the R on I-40	6.2	5		26
78	Exit I-40 on exit 133	0.2	4		20
79	VR on US95/R66	6.2	4		20
85	L on Goffs Rd/CR68/R66	13.6	3		14
98	*Goffs (pop 23)				0
	Alternate County Road route				
	R on CR 1 after leaving Golden Shores	7.1			12
7	S on Courtwright Rd/CR227	3.7			5
11	*Arizona Village				2
11	L on SR 95 (enter California)	1.5			2
12	R on Needles Hwy/R66 to rejoin main route				

Route 66 Section 24

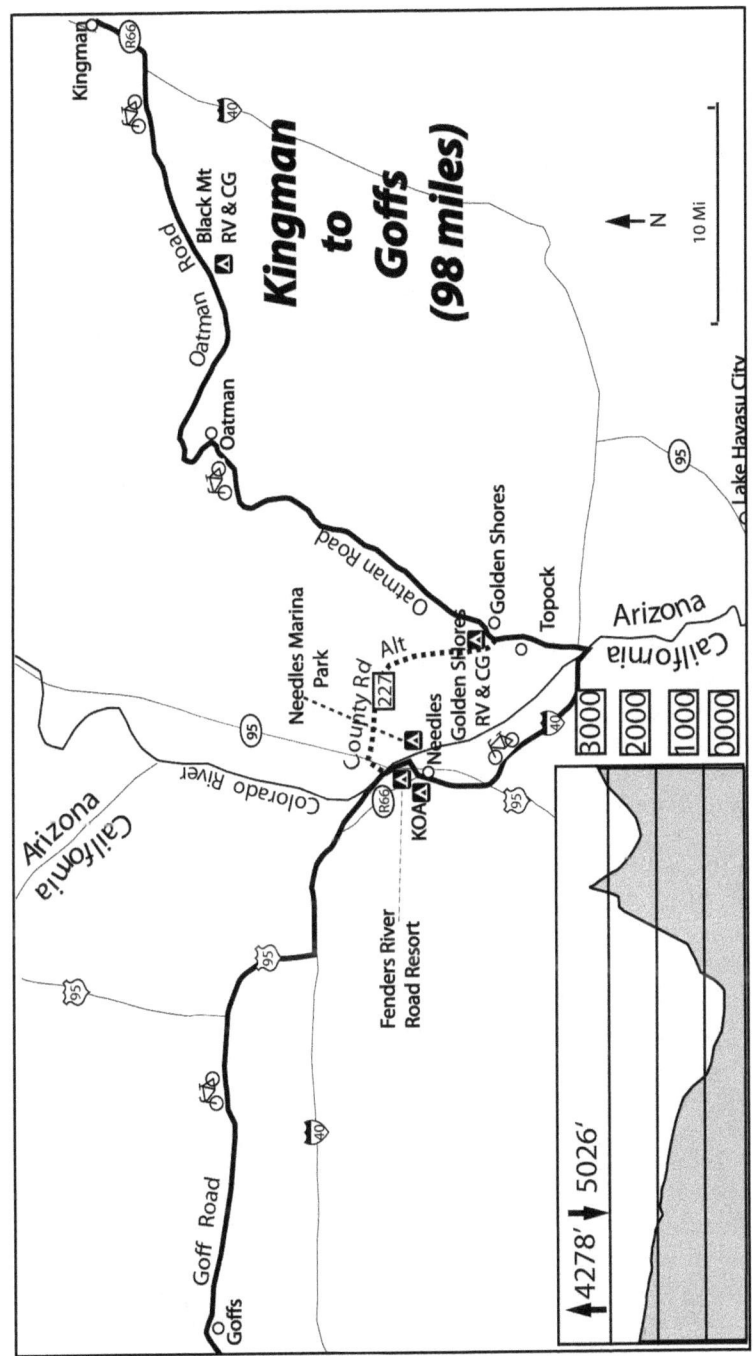

Route 66
SECTION 25

Goffs, CA to Ludlow, CA (76 miles)

As you are riding along Goffs Road in the hot dry desert heat, and you see what appears to be palm trees in the distance and as you get closer you hear what sounds like trickling water, don't panic, you're not hallucinating, you've just arrived at Hi, Sahara Oasis, in Fenner.

The Oasis has everything you need to prepare for the barren stretch of road ahead (except for bicycle parts). They have food supplies, a restaurant, water, sun screen, and just about anything else you can think of. They even let you pitch a tent on their lot for $10. Or, if you just want to take a break, you can relax in the shade under a palm tree beside the water fountain as you munch on a snack.

The 60-mile stretch of highway from Fenner to Ludlow is the most desolate section on Route 66 thus far. Also, this is the southern border of the Mojave Desert, so count on it being hot. Only one of the towns listed on the maps have services, and the others have no services, or even residents, for you to replenish water. So understand that you will be fully self-supported and be sure to top off "all" of your water containers when leaving Fenner.

Looking on the bright side of it however, because this is such a deserted stretch of highway you will probably have the road to yourself, and if you are properly prepared it can be enjoyable. I don't normally listen to music while riding my bicycle, because I like to be aware of my surroundings, but the highway here is straight and what few motorists there are can literally see from you miles away. So I made an exception on this section. I tuned in and escaped into my inner Zen.

A few miles after leaving Fenner you join the old National Trails Highway (NTH), a precursor to Route 66. However, although NTH preceded the Mother Road, it wasn't America's first attempt at creating an interstate highway system. NTH was preceded by the American Auto Trails, begun in 1911, which itself grew from the Good Road Movements, founded in 1880, which was created by bicyclists and bicycle manufacturers after forming the League of American Wheelmen. However, with the rise of the popularity of the automobile, in the 1900s the Good Roads enthusiasts' priorities had shifted from bicycles to motorized travel and support on the national level was developed. This led to the creation of the Federal Highway System.

Our approach to Cadiz Summit is a gradual ascent; however, eastbound cyclists begin their climb to the 1302' peak at almost ground level, so it's a little more of a challenge for them.

If you had been cycling through here back in 1942 you would have encountered a lot more activity. This was the area where General George S. Patton established his Desert Training Center to prepare U.S. troops to fight General Erwin Rommel's (the Desert Fox) German troops in North Africa.

I paused at the top of the Cadiz Summit to sit on a boulder and peer across the wide desolate valley below, trying to imagine what that scene would have been like when General Patton and his troops were here. Thousands of soldiers along with hundreds of tanks and other artillery equipment scattered across the desert floor, everyone working desperately to develop a strategy to defeat the ever increasing forces of the Axis powers. The U.S military had been badly beaten in their first encounter with the German lead forces in the disastrous Battle of the Kasserine Pass, so the pressure on General Patton to find a solution had to have been unimaginable. But thankfully, once again America, and the world, was saved by having the right person in charge at the right time.

Shortly after descending Cadiz Summit I entered the community of Chambliss where I saw a large sign advertising, "Bolo Station Water Company." Beside it was a tall fence around what appeared to be an open-air bar and dining area. "Cool," I thought to myself and pulled into the parking area to check it out.

When I asked a guy what the area was and if it was open to the public, all hell broke loose.

"What the f#@ are you doing here?" he yelled at me.

I attempted to explain that I was just bicycling through the area and wanted to see what the place was, but he interrupted me with more cussing, accompanied by more gestures for me to leave. So I left.

I don't know if I caught them on a bad day or what, but use your own judgement to determine if you want to stop here to top off your water bottles. If yours is a better experience than mine please let me know, because this would be a much needed stop for cyclists if we could work it out.

There are several interesting roadside attractions between Chambliss and Amboy. First, you pass the remains of what had once been a popular tourist stop, Road Runner's Retreat, with a pretty cool sign still standing out front. Then, there are the interesting rock art patterns alongside the highway, with names, memorials, and other messages written out using rows of rocks. You also pass what I call the "Mojave Glacier." I know it's not really ice, and is probably just a massive pile of lime that has accumulated on the mountainside, but it reminded me of an iceberg. And then, in an open field about 40' from the highway, there is a matching pair of seven-foot-tall Chinese Guardian Lions patiently standing watch over their territory. The only thing I could find out about these "Foo Dogs" was that they just appeared in 2013 and no one had any idea where they came from. They are beautiful works of art, and you would think someone would have stolen them by now. But I guess no one wants to risk the bad voodoo they might invoke from stealing these spiritual icons.

Next is the legendary Roy's Café & Motel. And, great news, Roy's is once again satisfying the needs of Route 66 travelers, as it has been doing since the route was first established. Albert Okura purchased the entire town of Amboy in 2005 and is currently in the process of restoring the place to its former glory. The café and motel were not fully functioning when I rode through, however they do sell gasoline and also have sodas and snacks. I was also told that any cyclist who came by would be assured of either a place to pitch their tent or a room to sleep in. Okura also owns the first McDonald's Restaurant in San Bernardino, which now operates as a museum. So, be sure to let him know how much you appreciate his work to keep this piece of Americana alive for future generations to enjoy.

Just outside of Amboy, the highway is bordered on both shoulders by black crusted lava that flowed some 79,000 years ago from nearby Amboy Crater. The 250' high cinder cone of the crater can be seen from the highway. There is a parking lot .5 miles off the highway, where you can hike a 1.5 mile trail all the way up to the rim of the crater. There are also restrooms located at the trailhead.

The roadside into Ludlow is littered with abandoned homes, businesses, and trailers. If you turn to the left, across from the listed right turn over I-40, you can visit the remains of the old Ludlow Mercantile Building.

There are convenience stores on both sides of I-40 at Ludlow, but the one on the north side has a Dairy Queen, where you can get a cool refreshing milk shake.

After Ludlow, the National Trails acts pretty much as a frontage road for I-40 the remainder of this section.

Camping

*Hi Sahara Oasis
31251 Goffs Rd
Fenner, CA 92332
760-694-0181
(pitch tent on lot)

*Roy's Motel & Cafe
87520 National Trail Hwy
Amboy, CA 92304
760-733-1066
(pitch tent or stay in room)

Lodging

*Ludlow Motel/Cafe
68315 National Trail Hwy
Ludlow, CA 92338
760-733-4501

Bike Shops

N/A

Foo Dog standing guard over Route 66 Adventurers.

Goffs to Ludlow (76 miles)

Miles E/W	Directions	Dist	R	Service	Miles W/E
	*Goffs (pop 23)				
0	S on Goffs Rd/CR68/R66	9.5	3		76
10	*Fenner			CQR	67
10	S on Goffs Rd/CR68/R66	5.3	3		67
15	R on National Trails Hwy/R66	1.7	3		61
17	*Essex (pop 89)				60
17	S on National Trails Hwy/R66	8.9	3		60
25	*Cadiz Summit				51
25	S on National Trails Hwy/R66	3.4	3		51
29	*Chambliss (pop 6)				47
29	S on National Trails Hwy/R66	10.7	3		47
40	*Amboy (pop 4)			CQ	37
40	S on National Trails Hwy/R66	8.0	3		37
48	*Bagdad				29
48	S on National Trails Hwy/R66	20.2	3		29
68	*Ludlow (pop 10)			LQR	8
68	R at SS on Crucero Rd to cross I-40	0.2	3		8
68	L on National Trails Hwy/R66	8.1	3	QR	8
76	L on Lavic Rd to cross I-40				0

Route 66 Section 25

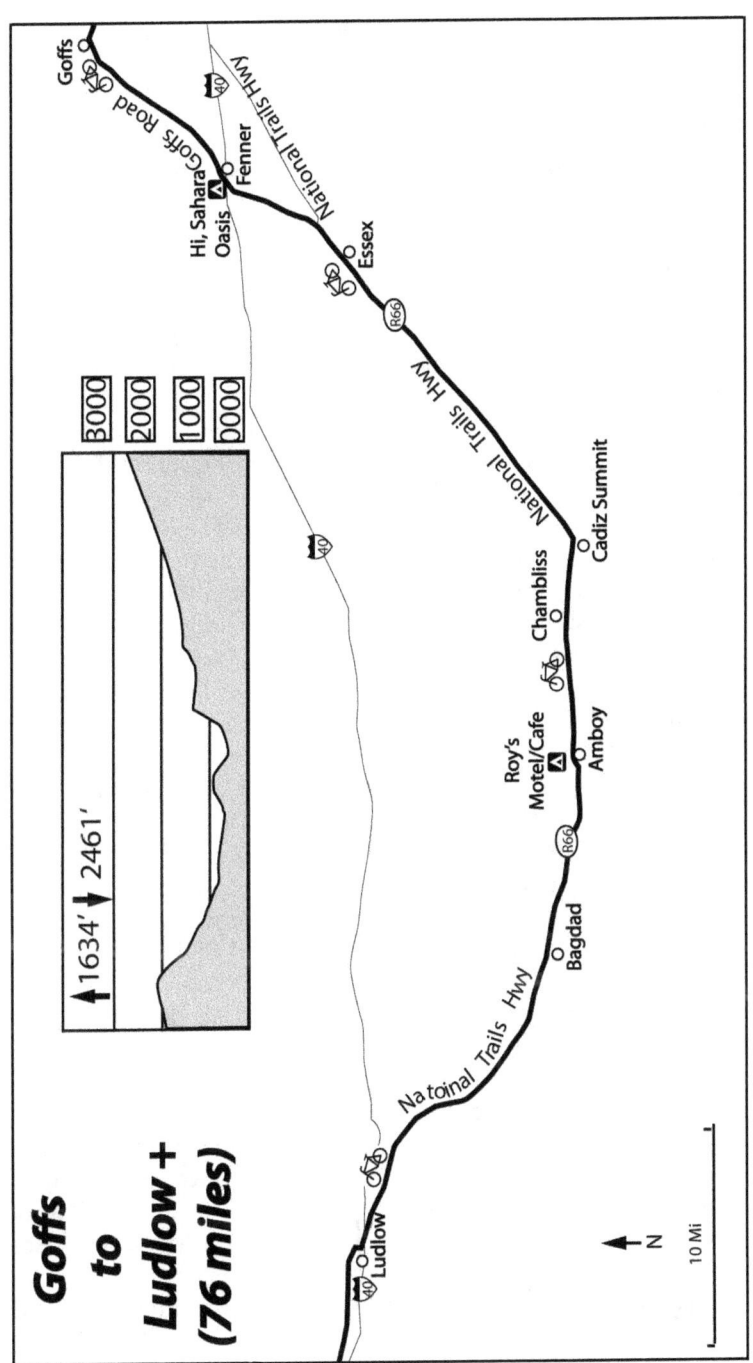

Route 66
SECTION 26

Ludlow, CA to Hesperia, CA (85 miles)

This section has several significant milestones in it: (1) you will complete our bicycle ride across the Mohave Desert (2) you will reach the end (or beginning, depends on which direction you are riding) of your companion across four states, Interstate 40 (3) puts you within striking distance to the end of our Route 66 Adventure.

We ended Section 25 in the middle of nowhere, and so we shall also begin this section in the middle of nowhere, the Lavic Road crossing over I-40.

I imagine the unrelenting heat of the Mohave Desert had something to do with it, but the pavement at the beginning of this section is the roughest I've seen. It was so rough that I often rode on the gravel shoulder. So secure all of you equipment and take your time, it does get better after about fifteen miles.

The route takes you past the Pisgah Lava Field early in this section. I don't know if all the lava is from the same volcano but the lava stretches on for several miles.

A day of riding in this heat will make you appreciate the pool at the Newberry Mountain RV Park near the Fort Cody Road crossing.

There were a lot of abandoned businesses in Section 25 and in this section as well. When I-40 opened up there just wasn't a reason for people to continue driving these roads, and all the businesses at that time were driven by the tourist industry. So be sure to support the businesses that still struggle by. Maybe with the new ACA maps the bicycle tourists will make the difference for their survival. We need them as much as they need us.

Before reaching Newberry Springs, you pass the café where the Bagdad Café movie was filmed. At the time the movie was made the café was called Sidewinder Café, but it has since been changed to Bagdad Café. When you stop off for a bite to eat and cold drink be sure to check out the pictures they have from when they were shooting the film.

Following Newberry Springs the highway is in pretty good condition and there is even a shoulder. Plus some of the homes through there have some really healthy palm trees. I could really get used to having some cool palm trees in my yard.

In Daggett they found the right crop for their environment, solar farming. Literally a match made in the heavens.

The town of Daggett has a few interesting attractions that make it a good place to park your bike and stretch your legs. There's the Ski Sloped House (you'll understand the name when you see the house), Mugwumps station, the Stone Hotel (where both John Muir and Tom Mix have stayed), and the still-open Desert Market. Most are just abandoned buildings now, but try to view them in your imagination's eye during their heyday.

In Barstow we take our last ride on I-40. It's just a short two mile ride that circumvents the Marine Corps Logistics Base. We take exit #2, and two miles later I-40 unceremoniously becomes I-15. So long, I-40!

Barstow would be a good place to layover for a couple days before making your final push to Santa Monica Pier (I'm giddy just writing about the end being so near). It is a nice clean town with numerous attractions to check out.

The Visitor Information Center would be a great place to start, not just to collect information to help you plan your tour, but the building itself would be near the top of the list of the town's main attractions. The building was originally the Casa Del Desierto, constructed in 1911, and later becoming the Harvey House Railroad Depot. The building is described as a fusion of Spanish Renaissance and Classical Revival styles. It uses an interesting mix of a concrete frame and red tapestry brick, with a red clay tile roof effectively bringing all these designs together.

The Western American Railroad Museum and the Route 66 "Mother Road" Museum are also located in the building.

Once you have finished your visit at the museums, take a tour of the downtown to walk among the healthy palm trees and view the colorful murals that document the interesting history of the area. I couldn't get enough of the palm trees.

There are plenty of lodging and eating options to choose from in Barstow. The city is also keeping the Mother Road theme alive through the preservation of vintage signs and classic motels.

Lenwood has become pretty much a suburb of Barstow, with their borders merging together. But once you leave Lenwood you are back in the desert once again. And what a big desert it is. As far as the eye can see to the north, which is a long way when there are no trees or manmade obstacles to block your view, just dry barren open desert nothingness. When I return home I'll be experiencing color overload.

Most of the businesses in Helendale are off-route about a mile via Vista Road. But there is a nice shopping center with a market and deli once you reach it. The Inn at Silver Lakes is about another two miles beyond the shopping center.

Dempsey's Pub is located at the turn onto Vista Road, which has hot wings, along with other snacks, and cold beer.

But if you are in the mood for some good home-style cooking, continue a couple miles further on our route to reach Molly Brown's Country Café. Good food, good service, and a clean establishment.

After you've had your fill at Molly's, pedal a couple more miles down Route 66 and then let your food settle as you stroll among the outdoor art at The Bottle Ranch, another CRA. This is two acres of folk art made from welded metal pipe, with colorful classic antique glass bottles mounted on every possible appendage. And it doesn't stop with pipes and bottles. Elmer Long has incorporated industrial equipment, vehicle parts, and any other quirky object he can find that he thinks will contribute character to his masterpiece. As you walk among the structures listen to the gentle tinkle as the wind jostles the glass bottles on their metal perch.

As I rode past the Iron Hog Restaurant & Saloon, with an overflowing parking lot, I realized that most of the businesses that are surviving along Route 66 in this area are associated with liquor.

Oro Grande is a quaint old town, with all of the buildings in their limited downtown occupied with antique stores, a sweet shop, and a pizza parlor. I particularly liked the brightly painted cow atop one of the buildings.

Following Oro Grande, the traffic begins to pick up, so use caution. After riding so many miles on the deserted highways during the past days, it takes some time to become accustomed once again to having cars flying past you.

Victorville greets travelers with one of the most impressive Route 66 arches I've seen on the entire tour. It appears to be a new sign. It's great to see the Mother Road still growing.

Riding a bicycle, Shady Oasis Campground is a little challenging to reach, because we can't ride on I-15. To reach it, rather that turn right 7th Street as the Mileage Log specifies, continue straight on State Road 18 another half-a-mile, then turn left on Stoddard Wells Road to ride another mile. The entrance will be on your left.

Route 66 Section 26

Camping

*Newberry Mountain RV Park
47800 National Trails Hwy
Newberry Springs, CA 92365
760-257-0066

Shady Oasis Kampground
16530 Stoddard Wells Rd
Victorville, CA 92395
760-252-6100
(2 miles off-route)

Desert Springs Rv Park & Bar/Grill
34805 Daggett Yermo Rd
Daggett, CA 92327
760-254-2000

Mojave Narrows Reg Park
18000 Yates Rd
Victorville, CA 92392
760-245-2226
(7 miles off-route)

Mid Hills NPS Campground
2701 Barstow Rd
Barstow, CA 92311
760-252-6100
(2 miles off-route)

Lodging

*California Inn
1431 E Main St
Barstow, CA 92311
760-256-0661

The Inn At Silver Lakes
14818 Clubhouse Drive
Helendale, CA 92342
760- 243-4800

*Route 66 Motel
195 Main St
Barstow, CA 92311
760-256-7866

*Travel Inn & Suites
14998 7th Street
Victorville, CA 92395
760-245-8627

*Americas Best Value Inn
1350 W. Main St.
Barstow, CA 92311
760-256-8921

*New Corral Motel
14643 7th St
Victorville, CA 92395
760-245-9378

Elmer Long's famous Bottle Ranch.

Route 66 Section 26

*SpringHill Suites Hesperia
9625 Mariposa Road
Hesperia, CA 92345
760- 948-8982

*Best Western
9625 Mariposa Rd
Hesperia, CA 92344
760-948-8984

*Courtyard By Marriott
9619 Mariposa Road
Hesperia, CA 92345
760-956-3876

Bike Shops

Cycle Pros
820 E Williams St
Barstow, CA 92311
760-255-1816

Victorville Cycles
12120 Ridgecrest Rd #208,
Victorville, CA
760-245-5900

Victorville Cycles
12120 Ridgecrest Rd #208,
Victorville, CA
760-245-5900

Miles E/W	Directions	Dist	R	Service	Miles W/E
0	L on Lavic Rd to cross I-40	0.2	3		85
0	S on National Trails Hwy/R66	18.2	3		85
18	*Cross Fort Cody Rd			C	67
18	S on National Trails Hwy/R66	4.6	3	R	67
23	*Newberry Springs (pop 2,895)			QR	62
23	S on National Trails Hwy/R66	9.6	3		62
33	*Daggett (pop 200)			C	52
33	S on National Trails Hwy/R66	2.4	3		52
35	VL on Nebo St	0.2			50
35	R to enter I-40	2.0	5		50
37	Exit I-40 on exit #2	0.2	4		48
37	L at SS on Main St after riding under I-40 VR	0.2	3		48
38	S at SS on Main St to cross the I-40 exit then VR	1.4	3	Q	47
39	*Barstow (pop 22,639)			CGLQR	46
39	R at SL on Main St/National Trails Hwy/R66	6.6	4	GLQR	46
46	*Lenwood (pop 3,543)			GR	39
46	S on Main St/National Trails Hwy/R66	5.6	4	G	39
51	*Hodge (pop 431)				34
51	S on Main St/National Trails Hwy/R66	11.2	3	Q	34
62	*Helendale (pop 5,623)			GLQR	23
62	S on Main St/National Trails Hwy/HR66	8.8	3	R	23
71	*Oro Grande (pop 1,030)			QR	14
71	S on Main St/National Trails Hwy/R66/D St/SR18	5.3	4	R	14
77	*Victorville (pop 115,903)			CGLQR	9
77	R at SL on 7th St/R66	2.5	5	LQR	9
79	L at SL on Mariposa Rd	6.0	4		6
85	*Hesperia (pop 90,173)			GLQR	0

Route 66 Section 26

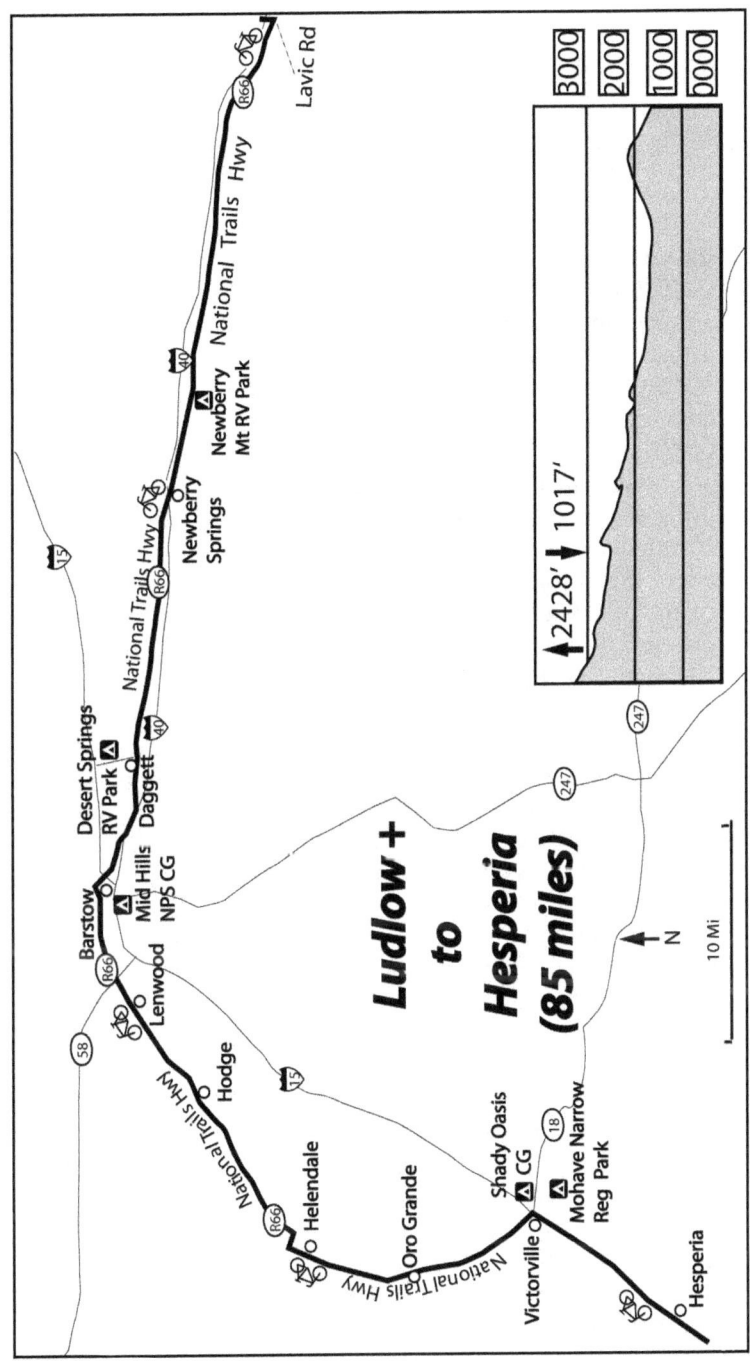

177

Route 66
SECTION 27

Hesperia, CA to Duarte, CA (79 miles)

Just before entering the town of Hesperia you cross an example of good old American ingenuity, the California Aqueduct. Begun in the late 1950s, through the use of massive pump stations, tunnels, and canals, this man-made waterway defies nature to direct water for a distance of over 400 miles, from sea level to elevations of over 1,300 feet, in an effort to route water to Southern California. Pretty mind boggling when you think about it.

Mariposa Road is pretty much a frontage road for I-15. Soon even it peters out and then you'll be riding on the Interstate. It was funny to see where they had crossed out the "No Bicycles" on the sign at the entrance to accommodate cyclists following Route 66. I believe this is something Adventure Cycling Association worked out with the state of California so we wouldn't have to shuttle across this stretch. Thank you ACA!

Before entering the Interstate, you can continue straight another tenth of a mile on Mariposa Road, past the turn on Oak Hill Road, to eat at a CRA, the Summit Inn. This place has been serving up comfort food to Route 66 travelers since 1952. You can even order their famous Ostrich Burger, made from birds raised on their own farm. Take a walk around the restaurant and see photos of famous celebrities on the walls who have eaten there; even Elvis frequented the place. There is also a gift store with tons of Route 66 memorabilia and an antique store with a lot of interesting one-of-a-kind treasures related to Route 66.

When I came through, the shoulder on the Interstate was pretty clean, and I'm sure the California Highway Department will keep it that way for cyclists. It's just a short seven mile ride on the Interstate, and most of it is downhill. The downhill is so steep they have a runaway truck ramp. It would take a lot of courage to make that turn off the highway onto the ramp.

Just another reminder, it is usually safer to take the exit ramp and return on the other side rather than attempting to ride across the exit with vehicles exiting at high speeds.

While riding on I-15 you cross paths with another epic route, the Pacific Crest Trail. This is a hiking trail that extends from the

Route 66 Section 27

Mexican border to the Canadian border. You really can't tell much about it from the Interstate, but if you want to get a closer look, take the Cajon Junction exit, head east on State Road 138 to ride over I-15, then turn right on Wagon Trail Road and ride it to the end. Round trip, it will be about two miles off-route. While there, you can also see a memorial for the Santa Fe and Salt Lake wagon trails.

Once you exit I-15 you'll have a better opportunity to check out the beautiful San Bernardino and San Gabriel Mountains bordering the highway. That tall pyramid looking peak to the north is Mount Baldy, at 10,064 feet elevation.

Note: For the camping listed for this area, the directions can be used for either campground. Bonita Ranch CG is just 1.6 mile south of Applewhite CG on Lytle Creek Road.

When you crossed the Colorado River into California you entered San Bernardino County, and you will be riding across it almost all the way to the ocean. San Bernardino County is larger than the nine smallest states in the US. What San Bernardino Country is size-wise, Los Angeles County is in population, with more people than 43 of the states in the US.

I tell you this to help prepare you for what's ahead. Most of this section you will be riding through the Megalopolis of Los Angeles. Until you experience it there is no comprehension of how far this metropolis' boundaries extend. It begins miles from downtown Los Angeles and feels like all of the cities merge together to form one gigantic city. It's difficult to determine where one city ends and another begins. And People, Los Angeles County contains one quarter of the entire population of the state of California.

So just be patient, watch the traffic, and you will come away with some memorable "Only in California" stories to share with your cycling buds back home when talking about your Route 66 Adventure.

Fortunately, motorists are accustomed to sharing the roads with bicyclists. It was comforting to see signs in some of the neighborhoods promoting themselves as being bicycle friendly. Plus, a large chunk of the route through here will be following the Pacific Electric Bike Trail (PEBT).

After leaving the Interstate many of the roads you will be following have painted bike lanes, and even when there isn't a bike lane there is usually room to ride on the shoulder.

You are still in a rural area during the first part of this section. When riding down Kenwood Avenue stop off at Mon's Store to pick up a snack and soda to enjoy a little peace before continuing into the Megalopolis. After your visit at Mom's the route takes you through a mix of industrial and older residential areas.

A few blocks after you begin riding Mount Vernon Avenue, you will be within a couple miles of visiting a cultural icon, the site of the original McDonald's Restaurant, at 1398 N E Street, San Bernardino. This is the where Richard and Maurice McDonald opened the first McDonald Barbecue Restaurant in 1940. It wasn't until eight years later they reduced their menus to burgers and fries, and revolutionized the restaurant industry. Even if you don't patronize the restaurant itself, you'll enjoy seeing all the historic memorabilia they have on display about the making of the famous franchise. This particular restaurant is now a museum and no longer serves food. To get there, turn left off of Mount Vernon Avenue onto West 16th Street to ride a mile, then right on North E Street and ride another two tenths of a mile.

Also, when you are riding along Pepper Avenue, at the Foothills Boulevard crossing, you are only block away from one of the CRAs that is most associated with Route 66, the Wigwam Motel. If you missed your chance to sleep in one of these classic teepees in Holbrook, Arizona then now's your chance. Although the environment has changed a lot since their construction in 1949, when they were surrounded by citrus groves, they still offer a truly unique experience. Just turn left at the intersection.

The traffic can be pretty heavy through San Bernardino. Also, when you are riding Merrill Avenue, watch the drainage culverts that run across the highway. If you're not careful the dip could pop a spoke.

The Pacific Electric Bike Trail (PEBT) is constructed on the former San Bernardino Line. This rail system was a major player in the Great American Streetcar Scandal, in which General Motors, along with other companies, plotted to dismantle the nation's streetcar system to eliminate their competition for land based travel. The plot in the movie Who Framed Roger Rabbit was actually modeled on the alleged conspiracy to dismantle the streetcar lines in Los Angeles. When I read about this I was reminded of the 2006 documentary film, Who Killed the Electric Car.

The PEBT is a very welcome environment after riding on the busy streets you ride to reach it. There are water fountains along the trail, benches, exercise stations, art, and plenty more to make it a pleasurable bike ride.

Shortly after you begin riding the trail you ride past an inviting park in Fontana, with water fountains and tall shade trees. It makes a great place to take a break. Following this, the trail routes you

Route 66 Section 27

past the Fontana Art Depot, with a pretty rose garden and more trees. The gallery itself is the original 1915 freight train depot. It now showcases visual art programs for area artists.

Further along the PEBT a street that used to cut across the bike path has been closed so they could put park benches and chess tables at the crossing. In another section of the trail a neighborhood has planted a garden in the green space along the trail.

It is like each of the neighborhoods the PEBT passes through tries to outdo the others to make it more appealing. There are sections of the trial that have crushed gravel paralleling the paved path for runners, so bikers and runners aren't running into one another.

At the street crossings where there are no direct signal lights, be sure to follow the directions that route you to a nearby light controlled crossing. Notice also, that at the crossings that do have lights there are lower buttons for pedestrians to control the lights and another set higher for people on horseback. One of the many "Only in California" oddities you will experience enroute to the Santa Monica Pier.

While riding the PEBT you see some of the concrete drainages that you've seen in action movies where they shoot car chase scenes. These things are even larger in life than they seem in the movies.

About three miles into your PEBT ride, at the Foothills Boulevard crossing, you can turn left and ride a "California" block to see one of the large orange vendors that were once a popular stop for Route 66 tourists. This particular stand was built in 1936 and called Bono's Historic Orange. The stand looked like it no longer sold juice when I came through, but it is worth the detour because it is shaped like a large orange.

There are way too many attractions to see on this final leg of your Route 66 Adventure to include in this book. If you would like to learn more about what is in the area, stop at the newly opened California Welcome Center, located on the west side of the Ontario Mills Mall. To reach the mall, about three miles after the PEBT crosses over I-15, turn left on Milliken Avenue. After three miles you will reach the mall.

At the Vineyard Avenue crossing you can turn left and ride less than half-a-mile to reach the location of the oldest winery in California, and also the second oldest in the U.S., the Thomas Winery (Yes, a double "-est"). The winery continued production into the mid-1960s, until development overran the vineyards. The Thomas Winery building is a California Historic Landmark and now operates as The Wine Taylor, which is an actual winery that makes all the wines they sell. Stop by for a wine tasting and tour of the historic building.

You will have plenty of other opportunities on your ride to grab some good food and drink, because all the way to Santa Monica Pier there are strip malls and eateries bordering, or close to the route, that will test your willpower. Plus, with people from 140 countries calling the Los Angeles area home, there is a great selection of ethnic foods. Don't fight it, give yourself a treat, you've earned it.

Speaking of good food, if you are a big pastrami lover, just prior to the end of the PEBT, if you turn right on Central Avenue and ride half-a-mile you can experience the "World Famous Pastrami" dip sandwiches at The Hat. They've been serving them up since 1951. Although this isn't the original restaurant, it does follow the same delicious recipe, plus it has the familiar retro neon sign.

I enjoyed riding along the tree lined streets they have through a lot of the neighborhoods in this section, and when you throw in the San Gabriel Mountains in the background it makes for a pretty sweet ride. It makes sense that there would be such heathy plant life in Southern California because they have summer year round.

There is a tricky intersection along Foothills Boulevard after about six miles, where they call a short piece of the road Alosta Avenue. This will probably not be a problem for westbound cyclists because one highway just flows into the other and you probably won't even notice the change. However, for eastbound cyclists, Alosta Avenue curves to the right and Foothills Boulevard continues straight, and after about half-a-mile T-bones Citrus Avenue and ends. Weird! So, for eastbound cyclists, after about six miles, watch for where Alosta Avenue curves to the right and follow it, rather than continuing straight on Foothills Boulevard. You could also watch for the old Foothill Drive-In Theater sign, which is located at this turn. This drive-in theater opened in 1961, and closed in 2001. The retro marquee sign towering over this intersection is the only thing remaining of this classic drive-in theater.

You have a good selection of lodging along Huntington Drive in the Duarte area. I like the Rancho Inn Motel because it had a retro look about it. Get yourself a room and rest up for the final push tomorrow.

Route 66 Section 27

Camping

Applewhite CG (USFS)
Fontana, CA 92331
909-382-2851
(after exiting I-15, 1.7 mi
on Cajon Blvd, R 2.8 on
Swarthout Canyon Rd, L 1.3
mi on Sheep Creek Truck Trl,
L 1 mi on Sheep Canyon Rd,
L .3 mi on Lytle Creek Rd, L
to CG, partial dirt rd)

Bonita Ranch
900 S Fork Rd
Lytle Creek, CA 92358
909-887-3643
(at Devore Rd & Cajon Blvd
cont S on Glen Hellen Pkwy
3.6 mi, turn R on Lytle Creek
Rd for 5.7 mi, .2 mi on S.
Fork Rd, pvaed all the way)

Cucamonga-Guasti Reg Park
800 N. Archibald Avenue
Ontario, CA 91764
909-481-4205
(L off PEBT 3.5 mi on
Archibald Ave)

Fairplex KOA
2200 N White Ave
Pomona, CA 91768
888-562-4230
(.7 mile off Bonita Ave)

Lodging

Days Inn San Bernardino
2000 Ostrems Way
San Bernardino, CA 92407
909-880-8425

Wigwam Motel
2728 E Foothill Blvd
San Bernardino, CA 92376
909-875-3005

Americas Best Value Inn
425 W Foothill Blvd
Rialto, CA 92376
909-820-0705

Forty Winks Motel
15210 E Foothill Blvd,
Fontana, CA 92335
909-823-1087

New Kansan Motel
9300 Foothill Boulevard
Rancho Cucamonga, CA
909-944-0221

Claremont West Suites
360 S Benson Ave
Upland, CA 91786
909-626-0211

Hotel Casa 425
425 W 1st St
Claremont, CA 91711
866-450-0425

*20th Century Motor Lodge
1345 E Route 66
Glendora, CA 91740
626-335-3348

*Best Western Plus Route 66
625 E Rte 66
Glendora, CA 91740
626-335-2817

*Stardust Motel Azusa
666 E Foothill Blvd
Azusa, CA 91702
626-334-0251

*Colonial Motel
534 E Foothill Blvd
Azusa, CA 91702
626-969-1895

Santa Monica HI Hostel
1434 2nd St
Santa Monica, CA 90401
310-393-6263

Bike Shops

REI
12218 Foothill Blvd Rancho
Cucamonga, CA 91739
909-646-8360
(1 mile off-route)

Performance Bicycle
4400 Ontario Mills Parkway
Ontario, CA 91764
909-483-8154
(4 miles off-route)

Roy's Giant Cyclery
106 E 9th St
Upland, CA 91786
909-982-8849
(.1 mile off-route)

Rad Stop Cycle
297 E Stowell St
Upland, CA 91786
909-946-8300
(.1 miles off-route)

Competitive Edge Cyclery
65 E Foothill Blvd
Upland, CA 91786
909-985-2453
(.5 miles off-route)

Jax Bicycle Center
217 W 1st St
Claremont, CA 91711
909-621-5827
(.1 mile off-route)

Coates Cyclery
760 E Foothill Blvd
Pomona, CA 91767
909-624-0612
(1.6 miles off-route)

Bicycle Central
942 S Grand Ave
Glendora, CA 91740
626-963-2312
(.5 miles off-route)

Lloyd's Custom Bicycle Shop
816 Highland Ave
Duarte, CA 91010
626-357-3509
(.2 mile off-route)

Route 66 Section 27
Hesperia to Duarte (79 miles)

Miles E/W	Directions	Dist	R	Service	Miles W/E
	*Hesperia (pop 90,173)			GLQR	
0	S on Mariposa Rd	5.6	3		79
6	R at SS on Oak Hill Rd	0.2	3		74
6	L to enter I-15	6.8	5	QR	74
13	Exit I-15 on exit #129	0.2	4		67
13	R at SS on Cleghorn Rd/Cajon Blvd/R66	6.1	4	C	67
19	L at SL on Kenwood Ave to go under I-15	1.4	3	Q	60
20	*Devore				59
20	R on Devore Rd	1.0	3	Q	59
21	L at SS on Cajon Blvd/R66	7.7	3		58
29	R at SL on 21st St then L on Mt Vernon Ave	0.9	3	L	50
30	R at SL on Baseline Rd	2.2	5	GQR	49
32	*San Bernardino (pop 209,924)				47
32	L at SL on Pepper Ave	2.0	5	R	47
34	R at SL on Mill St/Merrill Ave	3.0	5	QR	45
37	*Fontana (pop 196,069)				42
37	R at SL on Locust Ave	0.5	4	Q	42
38	L on Pacific Electric Bike Tr	18.7	P	C	42
56	R on Huntington Dr (unsigned) then L on 1st St	0.6	3		23
57	R at SS on College Ave	0.1	3		22
57	L at SS on Bonita Ave	0.3	3		22
57	*Claremont (pop 34,926)			QR	22
57	S on Bonita Ave	4.3	4	R	22
62	R at SL on San Dimas Canyon Rd	1.0	4		18
63	L at SL on Foothill Blvd/R66/Huntington Dr	8.9	4	LQR	17
72	*Duarte (pop 21,321)			LGQR	8
72	S on Foothill Blvd/R66/Huntington Dr	3.8	4	LQR	8
75	R at SL on Mayflower Ave	0.3	3		4
76	L at SS on Colorado Blvd	1.8	3	QR	4
77	BR at SL on Colorado St/Colorado Blvd/R66	1.9	4	LQR	2
79	L at SL on Rosemead BLvd				0

Classic fresh orange juice stand in Southern California.

Route 66 Section 27

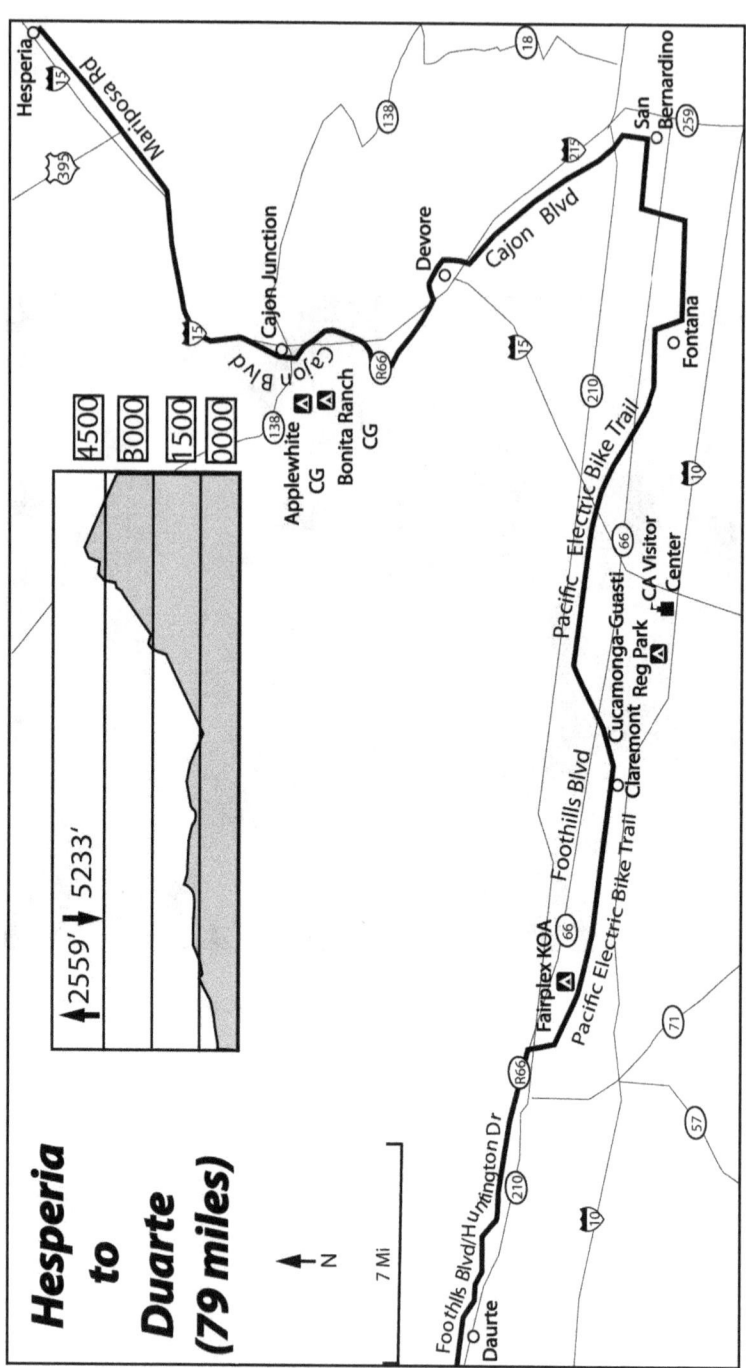

Route 66
SECTION 28

Durate, CA to Santa Monca Pier, CA (37 miles)

Only thirty seven miles remaining and most of that is downhill. This is a walk in the park after what you've been through. This is the equivalent of the final stage of the Tour de France, all the hard work is behind you, now you can relax for your victory lap. Njoy, you've earned it.

I'll include information about a lot of the attractions along the remaining route, but believe me, if I put in everything I don't think you would have wanted to lug the huge book it would have resulted in across the country. If you want to spend some time in Los Angeles and see everything the area has to offer, pick up the literature at the California Visitor Center I directed you to earlier.

Even though you are slowly pedaling deeper into the bowels of the Megalopolis, there still remains a mix of residential housing along with the business related structures. You'll find a sprinkling of private homes almost all way to the Santa Monica Pier. I would have thought the real estate values would have driven residents off their homesteads long ago.

One of the first things you might consider stopping at in this section is the Historic Bungalow Heaven. It's about six miles off-route, but with the neighborhood listed as one of the "10 great places in America" by the
American Planning Association, you know it is something special.

These relatively small homes were built during the Arts and Crafts period of the 20th century. From its beginning the area stood in opposition to increasing industrialization, emphasizing artistry of craftsmanship over mass production. The neighborhood is a historic gem which preserves Pasadena's innovative origins. To reach the southeast corner of this designated Landmark District, turn right off Del Mar Boulevard onto Hill Avenue, and then ride approximately six miles to Orange Grove Boulevard.

Section 28 would be a great one to schedule for a weekend ride, to avoid some of the heavy traffic. It's a beautiful ride, with palm tree lined highways and the San Gabriel Mountains towering over the outskirts of the city, but the traffic can be pretty intense.

However, if the timing doesn't work out for the weekend, with bike lanes and bike sharrows scattered throughout the route, it's still one sweet ride.

On your ride along Fair Oaks Avenue you ride pass another CRA, the Rialto Theatre. The theatre opened in 1925 for live vaudeville performances, and also showed movies. For its farewell performance in 2007 it showed "The Rocky Horror Picture Show". What an exciting experience that must have been. I was told the Rialto was purchased by an LA developer in 2015, so maybe there is still another chapter to be written in the story of this grand old theatre.

As you turn onto Huntington Drive, check out the globe advertisement atop the Dry Cleaner building. I thought it showed the Route 66 art deco style.

Also on Huntington Drive you pass a sign announcing that you are "Entering Los Angeles". It's official now. Shortly after the city limits sign you ride through the first of many ethnic neighborhoods, this one being Latino.

While riding along Mission Road you pass Lincoln Park, created in 1881, it is one of Los Angeles' oldest parks. With a lake, trees, benches, and restrooms it makes for a great place to take a break. Following the park, as you ride over a railroad bridge, you get a glimpse of the Los Angeles skyline. Impressive! Speaking of railroads, Cesar E. Chavez Avenue routes you right through Union Station. It's huge!

Shortly after passing the train station, take a left onto Spring Street and ride .3 miles off-route to reach Los Angeles City Hall. The art deco building is pretty impressive in itself, but the real attraction here is that you can take a series of elevators to reach an observation deck on the 27th floor for a great 360-degree view of Greater Los Angeles. It's a great vantage point and it's free.

Just a short distance further on Sunset Boulevard, you can turn right and ride about half-a-mile to visit the home of the Los Angeles Dodgers. In the mid-1950s, when the Brooklyn Dodgers' president tried to build a domed stadium in New York City and he couldn't reach a deal with city officials, he moved the entire operation to Los Angeles, and the rest is history.

Another CRA is a little further along the route in the Echo Park neighborhood. Located at the Logan Street intersection, there is a one-of-a-kind animated neon sign that sits atop the Jensen Recreation Center. The sign shows a bowler throwing a ball and it rolling twenty-eight feet to smash into a set of pins. It is the only sign like it in the US, so be sure to keep an eye out for it.

Route 66 Section 28

What a mix of cultures on just this short ride. You ride through a Latino community, Chinatown, and then past a beautiful Jewish Synagogue. As I was riding through all of this, with palm trees lining the highway and blue sky above, the lyrics to Randy Newman's song rang in my head, "LA, we love it!"

The only downside of it is the traffic. I don't love it.

If you continue straight a couple blocks on Van Ness Avenue, past the La Mirada Avenue turn, you can visit Hollywood Forever Cemetery. This is a beautiful setting with a rich and interesting history. Be sure to locate the classic headstone of Johnny Ramone, complete with guitar in hand.

It was such a novel experience bicycling down Fountain Avenue in Hollywood, California. The architecture is a well balanced mix of old and new, with an added touch of Greek influence. Peel off any street through here, or any other area for that matter, that attracts your attention and I'm sure you will discover something interesting and beautiful.

You can't be in this area without paying a visit to a one of America's most popular monuments, the Hollywood Walk of Fame. To reach these brass memorials, turn right off Fountain Avenue onto Highland Avenue to ride half-a-mile to reach Hollywood Boulevard. At this point you can turn left to view the five-pointed star tributes to Hollywood's famous stars, where you will reach this western end of the Walk. At that point you can then turn left on La Brea Avenue to return to Fountain Avenue, and resume the ride. Or, you can turn right on Hollywood Boulevard and ride about a mile to Gower Street, if you're one of those people who just have to see the entire walk.

Note: If you are interested in checking out the attraction in the next paragraph, as you are riding on La Brea Avenue, you can turn right on Sunset Boulevard to ride a little over a mile and you will be at the Crescent Highlands Boulevard intersection, the start of this next attraction.

Further along Fountain Avenue you are a quarter-of-a-mile from another Hollywood icon, Sunset Strip. This stretch of the city has undergone numerous periods of reinventing itself that began back in the 1920s. At that time, being located just on the outskirts of Los Angeles, the heavy handed laws of LA ended at the city limits sign. As a result, a number of nightclubs and casinos moved in along the strip. This beginning set a reputation for glamour and glitz that has carried over for the locale that exists to this day.

To reach Sunset Strip; while riding on Fountain Ave, turn right on North Crescent Heights Boulevard to ride .3 miles then turn

Route 66 Section 28

left on Sunset Boulevard to begin your cruise down The Strip. You pass many establishments that you have heard about all your life: The Laugh Factory, Whisky A Go Go, the Viper Room, the Roxy Theatre, and many others. When finished with cruising The Strip, you don't have to backtrack if you don't want to, just turn left on Doheny Drive to ride .6 miles and the turn right on Santa Monica Boulevard to rejoin the Route 66 route.

The Flores Street turn is easy to miss, or at least it was for me. Just watch for the building on the left with the castle turrets. Then enjoy your tree covered canopy ride along Flores Street.

Santa Monica Boulevard is lined with a variety of expensive shopping centers and places to eat. Stop at the Millions of Mike Shakes to enjoy one of the celebrity-named milkshakes and participate in one of the area's most popular pastimes, people watching. This was probably where people watching was invented because there are some really "interesting" individuals.

Following this you are in for a real treat, you get to ride through Beverly Hills. Wow! It is a nice break to escape the busy highways and cruise through the neighborhoods where the beautiful people live. I think I could be comfortable in one of these huge mansions with the meticulously manicured landscaping, as long as I didn't have to do the lawn work myself.

Once you return to busy Santa Monica Boulevard check out the gigantic Pacific Design Buildings with the pulsating water fountains.

The left onto Ohio Avenue is another turn that is easy to miss.

When Ohio Avenue transitions into Broadway and you are riding past busy upscale apartment complexes and ritzy shopping areas, check out the rusty old military Quonset Hut that houses Pono Burger. Using only locally grown and organic (of course, after all it is LA) ingredients, Chef Makani serves up a delicious burger. The contractor, who built the plush apartments that surround this pre-fab decades old structure, went to a lot of effort to preserve this piece of area history. Like I said before, what a mix of architecture.

Third Street Promenade is a good place to stop and walk around, what with the permanently blocked off street, lined by plenty of trendy shops and eating places, this makes for a favorable environment for more people watching.

The Hi Los Angeles Santa Monica Hostel is just one block off Broadway to your right. Which turns out to be very convenient for you, because as you near the end of Broadway, that breeze in your

Route 66 Section 28

face is salt air and that blue horizon ahead of you is the water of the Pacific Ocean. You have made it to the end of your Route 66 Adventure!

Turn left on Ocean Avenue to soak up the atmosphere for these final few blocks, then steer your bike under the Santa Monica Pier sign. Next, stroll along the quarter-mile-long linear amusement park known as Santa Monica Pier.

Today's pier is actually two piers combined. One pier, built in 1909, was used to pipe sewage out beyond the breakers (those were the good old days) and the second was built in 1916 by an amusement park owner who set the theme for what is present today.

With the 1920s Hippodrome-housed carousel, an aquarium, a solar powered Ferris wheel, video arcades, restaurants, pubs, live music, a trapeze school, and many other fun things to do, this place is a one-of-a-kind attraction that I'm sure you will agree was worth bicycling across the country to visit in person.

THE END!!!!

Congratulations on your accomplishment!!!! Just a reminder to email me at bob@spiritscreek.com to receive your "Certificate of Completion" for bicycling the entire *Route 66* route.

Maybe we will meet on a ride sometime to share our Route 66 Adventures around a campfire.

Bob Robinson

Route 66 Section 28

Camping

N/A

Lodging (There are many more lodging options than listed here)

Pasadena Inn
400 South Arroyo Parkway
Pasadena, CA 91105
626-795-8401
(1/2 blk off Del Mar Blvd)

*Titta Inn
5533 Huntington Dr N
Los Angeles, CA 90032
323-221-8828

*Lincoln Park Motel
2101 Parkside Ave
Los Angeles, CA 90031
323-225-3101
(just off Mission Rd)

*Paradise Motel
1116 W Sunset Blvd
Los Angeles, CA 90012
213-250-9094

*Comfort Inn
2717 West Sunset Blvd.
Los Angeles, CA 90026
213-413-8222

The Grafton On Sunset
8462 West Sunset Boulevard
West Hollywood, CA 90069
323-654-4600
(on Sunset Strip)

Alta Cienega Motel
1005 N La Cienega Blvd
Los Angeles, CA 90069
310-652-5797
(just off Santa Monica Blvd)

West End Hotel
1538 Sawtelle Blvd
Los Angeles, CA 90025
310-479-1823
(just off Ohio Ave)

Hotel Wilshire
1516 S Bundy Dr
Los Angeles, CA 90025
323-852-6001
(just off Broadway)

*Hotel Carmel
201 Broadway
Santa Monica, CA 90401
310-451-2469

*Ocean View Hotel
1447 Ocean Avenue
Santa Monica, CA 90401
310-458-4888

HI Los Angeles Santa Monica
1434 2nd St
Santa Monica, CA 90401
310-393-6263

Bike Shops

Velo Pasadena Inc
2562 E Colorado Blvd,
Pasadena, CA
626-304-0064
(.3 off Del Mar Blvd)

Open Road Bicycle Shop
60 N Sierra Madre Blvd,
Pasadena, CA 9110732
626-683-9986
(.4 off Del Mar Blvd)

*Gabe's Bike Shop
5346 Huntington Dr S
Los Angeles, CA 90032
323-226-1921

*The Bicycle Kitchen
4429 Fountain Ave
Los Angeles, CA
323) 662-2776
(tools to work on your bike)

Beverly Hills Bike Shop
10546 W Pico Blvd
Los Angeles, CA 90064
310-275-2453
(.8 off Santa Monica Blvd)

*Zone 3 Multisport
3216 Santa Monica Blvd
Santa Monica, CA 90404
310-828-0313

*Helen's Cycles
2501 Broadway
Santa Monica, CA
310-829-1836

*Bike Effect
910 Broadway #100
Santa Monica, CA
310-393-4348

REI
402 Santa Monica Blvd,
Santa Monica
310-458-4370
(blk off Broadway)

Route 66 Section 28
Duarte to Santa Monica Pier (37 miles)

Miles E/W	Directions	Dist	R	Service	Miles W/E
0	L on Rosemead BLvd	0.3	4	QR	37
0	R at SL on Del Mar Blvd	4.0	4	LR	37
4	*Pasadena (pop 137,112)			GLQR	33
4	L at SL on Fair Oaks Ave	2.4	4	QR	33
7	R at SL on Huntington Dr/R66	3.4	4	QR	30
10	*Los Angeles (pop 3,792,621)			GLQR	27
10	BR on Mission Rd	2.4	4	QR	27
13	R ar SL on Cesar E. Chavez Ave	1.3			25
14	S SL on Sunset Blvd/R66	3.4	4	LR	23
17	L at SL on Fountain Ave	1.7	4	LR	20
19	L at SS on Van Ness Ave then R on La Mirada Ave	0.1			18
19	R at SS on Bronson Ave	0.1			18
19	*Hollywood (pop 123,435)			GLQR	18
19	L SL on Fountain Ave	3.3		QR	18
22	L on Flores St	0.2	4	R	15
23	R at SL on Santa Monica Blvd	1.6	4	R	15
24	R on Sierra Dr	0.1	3		13
24	*Beverly Hills (pop 34,109)			GLQR	13
24	L at SS on Carmelita Ave	1.3	3		13
26	L at SS on Linden Dr	0.2	3		12
26	R at SS on Santa Monica Blvd	2.0	4	QR	11
28	R at SL on Westwood Blvd	0.5	4		9
28	L at SL on Ohio Ave	1.2	4		9
30	L at SS on Westgate Ave then R at SL on Santa Monica Blvd	2.0	4		8
32	L on Ohio Ave/Broadway	2.5	4	LQR	6
34	*Santa Monica (pop 89,736)			GLQR	3
34	L at SL on Ocean Ave	0.1		LR	3
34	R on Santa Monica Pier	3.0		R	3
37	End of Route 66!				0

The End of the Road!

Route 66 Section 28

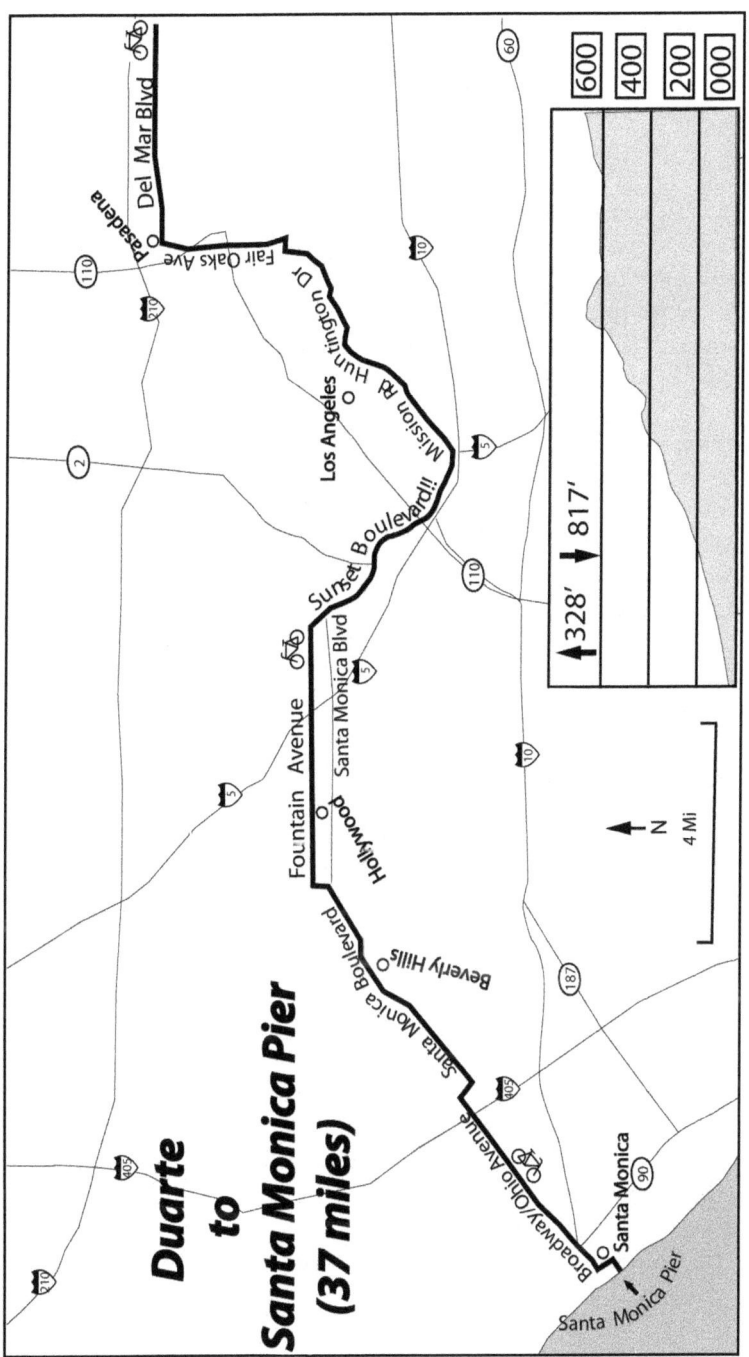

INDEX

A
100th Meridian Museum 87
Acoma Pueblo 120
Amarillo 18, 94, 95
Amboy, CA 167, 168
Arroyo de Los Chamois Trail 113, 114

B
Ballhagen's Puzzles 49
Big Texan Steak House 94
Blue Whale 68
Bottle Ranch 174
Buckingham Fountain 10, 11
Burnham Greenway Trail 11

C
Cadillac Ranch 94, 95, 96
Carthage, MO 55, 56, 57
Centennial Land Run Monument 76
Chain of Rocks 31, 32, 36
Chicago, IL 10, 11, 13
Coleman Theater 63
Colorado River 153, 161, 179
Constitution Trail 20, 24
Cyrus Avery 18, 62, 68, 69, 100

D
Daughters of the American Revolution 119

E
El Malpais National Monument 125
El Morro National Monument 126, 127
El Rancho Hotel 131
El Vado Motel 120
Elbow Inn 44, 45
Elvis Presley 17, 83, 152, 154, 178

F
Flagstaff 142, 145, 146, 147, 155
Fred Harvey 134, 162
Fried onion burger 76

G
Galena, KS 57
Gallup 127, 131, 132
Gateway Arch 36
Gettysburg of the West 112
Good Roads Movement 6, 62
Grand Canyon National Park 146, 147

H
Haak'u Museum 120
Historic Fort Reno 76
Holbrook, AZ 138, 180
Hollywood, CA 189
Homolovi Ruins State Park 140

I
Inscription Rock 127

J
Jackrabbit Trading Post 139
James N. Quinn Memorial 118
Joplin, MO 57

K
Kingman, AZ 154, 155, 160

Index

L
Lake Overhosler Bridge 76
Lakefront Trail 10
Leaning Tower of Texas 93
Los Angeles, CA 179, 180, 182, 187, 188
Lowell Observatory 145
Lucille's Roadhouse 80, 81

M
Madison County Transit Quercus Gro Trail 31
Marathon Service Station 63
Meramec Caverns 19, 38
Mickey Mantle 62, 63
Midpoint Café 101
Mojave Desert 159, 166
Muffler Man 6, 17, 24
National Cowboy Western Heritage Museum 75

N
National Route 66 Museum 84
Needles, CA 161, 162

O
Ozark Mountains 38, 49, 55
Ozark Trail 62, 69, 100

P
Pacific Electric Bike Trail 179, 180, 18 182
Painted Desert 134
Peace Park 94
Pecos River, NM 108, 112
Petrified Forest 134
Pixar Moive 57, 70, 101, 106
Pops Soda Ranch 75
Port of Catoosa 68
Pryor Creek Bridge 63

R
Rabbit Ranch 31
Rainbow Bridge 57
Riverfront Trail 36
Rock Creek Bridge 69
Rock Creek Bridge 70
Round Barn 75
Route 66 Interpretative Center 74
Route 66 Mural City 43

S
Santa Fe Trail 112, 119,
Santa Fe, NM 107, 108, 112, 113, 11
Santa Monica Pier 173, 181, 187, 19´
Santa Rosa, NM 107, 108
Shamrock, TX 83, 88
Sinclair Service Station 70
Sitgreaves Pass 159
Six Flags Park 37
Sky Center Cultural Center 120
Slug Bug Ranch 94
Soldier Field 10
Springfield, IL 25, 44, 50, 51
St. James Winery 44
St. Louis 18, 19, 31, 36, 37
Stonehenge 44
Sunset Strip 189

T
Tepee Curios Shop 101
The Cross 93
The Grapes of Wrath 87
Thorn Creek Trail 12

Index

Tucumcari, NM 103, 106
Tulsa, OK 18, 19, 62, 68, 69,
Turquoise Trail 118

U
U-Drop Inn 88
Ugly crust pie 101

V
Villa De Cubero Trading Post 121

W
Wigwam Motel 138, 180
Will Rogers 6, 57, 63, 68
Winslow, AZ 139, 140
World's Largest Totem Pole 64

About the Author

Bob Robinson has been an avid cyclist for over 35 years. During this period he has raced both road and mountain bikes, organized races for both road and mountain bikes, built mountain bike trails, served as cycling club president, organized bicycle tours, and worked as a committee member for the National Trails Symposium. He has also ridden many extended self-supported bicycle tours. Bob knows firsthand the requirements for a safe and enjoyable cycling adventure, and designs his guidebooks to fulfill those needs.

Bob's two current bicycle guidebooks, Bicycling Guide to the Mississippi River Trail and Bicycling Guide to the Lake Michigan Trail, have been well received by the cycling community and have sold several thousand copies in the United States, Canada, Australia, Germany, Switzerland, England, France, and other countries.

The author enjoying a cold Route 66 cream soda during another fine day on the road.

In researching this guidebook Bob followed Adventure Cycling Association's Bicycle Route 66 map set. He looks forward to meeting cyclists, and sharing stories with them around the campfire on future rides.

www.ingramcontent.com/pod-product-compliance
Lightning Source LLC
Chambersburg PA
CBHW061759110426
42742CB00012BB/2086